Mule Deer Quest

Mule Deer Quest

THIRTY-FIVE YEARS OF OBSERVATION
AND HUNTING MULE DEER FROM
SONORA TO SASKATCHEWAN

Walt Prothero

SAFARI PRESS INC.

Prothero, Walt

Safari Press Inc.
Long Beach, California

First Edition 2002

ISBN 1-57157-220-1

Library of Congress Catalog Card Number: 2001087325

10 9 8 7 6 5 4 3 2 1

Readers wishing to receive the Safari Press catalog, featuring many fine books on big-game hunting, wingshooting, and sporting firearms, should write to Safari Press Inc., P.O. Box 3095, Long Beach, CA 90803, USA. Tel: (714) 894-9080 or visit our Web site at www.safaripress.com.

TABLE OF CONTENTS

Preface

Jack O'Connor, in his foreword to *Sheep and Sheep Hunting*, says, "I must confess that I have had a hell of a time with this book. In the first place, I had difficulty deciding how to divide it up and organize it so it would not be too repetitious, and yet make each chapter relatively complete for those readers who skip chapters on subjects that don't interest them." With this mule deer book, I've had exactly the same problem. I wish O'Connor were alive today so that I might commiserate with him. Since he isn't, I'll whine a little in this preface. It was simply impossible to organize the book in such a manner as to get rid of any trace of redundancy. Some tactics, elements of deer biology or management, and food plants are so basic that it is impossible not to repeat them in various chapters dealing with different aspects of either hunting or biology. Since I skip chapters in expository books that I read, I fully expect that other readers will do the same here; if those readers are to completely understand a chapter, they will have to know basics that may have been presented earlier, so I was forced to include them again. And anyway, in my university teaching I have found that repetition is a good way to get important ideas across to undergraduates.

The first section of the book deals with mule deer biology. I studied this specific subject, especially the catchall areas of behavior and ecology, back in the '70s. Recently, I completed a dozen-year study of mule deer biology that began with winter survival and expanded to include rutting behavior as well as other deer habits including food preferences and general ecology. As a result, I know a little something about mule deer. In the biology section of the book, I tried to include only information that would be of interest to a general audience; I've collected all kinds of info that I hope eventually to include in scientific publications, but much of this deals with statistics and other esoteric biological materials. If I had wanted, I easily could have expanded the first section to four times its current length.

The second section is on the basics, and also includes more than a smattering of general biology. However, here the biology is given a practical slant to help readers understand mule deer habits, use them in hunting, and see how they work in herd management. Here, I'm certain, readers will find the first bits of redundancy. Certain elements of biology must be repeated in the context of practical use if they are to be fully understood.

Since this book is also about hunting, the "how-to" section tells hunters how to go about collecting a trophy buck. Many of these chapters have appeared in *Field & Stream* and *Outdoor Life* (I've been on the masthead of both publications) in one form or another; often in this book I've expanded them to include more information. Some chapters appear here for the first time anywhere.

Older hunters, myself included, prefer narratives or stories over the essentially didactic "how-to" essays. So I've included a collection of hunting narratives in the fourth section of this book. Here again, some of these have appeared in the magazines mentioned above. Some of these narratives were crafted to meet the requirements of the magazines, including article length.

The Afterword attempts to answer perhaps the most important question trophy buck hunters ask these days. You know what it is; for more information on this question, read it.

I don't mean to brag here, really, but I have hunted nearly every North American big-game species (I'm still waiting to bag a desert bighorn sheep), and have hunted throughout Africa (see my book *Safari: A Dangerous Affair* from Safari Press) and in half-a-dozen places in Asia. I mention this to establish my credentials so that I am more apt to be believed when I say that a trophy mule deer buck is one of *the* hardest animals to bag on the planet, and the hardest in North America.

If you've got the money, you can "buy" most other game species—trophy whitetails on highly managed, fenced ranches in the East (some only two thousand acres in area); huge rams on the most expensive concessions (not to mention governor's or other such permits that sell for $400,000 or more); 400-point-plus bull elk on Montana or Colorado ranches that are raised just like cattle, and given special antler-growing nutrients in their feed pellets and inoculations in the spring. Mule deer bucks, bless their hearts and spirits, have so far resisted large, enclosed ranches and antler-growing feeding programs and other schemes to turn them into a cash-producing crop. One good reason is that mule deer migrate (except on more southerly ranges, where winter snow plays no role in their life cycle). Another is that they simply do poorly in proximity to humankind and its various methods of intentionally and unintentionally killing them.

When I first started hunting mule deer, they were considered by many outdoor writers to be the whitetail's dumb relative. Magazines and writers propagated the myth that big bucks pause to look back before crossing a ridge and that the hunter could wait for this opportunity to shoot. To an extent, this was partly true—back then. But mule deer are quick learners and highly adaptable. Those bucks that paused in the open to watch their backtrail got killed off and didn't pass on their genes for that trait. The bucks that didn't pause to watch their backtrail survived to do most of the breeding and pass on genes that made them more secretive. Bucks have become essentially nocturnal, at least during hunting seasons. They don't pause in the open during daylight hours, and they won't even come out in the open unless it's dark. Most won't move unless they're certain they've been located. All of which makes them pretty tough to hunt. Throw in their unpredictability and their icy coolness compared to the whitetail (they seldom get rattled), and you need not only skill, persistence, and knowledge—you need luck.

I studied rutting behavior in elk during much of the '70s (with a thank-you to the National Science Foundation for its generous financing) as my research project for an advanced degree in wildlife biology. During that time, I observed nearly as many mule deer as I did elk, and collected data on them in Utah, Wyoming, and Yellowstone National Park. Though I have published several scientific works on elk, I have yet to publish anything on mule deer; some of the mule deer material is presented here. I studied mule deer biology from the late '80s until only a year or so ago. All told, I suppose I have spent tens of thousands of hours in the field observing deer and elk. I've observed mule deer in Arizona, Colorado, Idaho, Nevada, Utah, Wyoming, British Columbia and Alberta, and in Sonora, Mexico. I have kilos of notes on the animals and more kilos of statistics on behavior and other biology stashed away in cabinets in my offices. And I still enjoy getting out on snowshoes and cross-country skis on winter deer range, and each time, I learn something new.

I'm not only a biologist—I started hunting mule deer as a prepubescent kid back in the '60s. I bagged one of the fattest deer I've ever taken on the mountainside across the street from our house. It was pure luck, I knew even then, but I've been addicted to mule deer ever since.

Yes, trophy bucks are definitely more scarce today than they were back in the '60s, '80s, or '90s. With so many humans using up critical winter range and other range for Wal-Marts and campus parking lots, with more roads being built and SUVs using them, and with too many ATVs and snowmobiles disturbing deer at all seasons, few mule deer live long enough to produce trophy antlers; those that manage to live long enough do so by becoming ultra-secretive and staying away from human activities. Some big bucks do, or at least can, live long enough in overhunted ranges by adopting special hideouts. Two of the three best bucks I bagged in the 1980s were on relatively overhunted ranges (not to mention overgrazed and overused by snowmobiles). Some of the biggest bucks I've ever seen were spotted during the '90s in northern and southern Arizona, northern Sonora, and extreme southern Utah. But drawing a permit and/or booking a hunt in these areas won't guarantee you a trophy buck; you've still got to *hunt*. I've known too many hunters who drew permits in hot areas with the idea that they were assured a trophy buck, only to return with no buck or a mediocre deer they could have bettered closer to home. They didn't have a plan, hadn't researched or scouted the area, and just wandered around with the absurd notion that since they were in good buck country, a trophy would wander right out in front of them and pause while they turned off the ATV, uncased the rifle, and took aim. It ain't gonna happen.

This is a book for those fair-chase hunters who realize they have to hunt honestly and revert to the old bush skills to bag a trophy buck on whatever range they are hunting. Machine- and gadget-reliant hunters will collect a trophy mule deer only with luck.

Dedication

To Dad, Walter K. Prothero, and Mom, Dolores D. Prothero, who passed on to a better place, I hope, in the autumn of 2000. I wrote this and every other book for you and your approval.

Chapter 1

Mule Deer Biology

BIOLOGY

Back when I was a graduate student at Utah State University, working on an advanced degree in wildlife biology and studying elk behavior, I began gathering data on mule deer. My emphasis was on rutting (mating) behavior in elk, though I collected data on other behavior types (maternal-neonatal, agonistic, play, etc.). Much of the mule deer data I collected was qualitative rather than quantitative and consisted of hurried notes scribbled into notebooks, and most of it was simply filed away for future use.

Much later, while observing mule deer on winter range in the mid-1980s, I became alarmed at winter mortality in mature bucks. Since I was also a very serious trophy buck hunter at the time and had been for two decades, I'd previously noted the big drop in mature bucks over the previous decade and had begun to notice another drop. I wanted to isolate the causes of such intense winter mortality. After the first winter of observation, I hypothesized that mule deer mortality is caused by the following factors:

1. Disappearance or destruction of winter range because of housing tracts, golf courses, etc.,
2. Severity of winter weather,

3. Disturbance by snowmobile and ATV activity,
4. Disturbance by dogs accompanying recreationists or free-ranging dogs,
5. Disturbance by recreationists simply approaching deer too closely.

The ordering of these factors depends on the environment. For example, in North Ogden, Utah, where I first became alarmed by buck mortality, much of the mortality was caused directly by human activity, especially ATV use and dogs either free-ranging or accompanying hikers or skiers. Since North Ogden itself is largely built upon historic winter deer range, the ultimate cause was simply human occupation of critical deer range. Additional mortality was caused by automobiles.

One critical afternoon sparked my interest in gathering data on winterkills. I live on the opposite—east—side of a mountain range, the Wasatch Front, from North Ogden. I started early from my house one morning on snowshoes to cross the range and drop down into North Ogden, where I'd be picked up by my better half. As I made my way down a slope above the town, I spotted an enormous buck bedded in scrub oak six hundred yards away. I sat in the snow and watched, since bucks of that size are as rare in northern Utah as half-pound sapphires. Before long, a cross-country skier with two free-ranging Labrador dogs skied along a road below the buck. The dogs scented the buck and, methodically working uphill, jumped it from its bed. The buck lunged uphill through deep snow several hundred yards until the dogs gave up. He stood for a while, and through the binoculars I noted that he was panting slightly. He then found another suitable bedding place nearby and again lay down.

The next day I drove as near as I could to the place and watched the buck through the spotting scope. He hadn't moved from his bed, and though his head was upright, he'd stretched his chin along the snow and seemed to be resting his neck. After an hour of watching, it occurred to me that the buck had not even flicked an ear. After watching more, I was convinced the buck was dead.

I climbed up the steep slope through the snow to confirm my conviction. The buck was indeed dead. He had no external injuries, which probably meant he had no internal injuries—he hadn't been hit by a car or injured in a rut battle or by a predator. He was thin—typical of post-rut mule deer bucks—but otherwise seemed in normal condition. Apparently, given the severe winter and the rigors of rutting, the buck simply didn't have enough energy reserves to run from dogs. Those he had squandered doing so were the reserves necessary to maintain body temperature in the cold. Post-rut mature bucks are at the season's physiologic low point; they can't afford any wasted energy because survival demands are peaking at the same time their physiological condition is at a low point. All it took was for those dogs to chase the buck a few hundred yards up a steep, snowy slope. I was infuriated.

Later that week I was at the base of west and south facing slopes above monastery farmlands in Ogden Valley, at an elevation of approximately 5,500 feet. Elk, deer, and a few moose were scattered across the snow-covered sagebrush and grass slopes on the southern and western exposures (these get more sun and have less snow for animals to dig through to reach vegetation). In my pickup half a mile away, I used a spotting scope to quickly locate winter kills—dark or reddish smears on the distant snowy hillsides, many with golden eagles or coyotes nearby. Bucks hadn't yet shed antlers—it was early January—and I spotted antlers on several carcasses. As I watched, two snowmobiles rushed down the slope from above and isolated a small band of bucks and then buzzed up close. The bucks bounded up through the snow and then stopped, apparently too exhausted to run farther. The snowmobilers left, and the bucks stood in the same spot for over an hour before walking around the curve of the slope and bedding in shintangle out of the wind. The next morning, one of those bucks was dead and another so weak it could not move away when I approached. It could hold its head up only for a few minutes at a time. If I'd had a gun, I would have put the buck out of its misery. Later that day, the coyotes did, eating on the buck before it was dead.

Though I'm certain that neither the skier with the dogs nor the snowmobilers had intended to harm the bucks, their ignorance and lack of consideration for another species had killed the animals just as surely as a poacher with a rifle might have. In subsequent years, I've watched similar dramas involving free-ranging dogs in Eden, Pleasant View, and North Ogden, Utah, and near Kemmerer and Cokeville, Wyoming. I've also noted too many similar incidents with motorcycles, ATVs, and snowmobiles. People should stay completely away from deer attempting to survive winter, because often it takes only a bit of disturbance to tip the scales against survival.

Of course, humans have less effect on the winter survival of mule deer in wilderness or other remote country. But since wild areas are normally higher, more remote, and of less value to humans, humans have usurped lower river bottoms where deer would normally winter. However, deer do at times winter in

This young buck has shed his antlers and will die of starvation and hypothermia before the day is out. There simply isn't much feed on a golf course, which displaced the range where his ancestors had browsed in hard winters for millennia.

wild areas, and there the causes of mortality differ. Overgrazing, by both domestic stock and wildlife, seems to be the Number 1 cause of winter mortality in various places in Utah, Nevada, Wyoming, and Idaho. Here, if bucks are undisturbed by snowmobiles, ATVs, and dogs, survival even in harsh winters is higher than survival near human activities. It's difficult to quantify such findings without knowing the precise number of mature bucks wintering in an area, which is nearly impossible to determine. Bucks migrate up to fifty miles to reach wintering range, so my findings are mostly qualitative.

In remote country, winter mortality is more affected by predation. Coyotes are the main predator. On flat or gently sloping terrain—which makes up much of winter range—coyotes run faster than mule deer, especially over packed snow. However, my data indicates that coyotes often kill deer that may be too weakened to survive anyway. Again, this is only impression based upon years in the field. If coyotes move onto a winter range, deer move out if they are not isolated by high mountains or other natural obstacles. Of course, this movement uses critical energy that is necessary simply to survive, and may cause significant additional mortality, especially of mature bucks.

Mountain lions, or cougars, are quick to take advantage of such stressed deer, as are coyotes. Above my house in northern Utah there's a high, south-facing, windblown slope. Much of the snow is usually blown free, and on this exposure deer can easily get to vegetation and soak up the sun. I'd watched three bands of deer along the big ridge for two weeks. I kept my distance and observed through binoculars or the spotting scope. After two weeks, a lion moved onto the slope and immediately killed a 4½-year-old buck and, a week later, a doe in very poor condition. The rest of the deer moved completely out of the area, and in spite of diligent searching on snowshoes and covering perhaps forty square miles, I could not relocate them. Should we control predators on winter range? I can't answer that, but my biological bias is to leave things be. With mule deer, however, the answer may not be that easy.

It's still my impression—backed up by statistics—that by far the most winter mortality in mule deer is caused by man on his ATV or snowmobiles or accompanied by his dogs, which usurps or destroys critical winter mule deer habitat. It seems easier to control human activities than to alter evolution, but I may be deluding myself.

It's difficult to prevent humans from building housing tracts and golf courses on winter range. However, it's possible to strictly curtail human activity and enforce or enact leash laws. After a dozen years of closely watching mule deer in winter, I'm convinced that mortality caused by human activity on critical winter ranges contributes substantially to total mortality, especially in mature bucks that enter the winter with physiological reserves depleted by rutting.

Valerius Geist, the widely known large-mammal behaviorist from Canada, believes the mule deer is an evolutionary failure and on the way out. Unfortunately, I agree. He believes the biggest reason for this lack of evolutionary success is that the mule deer is crossbreeding with the whitetail and the resultant hybrids are poor survivors—e.g., they can neither bound nor run well and become confused by obstacles while retreating, thus becoming easy prey. I question this hypothesis. While I agree that the mule deer is on the way out, I see human activity as the primary cause because mule deer are declining in places where no white-tailed deer exist. The whitetail, like humans, cockroaches, and starlings, is a "weed" species able to thrive in a variety of environments and adapt rapidly to change. It's a highly successful competitor, in other words.

In light of my dozen-year study of mule deer behavior and ecology, let's begin a general discussion of mule deer biology with winter, the season when my odyssey began.

WINTER

The mule deer rut generally begins in late autumn. Except in the southern ranges of southern Arizona, California, New Mexico, and northern Mexico, mule deer rutting begins in earnest

Deer are too often forced down onto traditional winter range usurped by man. This puts them in danger from autos, dogs, and starvation.

sometime in mid-November and runs through mid-December. Though the calendar says this is autumn, climatic conditions often say it's full winter. Snow may cover the ground to considerable depths, and temperatures can reach below zero.

Older hypotheses said that battles during the rut put mule deer in such poor condition. I'm finding fewer and fewer mature bucks in the general population, so there is less fighting, and yet adult bucks still enter winter in the same poor condition. I doubt big bucks lose condition from battling, especially in much of Utah, where there are few other adult bucks to battle with. Loss of condition, then, is a result of bucks ranging far and wide to test widely separated doe groups and from actual rutting. Wandering great distances causes greater weight loss than does fighting other bucks. First, true battles between mule deer bucks are rare; I've witnessed less than a dozen, but three of these were such violent affairs that the loser sustained fatal wounds. Since fights are so violent and bucks may be killed or lose much energy from the brief encounters, it's an evolutionary disadvantage for fights to

This doe was hit by a truck as it attempted to negotiate an ancestral migration route from summer to winter range.

occur at all. As a result, the mule deer has other methods to determine dominance that require less energy and are less dangerous, such as pre-rut sparring matches that largely determine dominance in a given area.

Even without battling, mule deer enter the winter in poor condition. Mature bucks and fawns suffer the highest mortality in winter. Severe weather alone is tough for an adult buck to survive; throw in ATVs, snowmobiles, dogs, and highways, and odds are stacked heavily against mature-buck survival. In places where white-tailed deer coexist with mule deer, hybridization occurs more readily in the absence of mature mule deer bucks (mule deer easily intimidate whitetails, and in a population with sufficient mule deer bucks, little hybridization occurs; if adult mule deer bucks are scarce, whitetail bucks can intimidate smaller mule deer bucks and breed with mule deer does). But I'm getting ahead of myself.

In December, after the rut, bucks seek places protected from the elements, safe from disturbance and predators, and near food. These places are harder to find, given the increasing human population and our increased affluence, allowing for summer or winter cabin estates and additional recreational mechanization. The ideal places for wintering bucks are in brush on south or west-facing slopes about one-half to one-third of the way down from the ridgetop. Here there's little wind, there's cover, and if there's browse nearby, so much the better.

Bucks move away from doe groups after the rut, perhaps to lessen the chance of detection by predators. They prefer to spend the early winter alone or with one or two cohorts. They move about as little as possible, probably both to conserve energy and to avoid detection. If sufficient feed is nearby, a buck may walk no more than three hundred yards in a day. Energy conservation is critical to surviving low temperatures and maintaining body heat. Ideally, mature bucks may regain some of the weight lost during rutting. If not, it's important they do not lose additional weight. If the winter is severe, energy expended to excavate and search for food won't allow them to maintain their weight. In such winters, mature-buck mortality is high even without human interference or harrying by predators.

In northern Utah, western Wyoming, and northern Nevada, mule deer bucks tend to shed antlers in late February or early March. I've observed apparently healthy mature bucks with antlers as late as mid-March and bucks that have shed one or both antlers as early as mid-January. In my observations, all bucks still have antlers in early January.

After antler shedding, bucks join doe herds. From a survival and evolutionary standpoint, this makes sense. If there are twenty deer in a group, statistically the buck has only a one in twenty chance of getting selected by a predator. Since bucks have lost weight and condition and flee slower than does, they tend to lag behind a herd running from a predator. Predation is always highest among those that can't keep up.

Mule deer often congregate in large wintering herds on windswept terrain; however, they do not "yard" like white-tailed deer. These places are relatively free of snow, and feed is easier to get at. Mule deer are effective runners in snow and can bound through deep snow better than whitetails can run through it.

Favored winter foods include sagebrush, but deer prefer bitterbrush, the various mahogany species, serviceberry, chokecherry, and various frost-killed forbs (ensilage). A clear sign that wintering deer are in trouble is heavy browsing of juniper trees; pedestaled—little growth within the deer's reach but a pedestal of growth up high—indicates past tough winters. Juniper fills the paunch but apparently has little nutritional value.

In severe winters during the 1950s above North Ogden, Utah, hundreds of deer carcasses were loaded on wagons. Often their gut was full of juniper. Still, the deer had died of hypothermia brought on by malnutrition. Fats in the bone marrow had been depleted and the marrow took on the characteristic bright pink color.

Winter feed includes storm-toppled trees, especially upper buds and branches of pines, firs, spruce, and other evergreens, and the twigs of poplars, oaks, maples, and other deciduous trees. Storm-felled branches are a much-needed windfall (no pun intended).

Mule deer have the ability to detoxify otherwise poisonous plants and as a result can eat sagebrush, juniper, and evergreens. However, as important as sagebrush is in the life of mule deer, they do poorly on it alone. They require supplemental browse, and I've noted them thriving on a diet of sagebrush and serviceberry. Other foods include grasses; sedges; dried berries of chokecherry, serviceberry, snowberry, and rose hips; and various autumn-shed deciduous leaves that carpet the ground in forests (when the deer can get at them).

When weather conditions moderate late in the winter, bucks separate from doe herds and form small bachelor groups. When shadows are right, it's easy to see ribs and hips poking through the faded, scruffy fur.

Later still, as the snows melt, deer follow the snowline upward, cropping new growth as it appears. Curiously, I've

Young buck in winter.

noticed high deer mortality in March and sometimes into April, just as winter's back has been broken. A late-season heavy snow is the catalyst that causes this late mortality.

SPRING AND SUMMER

Spring in the mule deer's northern ranges is often characterized by lingering winter weather, and deer are still in a weakened state. Since snow has melted or even disappeared, deer can effectively outrace coyotes. Antlers have begun to bud above the eyes of older bucks and appear as dark, fur-covered nodes. Later in the spring—say in May, though this is variable—the weathered, pale, and bleached fur is gradually replaced by shorter, shiny, reddish summer pelage. By late May antler pedicels are more pronounced and fork into additional tines. Vegetation grows more exuberantly, and deer begin regaining weight. Does drift to places with thick cover and nearby feed to give birth. In northern Utah and similar latitudes, does begin dropping

Mule deer also rely heavily on dead forbs and grasses, particularly in autumn.

fawns in mid-May and may drop them until mid-June. During the first weeks of life, fawns remain motionless, or "frozen," in cover and won't run from a predator unless physically touched. Since they are essentially scentless early in life, this is the best survival strategy.

Here again, dogs, both feral and those accompanying recreationists, cause heavy mortality. Several years ago a pack of pet dogs killed two fawns in aspens a hundred yards from my house. In the early morning hours I was awakened by the din of hysterical dogs just down the slope. I fired a shot or two over their heads in the darkness and ran them off. In daylight I explored the scene of the carnage. Two-week-old fawns had been killed and partly eaten. A blood trail led down the creek; the doe had been injured, too. I'd previously noticed the dogs packing and complained to the Weber County animal control office; I got little verbal and no physical response. I tracked one of the dogs to a neighbor's house; her response was typical—dogs will be dogs, and it's too bad.

Of course, natural predators also cause mortality. New fawns have little odor and predators won't find them unless they happen upon one hiding. As the fawn grows, it develops more scent and becomes more vulnerable to mammalian predators. But during this time, it also becomes more mobile and adept at racing off. I've found little evidence that golden eagles prey upon fawns. In decades of observing local eagle nests, I've found fawn remains in only two. It's probably more likely that an eagle found a fawn carcass and scavenged it rather than killed it. Highways are a favorite scavenging site for raptors.

By late spring, say mid-June, bucks are often up on summer ranges. If not, they are working their way there. Some bucks may spend the entire summer and early autumn on the same range and move off only when autumn snow or the rut forces them down. Others may occupy various home ranges during the summer. I've noticed bucks that had three or four home ranges between late June and early November. A home range is that area where a buck lives, and includes feeding and bedding areas. It's not defended against others of the same species. By late June, bucks have pretty well shed winter coats and are wearing a sleek, short, reddish coat. During the summer, they put on weight as preparation for rigors of rutting and winter. Most antler growth occurs in June and July, periods of fresh and vigorous plant growth. Bucks seem to grow better antlers in places with abundant willow growth (this belief coincides with studies that show moose must have large quantities of willow for adequate antler development). By documenting antler growth on moose along the Yukon River, where I spent the summers and autumns for a decade, I found that 80 percent of antler growth occurs in June and July. Superficially, the same is true of mule deer.

Photoperiod, or day length, affects the antler growth cycle. Studies show that decreasing photoperiod initiates the shedding of velvet, and increasing day lengths cause antler shedding and eventually new antler growth. Since moose in northern latitudes have shorter antler-growing periods, it may be that antler development in more southern deer species such as mule deer is more spread out over the entire growth season. Though antler growth for most mule deer does occur in June and July, perhaps more than 20 percent of it occurs in other months.

Nutrition plays an important role in both the ultimate size of antlers and growth rates over short periods of time. Older studies show that antler growth is stimulated in areas with higher calcium concentrations in the soil. Most hunters have noticed that bucks from one place simply do not grow trophy antlers as often as bucks from another valley or state; the answer may lie both in the types of vegetation available and in the relative concentrations of nutrients in local soils. It seems logical that the more abundant the plant growth, the larger the antlers; however, this is not always the case. In extremely arid locations in northern Sonora, mule deer grow absolutely immense antlers in places that wouldn't seem to support large herbivores.

By late summer, August or so, most antler growth is complete, and by late in the month, antler velvet has dried noticeably and lost the dark shade caused by the intense vascularization of early summer. Most mule deer shed velvet early in September; however, I've noted many instances of velvet shedding in late August. Bucks shed velvet by rubbing antlers against shrubs and saplings.

Since plants grow more profusely in early summer, fawns also grow most in the summer. In spite of the rigors of producing milk for one to three fawns, does somehow manage to gain weight. They do so more rapidly as fawn demand for milk decreases, since they're able to use more of the vegetation for their own nutritional demands.

During the summer, mule deer eat a wide variety of vegetation. Much of it is toxic to other animals, including humans. Deer have the ability to detoxify many plants and can therefore use plants other animals can't eat, thereby reducing competition. I've noticed that summer fawns occasionally refuse to eat plants on which their mothers are browsing. It's possible that they have not yet developed the mothers' tolerance for toxic plants.

Mule deer browse during summer on grasses, grass seedheads, sagebrush, wild raspberry, manzanita, wild onion, sedges, a variety of wildflowers, fungi (mushrooms), wild holly, snowberry, chokecherry, serviceberry, bitterbrush, mahogany, Gambel's oak, wild rose, big-tooth maple, rock rose, rabbit brush, hawk's beard, phlox, Russian thistle, and a variety of forbs. Proportions and preferences depend on relative abundances and availability of other favored food plants on a given range.

Mule deer are more fastidious than elk in selection of food plants. They'll take time to find the right morsel while an elk in the same place seems to eat everything within reach.

As fawns mature late in the summer, they wander farther away from the mother. This increasing independence is necessary for the ultimate rupture of the mother-fawn bond during the coming winter or the next spring before the dam drops a new fawn. In general, mother and fawn migrate uphill as the summer progresses, though

Bucks feed on a variety of vegetation, including sagebrush, snowberry, and the grasses shown here.

they don't normally reach the alpine basins where mature bucks may summer. In good mule deer range, the higher you go, the lower the proportion of does and fawns you'll see.

AUTUMN

Autumn is my favorite time of year. Above all, I am a hunter (as are all *Homo sapiens*, even if some refuse to acknowledge it), and the frosty dawns and flaming leaves herald the hunt. It's my favorite season for other reasons, too. My first focused scientific study of large mammals involved the rutting behavior of elk, or wapiti, in autumn. I remember lying pleasantly in a frosty Yellowstone meadow as dawn chased the shadows from the lodge pole pine forest and watching a harem bull bugle, his steamy breath hanging in the cold air; and I remember the clash of antlers as two behemoth bulls lunged and jousted four yards from where I cowered in pine shintangle. I

A doe bedding in scrub oak in summer.

remember, too, observing rutting elk in my two twenty-acre enclosures from a U.S. Fish and Wildlife Service trailer while sipping hot tea. I was a graduate student then, studying wildlife biology at Utah State University, and the whole world was before me.

To me, autumn is the best season for observing mule deer, too. Bucks have put on weight, shed their summer-red coat for a gray-blue one, and their necks swell. They spar and are at their most impressive.

In many places elk rutting peaks about September 20, thus giving bulls time to regain some of the weight lost during the rut before the onset of winter, and thereby improving chances for survival. Mule deer begin rutting in earnest about mid-November and finish in mid-December—full winter in much of their range. They often leave the rut emaciated and injured, and step into the full-time job of surviving winter. Few mule deer bucks regain weight to help with survival, and among mature bucks winter mortality is high.

These days, most hunting seasons precede the rut. Bucks are adaptable and cunning during these early hunts, and mortality is relatively low. If hunting seasons occurred during the rut, bucks would be more vulnerable because they're searching for estrous does and are more visible and less occupied with watching out for hunters. Rut hunting during this age of declining mule deer populations is unacceptable. Hunter-caused mortality of mature bucks is negligible when compared to normal winter mortality and mortality caused by dogs, ATVs, snowmobiles, and highways.

As the rut nears, mature bucks begin battering shrubs and saplings with their antlers, perhaps to relieve pent-up aggression caused by rising testosterone levels. These "rubs" are good indicators of the presence of bucks, and can be used to guess at the size of local bucks. There's a strong correlation between the size of a buck and the size of saplings he beats up on. Larger, mature bucks prefer larger saplings and even trees, perhaps because the greater resistance is more satisfying. Yearling bucks rub most frequently against small-diameter shrubs or saplings and seldom spend much time working on larger saplings. When I'm hunting, one of the key indicators I use to determine whether a mature buck is in the vicinity is the presence of rubs on saplings greater than three inches in diameter. Bucks rub vegetation less if the buck population is high during the pre-rut; in those conditions, sparring between bucks takes the place of rubbing, to an extent.

While I was studying elk behavior at Utah State, the state and the university maintained a few mule deer in a too-small enclosure. A spindly deciduous tree grew in its center. Of course, a young buck rubbed it since there was nothing else to rub against. But he also pressed his preorbital gland, that opening below the eye, against hanging branches. He then dug a hollow beneath and often urinated into it. Since mule deer weren't supposed to "scrape" like whitetails, I assumed this activity was a throwback behavior or an anomaly brought about by confinement in a small enclosure. I forgot about it.

Years later, I noticed scrapes similar to those I'd seen in whitetail country, but in areas where only mule deer and elk lived. True, there weren't many, but occasionally I'd locate a cluster of them in a small area. When I did, I'd find that they increased in number as the rut neared; they'd also be fresher—bucks revisited them more often and I could smell the musky odor. Eventually, I learned to use these scrapes as indicators that a mature buck lived in the vicinity, and I'd use them as ambush sites when hunting. Though I've found bona fide mule deer "scrapes" less often than scrapes in whitetail terrain, they seem to serve the same function as whitetail scrapes. They advertise a buck's habitat and breeding condition and probably his overall health. I've noted mule deer does sniffing at them with interest in late October and through November.

I've been told by other biologists, game managers, and hunting guides that mule deer do not scrape, but a wise man changes his mind many times, a fool never. For three consecutive autumns, I found scrapes in a tangle of big-tooth maple at about 6,500 feet in elevation. As the rut neared, scraping activity increased. The scrapes increased in number, and the buck freshened them by urinating and sometimes defecating in them. Judging by the track size in the pungent mud of the scrape, the buck was not fully mature—probably 3½ years old. Unlike a whitetail scrape line, these scrapes were clustered together within a fifty-yard radius.

I'd noticed similar scrape clusters in Montana, Wyoming, and Arizona. They are made both by subadult bucks and mature animals. Not all mule deer bucks, and probably not a majority of them, make scrapes, and I have not found many in the years I've hunted. This lack of detection may be due in part to the firm belief held at the time by many observers that mule deer simply did not scrape. Perhaps I'd noticed them earlier, but did not consider the possibility. So much for dogma.

Bucks begin sparring shortly after velvet shedding in September. The most important reason for sparring is to size up the local male competition and try to establish dominance early on when aggression levels are low, thereby avoiding potential lethal conflicts later on. After all, there's no reason to challenge the stud buck when you already know he's tougher. Sparring also serves to strengthen neck muscles and improve coordination for future battles, should they occur. Among subadult bucks, sparring increases until the rut; among adults, it increases through October, but then decreases late in November as bucks become more aggressive. Adult bucks do not spar during the rut, because aggression levels are high and sparring matches turn into full-fledged battles. I've already noted the seriousness of these.

It's my observation that uneven, "nontypical" antlers are more common on deer ranges with abundant or adequate numbers of adult bucks. Often these uneven racks are a result of earlier injuries to antler pedicels or to the body during rutting battles. Typically, an injury to one side of the body causes a deformity in the opposite antler. Don't ask me why. I've heard several hypotheses, but none seems satisfactory. It just happens that way with enough regularity that I consider it a rule. If I see a buck with a deformed antler, I search for an injury on the opposite side, and usually I find one. I suspect that bucks with two deformed antlers have suffered injuries on both sides, though this seems less consistent. I once examined a large nontypical buck with two uneven antlers; it had two badly healed broken ribs on one side and an arrow broadhead embedded in scar tissue in the ham on the other. In spite of these injuries, the buck had massive antlers and seemed in exceptional condition—it probably weighed three hundred pounds on the hoof.

Bucks in the intermountain region of Utah, Colorado, Wyoming, Idaho, and Nevada begin rutting early in November. I've seen adult bucks seriously tending does nearing or in heat (estrus) as early as November 2; however, most serious rutting activity doesn't get underway until November 10. The onset and intensity of the rut are influenced by weather. Cold fronts and snow accelerate both, and hot, dry conditions tend to set the rut back. A cold, stormy weather system early in November may be the catalyst that kicks off intense rutting. I've witnessed several such events, and the same thing happens with elk.

A mule deer buck "tests" a doe by standing so near to her as she beds that she rises and moves off. He then sniffs where she'd been lying, often exhibiting lip-curl, or "flehmen." Flehmen is the facial expression resulting from interpretation of the female's scent. The Jacobsen's Organ, located on the buck's palate, directly enervates the olfactory center of the brain. During flehmen, the organ opens and allows scent in.

The buck also tests the doe by approaching in the low stretch position, common in many ungulates, in which the neck is outstretched while the buck laps his nostrils with the tongue and makes low, variable vocalizations. This may catch the doe's interest, and she'll stand and stare.

The buck tries to "chin" or touch the doe with his chin or throat. If the doe stands, he averts his stare. Normally, the doe will move off and the buck will follow and attempt the process again. With luck and patience, the doe will eventually squat and urinate; then

This buck is browsing on grasses and forbs.

the buck will sniff the urine and exhibit flehmen. If she's not approaching estrus, the buck loses interest.

Bucks stimulate does to urinate through aggressive behavior, too, as do elk and other large mammals. In this case, the buck's posture becomes stiff and he may walk toward the doe in an exaggerated manner, or he may rush the doe, often while vocalizing. The doe rushes off. If she doesn't, he's liable to injure her since the buck is in an aggressive mood. Older does frequently have antler scars from this type of encounter. The buck repeats until the doe finally urinates just to get rid of her persistent suitor.

Does may be severely harried by small bucks during the rut. If there's an adult buck around, does may seek his attention just to keep younger bucks away. Adult bucks will not tolerate other courting bucks, even small ones that stand little chance of breeding. However, the adult stud buck will not always be in attendance, and then subordinate bucks will resume courting.

A buck makes many mounting attempts or actual mounts before successful copulation. Probably these attempts stimulate does to ovulate. Copulation or ejaculation is usually accomplished with one pelvic thrust; the buck leaps up and forward and violently propels the doe ahead, causing the couple to separate. On several occasions I've witnessed the buck thrust two to five times, perhaps because he was unsuccessful the first time. In any case, copulation isn't a drawn-out affair.

Early in the season a "hot" female may have to court the male. This also occurs in other large mammals; I've witnessed the same thing in Alaskan moose, African lions, and less frequently in wapiti. Late in the rut, bucks may be so exhausted they show little interest in an estrous doe without active courting on her part.

Small, subordinate bucks may hang around a breeding pair and occasionally attempt to interrupt the proceedings. Usually, the breeding buck chases them off. Occasionally, the interloper is ignored until the business at hand is finished.

On ranges with an adequate population of adult bucks, most do not breed. The majority of matings are by one or perhaps two bucks. Most bucks are sufficiently intimidated in pre-rut encounters with the local stud bucks that they do not attempt breeding. Even if they do, they may become reintimidated by scenting the stud buck again

A young buck harrying does during the rut.

or by additional brief skirmishes with him. Some robust and healthy adult bucks never mate. They may have become so intimidated earlier in the season or in an earlier year that they become "psychological castrates." Possibly they were beaten in a battle years earlier and have opted out of the breeding-season melee altogether.

In my observations, there's a correlation between even, nicely formed antlers and breeding-season competition among adult bucks. If there's a preponderance of balanced antlers, chances are that range has few serious battles between adult bucks, which also may indicate a too-low population of adult males. Northern Utah is an example; few bucks there are nontypical. Over three decades, I've killed scores of adult bucks, and only one of them was nontypical in antler formation. He had eleven points on the right antler and six on the left; he also had a deep, old injury on the left shoulder, apparently from an antler tine. Predictably, the eleven-point antler was on the side opposite the injury. The area has a low population of adult bucks, primarily because of dense human population, human disturbances on winter range, and open hunting seasons with no limits on number of deer permits sold. In many places in Utah, deer have been a lucrative cash crop, and it was politically unpopular to limit hunting tags. The few adult bucks do not have to risk battling as often, and so there are fewer deformed antlers.

True mule deer battles are rare. As mentioned earlier, they are so violent that it costs both the victor and loser too much to be of evolutionary value. Would-be suitors are normally intimidated in pre-rut encounters such as sparring matches, in which bucks engage antlers and almost playfully shove each other about. Lesser bucks learn who the stronger one is and so do not waste energy and risk serious injury later on. Serious battles during the rut are most often caused by the appearance of a previously unknown and therefore untested buck from outside the area. Since the established buck has not yet intimidated the newcomer, a serious battle may result.

I've witnessed several bona fide mule deer battles that had fatal consequences. In all of them, the victim was gored in the chest or abdominal cavity and died either during the night or the next day from hemorrhage or possibly peritonitis. In Yellowstone I was

A doe browses new oak-scrub leaves in summer in Colorado.

photographing at close range a big buck that was courting a female. I was perhaps twenty yards from the immense buck when he turned and "roared" at me—it sounded much like the aggressive vocalization of an angry mother moose or the rutting roar of a red stag. I immediately looked for a tree to climb and, while making for one, noticed another adult buck walking down the slope toward the breeding buck, shifting from one foreleg to another in an exaggerated side-to-side manner. The courting buck had roared not at me but at the newcomer; I'd just been between the two. I still shinnied up a lodge pole pine, accidentally dropping my expensive single-lens reflex camera in a muddy seep.

The bucks circled each other slowly, keeping a sideways profile to show off their body size and antlers, as ungulates frequently do. They squared off and engaged antlers. After a vigorous shoving match that lasted about ten seconds, the newcomer disengaged, jumped off a few yards, and averted his gaze, thereby ending the encounter. He walked rapidly over the ridge, with the dominant buck following fifty yards behind.

I witnessed a more serious battle near Tower Junction, also in Yellowstone National Park. I was photographing one November when I spotted a big buck on a sagebrush slope. Another buck stood skylighted on the ridgeline. Judging by body language, the buck on the ridge was uncertain and obviously the newcomer. Eventually, he walked down to meet the stud buck and they engaged antlers with a rush and a clatter. After a vigorous, violent shoving match up and down the slope that lasted, I suppose, seven or eight minutes, with neither getting the better of it, the newcomer tripped over brush. While he was down, the resident buck disengaged antlers in a fraction of a second and gored the newcomer in the side for several moments before the victim could regain his feet and retreat. The loser loped down the slope, and by the time he reached the river he was trotting in a wobbly manner. The winner followed. I examined the blood on the snow, and it was bright orangish and frothy, indicating the buck had been gored in the lungs, a fatal injury.

Though the resident dominant buck breeds most does, outsider and usually younger bucks attempt and occasionally succeed in breeding. This, however, is the exception.

On ranges with adequate populations of adult bucks, careful late-rut and post-rut observations indicate a high proportion of broken antlers. Logically, in places with few adults, post-rut surveys indicate significantly fewer broken antlers on mature bucks. Still, broken antlers don't necessarily indicate other adult bucks on the range; the antlers may have been broken while the wearer battered brush. I once watched a Coues whitetail buck one December in the Huachuca Mountains of southern Arizona; he was so aggressive during the rut that other adults strictly avoided any contact with him. As a result, he took his aggression out by battering brush, cacti, and even large pine deadfalls. By the end of the rut in January, he'd broken off five of his eleven tines and put out one eye. I suppose the same thing may happen with mule deer.

Mule deer expend more energy during the rut than whitetails. They seem to lose more weight and appear exhausted by rut's end, even to the uninitiated. And they are. As noted earlier, mature bucks retreat from other deer and lay up in quiet places free from disturbance. If the retreat is close to high-quality browse, so much the better. The rut may have taken most of the buck's energy reserves, but winter will be the true ordeal.

In other parts of this book I talk about rutting behavior, so I won't repeat myself more than need be. Typically, the local dominant buck either visits various doe groups within his home range or "tends" a single doe group, living nearby and keeping a close watch over them. A mature buck may make a large circuit as he "tests" for receptive does, and may use one trail to complete the circuit every day or two. During this time, he feeds little. He'll stay in a home-range "center area" (more about this later) when not actually testing does. This center area may also be the recovery area after the rut.

When the rut is in full swing, bucks pay little attention to anything else. A friend lives on the upper bench of Ogden, Utah, a city of about one hundred thousand humans. He often sees adult bucks pursuing does down the street with little regard for human activity. I teach at Weber State University in the same city and have seen rutting deer in the predawn as I went to my office. On one occasion, a large buck chased a smaller one up the steps in front of the English building. Which, I guess, shows why adult mule deer bucks get so exhausted during the rut that they are disadvantaged entering the winter bottleneck (a term used in biology that describes the heavy mortality of winter).

Since mule deer have been pressured out of better, traditional winter ranges and into more marginal ranges, survival decreases. Deer are forced to live where there is poor food, less cover, more exposure to winter weather, and increased encounters with dogs and people. Mortality, particularly in mature bucks, can't help but increase.

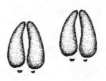

Chapter 2

General Ecology

RANGE MANAGEMENT

Given our discussion of winter survival, the winter bottleneck, and the effects of exposure to humans and their machines and dogs, it seems obvious that humans must preserve winter habitat if the decline in mule deer numbers is to be slowed. And we humans must not only preserve it in general but also preserve many pieces far enough away from human activity to allow for buck survival throughout the winter. This means keeping humans out and destroying dogs that get onto winter range before they have run deer, not after. It may mean patrolling for predators, too. All of which requires constant monitoring by conservation agencies, perhaps by air to minimize human impact.

Just any piece of range at the base of a mountain will not necessarily do. The range must have the right feed, exposure, and cover. Deer survive poorly on a winter diet consisting only of sagebrush; however, they do well on sagebrush combined with other browse such as serviceberry, bitterbrush, mountain and curleaf mahogany, and dead forbs and grasses. Deer should have both escape cover and protection from winter storms. Rough country helps mule deer survive predation, especially from coyotes; in gentle country, coyotes can run down mule deer, especially big bucks exhausted from rutting. On a steep, rough slope, even tired bucks can outpace a coyote.

I am generally against predator control, and I dislike mentioning it as a management tool. However, since the right winter range for mule deer is scarce, it may be prudent to manage predators on critical winter ranges. The best way to control mountain lions is by increasing hunting permits in the local area. I suppose trapping would be the most conscionable way to control coyotes. Poisons should be out of the question since they don't selectively kill only coyotes.

Some state conservation agencies are controlling human use of the land on critical winter ranges. In the Middle Fork (of the Ogden River) area of northern Utah where I live, the Division of Wildlife Resources has at long last closed this critical winter range to all human activity, even hiking and cross-country skiing. Previously it had been off-limits to motorized travel, but hikers, horse riders, and skiers frequently had dogs with them, and even the silliest lap dog is a hunter deep inside. I watched dogs harry deer and elk on several occasions. Once, a cow moose killed a dog.

While this coyote's menu is 90 percent rodents, he does occasionally kill a fawn or older deer stressed by the winter.

Deer may migrate as much as fifty miles to winter range. In the process, they cross highways, and we all have seen too many carcasses along roads. Some states have devised clever deer fences to slow migration in an area, force deer into a safer crossing, or funnel them underneath freeways. Wyoming is such a state. Mostly, however, this approach seems too costly to state legislatures. Only when increased human mortality or injury comes into the picture and the problem becomes politically correct is anything done. Unfortunately, too often the remedy is increasing deer hunting permits, which reduces even further a species that is, from an evolutionary standpoint, on the way out. This is like offering water to a drowning man.

Establishing sufficient winter range for existing deer populations seems out of the question. Humankind will not cease to breed or to build golf courses, shopping malls, tract housing, and university campuses, nor will we look elsewhere for our projects if winter deer range happens to be the cheaper land. We hold the mule deer's fate in our hands. Deer can be saved in pockets here and there, or disappear rapidly. Hunters have the most to lose and are the most committed to mule deer conservation; more commitment and more noise to legislators might preserve the mule deer.

BIRTH

Like elk, mature male mule deer breed earlier in the season than lesser bucks. The gestation period for mule deer runs between 189 and 210 days, according to several studies. My original elk study showed that the peak of rutting activity occurred about September 20 in an average year. The dominant bull gathered a harem and bred the cows that came into estrus during his tenure as harem master; however, the rigors of rutting took their toll and the dominant bull was often replaced by another bull within a week to ten days. The new dominant bull bred any cows that became receptive while he was there. On undisturbed range—Yellowstone, for example—as often as not a

These bucks were taken on opening day in the "old days" when northern Utah still had some big ones. The buck on the right is mine and has a spread of 33 inches.

third satellite bull took over the harem and bred what cows he could. All of this happens within two to three weeks. In a healthy elk herd with sufficient mature bulls, yearling and two-year-old bulls will not get a chance to mate. However, on much public land, hunting and natural mortality cull mature bulls. As a result, most breeding is accomplished by young bulls. The stickler here is that they breed approximately a month later, and so the young are born a month later in the spring and go into the winter in a less mature state, thereby decreasing winter survival.

Apparently, the same thing happens with mule deer: In overhunted ranges or areas where other causes of mortality have reduced mature buck survival, yearling bucks may do most or all of the breeding. The fawns are dropped later in the spring and are too small going into a severe winter to survive. State game agencies must manage mule deer herds to protect numbers of mature bucks in a population. This could be most effectively accomplished by lottery hunting, at least for mature deer. If the overall population is generally too dense and adversely affecting range quality, more does and small bucks could be culled.

In the intermountain region of the West, most mule deer fawns are born between mid-May and mid-June. In a mild spring, the earlier a deer is born the better, because that means it will be larger when entering the winter bottleneck. However, it's of no immediate advantage to be born too early since the early spring vegetation is still poor, there's less hiding cover, and late storms cause mortality. If a fawn is born too late—and I've found fawns born in late July—it is just too small to survive winter.

New fawns I've weighed ranged from seven to twelve pounds, and males weighed 20 to 25 percent more than females. Weight increases rapidly, and among the few cases where I was able to check the weights of known-age fawns, a week-old male weighed eighteen pounds (up from ten pounds at birth), a week-old female weighed sixteen pounds (8½ pounds at birth), and a ten-day-old female weighed nineteen pounds. Generally, fawns double their birth weight in two weeks and quadruple it in a month. Skeletal and muscle growth is rapid during the first growing season, but

This desert tom's scats were full of javelina hair and bones.

it stops during the winter; then, food intake is converted to fat for winter survival, or used directly for heat and metabolism.

LOCOMOTION

The mule deer is at home in rough country because he can use it to his advantage. As mentioned earlier, a coyote can run down a mule deer in gentle country, but throw in rocks, downed trees, and steep slopes, and no North American predator has a chance. The mule deer's ease in rough country is at least partly the result of a peculiar gait that has unfortunately become known as the stot. The stot was first described in African antelope species, such as the springbok of southern Africa and the Thomson gazelle of eastern Africa.

In these species, the animal prances about and exhibits spectacular bounds straight into the air, often with exaggerated

Likable rogue Homero Canedo Carballo with a buck taken off a Sonora ranch, probably without the owner's knowledge. That way, Homero didn't have to pay a harvest fee to the owner.

attitudes of the head and neck. The stot in African antelope is not used to move over rough country in a hurry; rather, it is used in a few courtship displays or in the presence of a predator, of which Africa has its fair share. For example, a healthy male Tommy will bound into the air in the presence of a cheetah as if to say, "Look at me—see how high I can jump! You don't stand a chance of catching such a healthy, prime animal!" I've seen springbok, a slightly larger antelope, do the same thing in the presence of a cheetah in Namibia. Other antelope species perform similarly in Africa.

Hunting writers, and now even biologists, have taken to using the term stot to describe the mule deer's stiff-legged bound (my term, which is, I admit, less poetic), a gait used to get over rough country in a hurry, not to impress predators or to court females. Perhaps "stot" should not be used for both (or all three) situations. For example, African antelope never stot to flee, in my observations.

The mule deer's stiff-legged bound (or stot, if you prefer) is critical for survival. It allows the animal to live in rougher country away from competitive whitetails, which do not bound in such a way. It allows them to escape predators efficiently in that rough country. It's an extremely energy-costly gait, and an alarmed buck won't use it for any length of time. However, it will leave a coyote or wolf behind almost immediately on rocky and steep slopes or in thick blowdown forests. I won't go further into mule deer gaits, since they are dealt with in a later chapter about hunting.

BODY SIZE

A mature buck of 4½ years of age will weigh at least 200 pounds on the hoof, and usually at least that weight field-dressed. I've killed more than sixty mature mule deer bucks in Canada, Mexico, and six western states in three-plus decades of hunting deer. More than a few were collected in remote country and had to be cut up and packed out on my back; these, of course, I could not weigh. However, nearly half did get weighed. All of these deer were at least 4½ years old, and one was 10½. Except for two bucks, a 4½-year-old from Nevada's Ruby Mountains and a 4½-year-old from Weber County, Utah, all weighed over 200 pounds field-dressed. One, aged at 7½ years old, weighed 268 pounds field-dressed after a day and a half of drying. He probably weighed at least 340 pounds on the hoof. The average field-dressed weight of those bucks was 213 pounds.

In 1986 I killed one monstrous buck in northern Utah. Unfortunately, I had to cut the buck into pieces and pack him out of a huge gorge on my back. I strongly suspect that buck weighed well over 360 pounds on the hoof, and probably closer to 400. He had huge antlers, too.

The few does I have weighed averaged 118 pounds field-dressed. Most of these were mature animals, and most were collected in northern Utah. As a student majoring in wildlife biology, I worked at a state checking station during deer season. My undergraduate project at the time involved deer and elk weights, so I had the guys at the station weigh as many deer as they could. Unfortunately, we simply did not have time to accurately age the deer, though our estimations

In bounding mule deer, hind hoofs print ahead of forehoofs and the left prints slightly ahead of the right.

were pretty good. So I can say with confidence that the average mature mule deer doe weighs over 150 pounds on the hoof.

I once killed a 2½-year-old buck in western Colorado that field-dressed at 221 pounds. He'd been feeding in alfalfa fields all summer. His antlers were normal for a buck of his age.

DIGESTION

All deer are ruminants, as are mountain sheep, elk, caribou, antelope, and goats. They're cud-chewers and possess a four-chambered gut. The complex digestive system helps process healthy quantities of coarse, nearly indigestible vegetation.

The four chambers are the rumen, reticulum, omasum, and abomasum. Freshly cropped browse goes first to the rumen, which holds approximately two gallons of undigested material. Fermentation begins here. Once the deer has filled the first chamber, it seeks out cover and hides, to digest the browse in comparative safety and comfort. In hiding, the deer regurgitates the material in the rumen and rechews it. The regurgitated portion is called the cud. A deer may chew its cud even while dozing. It's an automatic process, though cud-chewing ceases when the deer is threatened.

The abomasum has a smooth lining and a few elongated folds to increase absorptive area. Food materials in the abomasum are digested into a "soup" that is absorbed as it passes through more than sixty-two feet of intestines. The indigestible portion is compacted by muscular action and formed into feces, or droppings. It takes a bit more than twenty-four hours for cropped vegetation to pass completely through the mule deer.

Most members of the deer family, Cervidae, lack a gall bladder. Some physiologists believe this lack of gall allows deer to eat a variety of plants toxic to other ruminants, notably domestic sheep and cattle.

The ruminant strategy has two big survival advantages. First, the complexity of the system allows the use of coarse, hard-to-digest vegetation. Second, ruminants can crop a paunch-full of

Bucks browsing in the open during daylight hours—you seldom see them this way unless they know hunting season is over.

vegetation in short order and retire to cover and safety to complete the digestion process.

Obviously, deer eat different things in different places. Desert mule deer feed almost exclusively on plants that more northerly mule deer never see, such as mesquite, certain species of manzanita, and cactus fruit. And bucks in central British Columbia browse different shrubs than do those in Colorado and Nevada. It's nearly impossible to catalog all the species of plants mule deer eat, and I've already mentioned in this tome a number of important varieties.

DISTRIBUTION

The whitetail is the oldest deer species in North America, with fossils dating back four million years. According to paleontologist Bjorn Kurteen, fossil forms of the whitetail are identical to modern forms.

Mule deer, on the other hand, are relative newcomers, first appearing on the planet about ten thousand years ago. DNA studies indicate they're a hybrid combining the whitetail and the coastal black-tailed deer.

The whitetail is a survivor, having made it through several great waves of North American extinctions. He's adaptable and, since he hasn't changed in four million years, nearly perfectly evolved (though not as perfectly as the crocodiles, which have changed little in 300 million years!).

During those extinctions, most of the large mammalian species disappeared—the mammoth and mastodon, the giant stags, dire wolves, saber-toothed cats, and scores of others. Those species that did survive the extinctions, having to deal with considerably less competition and fewer predators, thrived and spread across the continent. The blacktail spread east from the West Coast, and the whitetail spread west from the east. Where they hybridized, they produced a newcomer species, the mule deer. DNA studies show that the original successful hybridization was between female whitetails and male blacktails, traceable through the female's mitochondrial DNA. Now, ten thousand years sounds like forever to you and me, but it's scarcely a blink of an eye by evolutionary standards. The mule deer is the newest member of the deer family.

Allowing for its many and often questionable races, the mule deer's range is roughly from the southern Yukon Territory in northern Canada south to the northern two-thirds of Baja California and the western parts of Chihuahua in Mexico. In the east, the mule deer gets into western Nebraska, the Dakotas, and Kansas. In the west, it ranges into western California, where it is displaced by the coastal version, the black-tailed deer.

Mule deer live in the plains and sandhills of the Midwest—as long as they're only lightly pressured by coyotes—and in the alpine basins of the Rockies. They inhabit the flat deserts of northern Sonora and marshy forests in British Columbia.

The mule deer is larger than its close cousin, the coastal blacktail, which includes the Columbian and Sitka blacktails.

The mule deer produces larger antlers and, where ranges overlap, is dominant to black-tailed deer (as it is to whitetails).

I'm not going to dwell on the races of mule deer, simply because there's sound biological doubt that they are true races at all. For the most part, any race differences in mule deer seem to be based mainly on size. The California and the Inyo versions are deemed smaller than the Rocky Mountain mule deer. Other differences involve respective habitats, especially food plants and climate, but also soil nutrients. Slight differences exist in the amount of black on the tails. However, individual differences occur in any population. Angolans and Scandinavians all belong to the same species and subspecies, *Homo sapiens sapiens*. Likewise, a mule deer is a mule deer,

This buck seems to be posing.

This buck is "testing" a doe to see if she's in estrus, or heat.

whether from Mexico, southern California, or northern British Columbia. Blacktail varieties of the genus *Odocoileus* are probably legitimate subspecies, and almost certainly are the ancestors of all mule deer.

The blacktail is much smaller than the mule deer and has a blackish tail more similar to a whitetail's in external appearance, though not as large.

The desert mule deer is simply a desert-living Rocky Mountain mule deer. In some places they're smaller in body size, but this is a reflection of a drier climate and less plant growth than the animals enjoy farther north. They also seem lighter in pelage, but this, too, is a reflection of environment and more exposure to sunlight. Forest mule deer, too, are of darker pelage. Even among bucks in one basin in Wyoming, some animals may look as light as most desert mule deer while others in the same band are nearly as dark as a blacktail buck.

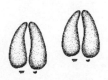

Chapter 3

Hunting Basics

GETTING READY

I view physical conditioning as the most important aspect of getting ready to stalk trophy mule deer—for several reasons: If I am doing it right, I normally shoot game at close range, so rifle accuracy isn't that important. It's tough to scour canyons and ridges day after day, searching for a respectable buck, if you're in poor physical condition. And finally, to be fully alert mentally, which is critical in close-in tracking or stalking, you can't be worried about a charley horse or cardiac arrhythmia (chess is a mental game, and most grand masters maintain a regular regime of physical and often intense exercise).

I exercise throughout the year because it makes me feel better and so that I won't have to endure the agony of concentrated workouts before hunting season. During the winter, I snowshoe or cross-country ski several times a week, usually onto big-game winter range where I can check for trophy bucks and otherwise enjoy myself. If the weather is too bad, I use the treadmill or stepping machine (I much prefer outdoor exercise, though others, my better half included, prefer indoor workouts while watching videos or listening to Shania Twain). I supplement the machine work with sets of pushups and sit-ups four or five times a week. In summer, I hike, run, and cut firewood. See your doctor for what's right for you.

I collected this buck while in high school. Mom beams proudly.

Other tips: If you're over forty and out of shape, let a physician decide on your exercise regime. It beats dying. After a summer and autumn of exercise, rest three days before a tough hunt; if you must do something then, go for easy walks. Load up on pasta before a rough day afield. Carbohydrates are full of energy.

The idea behind a hunting trip is to do what you enjoy most, and you won't enjoy it if you're massaging charley horses out of cramped thighs or waving away the black spots in front of your eyes. Better to plan ahead and get in shape. After a long summer, I brush up on bush skills by scouting where I plan to hunt. It's also time to enjoy camping, break in new hunting boots and toughen up your feet, and shake down other gear. Hunting time is too limited and precious to have to fool around with blisters or binoculars that fog up.

I wander the canyons and ridges, checking for deer spoor and other signs of their passage. I try not to disturb game while I scout. If I find a concentration of sign, I back away from the place. No need to see the animal and risk spooking him to know he's there (look elsewhere in this book for detailed info on deer sign).

I age tracks, since it does little good to get my hopes up over a two-month-old track. I age my own tracks to get a feel for how quickly sign ages in a given spot, given existing humidity and weather conditions. I search for nibbled twigs, cropped forbs, and cut grasses. They indicate where deer feed and may promise a good place for a potential ambush.

When I'm sure there's a nice buck in that stand of fir in the next canyon, I kick back and throw another piece of deadfall on the campfire and lean back and dream of the coming season.

Sight in your rifle. NEVER go hunting without checking out your rifle's zero. I've honed my hunting skills enough over the years that most of the bucks I kill are very near, and marksmanship isn't critical. Still, I make sure my deer rifle (these days I use a 7mm-08 for mule deer) is hitting 2½ inches high at 100 yards, which means I can hold in the center of the chest from point-blank range out to 300 yards without worrying about holding high or low for distance. If my gun won't hold under an inch-and-a-half group at 100 yards, I want

A Wyoming deer camp.

to know why. Once, I found that a stock had warped and was causing uneven vibrations; another time, the outside temperature was just too warm for the very light barrel on my Remington Model Seven to cool enough between spaced shots. After you've got the rifle shooting just so on the range, practice under field conditions. Since I often spend time tracking deer or surprising them in heavy timber, shooting is fast. I snapshoot in brush, so I've invented various types of moving targets. One of the best is a tire with a cardboard or plywood center rolled down a hill by a buddy. This snap-shooting, moving-target practice is far more valuable than splitting apples at 300 yards; I've never had the chance to shoot an apple at that distance while hunting deer.

Gun gurus, and there are thousands, have written everything there is to know about ballistics, guns, and shooting, and there's little left to say. So I won't say it here.

To improve your chances of collecting a big mule deer, at least know something about their biology. To a surprising degree, the best deer hunters are biologists or naturalists. Elsewhere in this volume, I've included information on mule deer biology that's important to the hunter, and some that's interesting to students of mule deer. Whichever category you fall into, it pays to correlate what you read with personal observations. National parks and other refuges in most western states and Canada offer excellent chances to see big mule deer just carrying on in life; often, this kind of observation will teach a hunter more than he'll learn in many hunting seasons.

TACTICS

If a particular tactic—tracking, for example—works well for one hunter, he tends to use only that method. Some hunters use only one tactic over their entire career. More may use two tactics, but few are well-rounded hunters. Such single-mindedness is fine if the tactic always worked, but sooner or

Deer quarters hang in the trees, and it's time to kick back and enjoy camp

later the hunter will run into conditions that require other tactics. Since that person is not versatile, he'll lose an opportunity to collect a buck.

Many guides are as rigid in hunting-method use as most dudes are. While hunting whitetails in Saskatchewan a decade or so ago, I had absolutely no luck by parking in tree stands or by driving. Rattling was slightly more successful—I brought in two small bucks. But I was after a trophy. One dawn after a fresh snow, we found immense tracks. The guide didn't think tracking would work. Either he had never tried it or it hadn't worked when he did. I'd had great luck trailing a variety of species. The guide encouraged me to hunt elsewhere, and since he was the pro and supposedly knew better, I acquiesced. In retrospect—which is always perfect hindsight—I'm convinced that if left to my own devices and inclinations, I'd at least have seen that big buck.

Years ago a neighbor seemed to collect a good buck every season. He would locate a trail through a saddle that led into a steep gorge to which deer retreated during hunting season. But one season his tactic failed. In later seasons it produced less consistently. The reason is that more hunters probed the area and fewer bucks survived to trophy proportions. Those that did were smart enough not to run through the saddle. By the second day of the hunt, his odds of seeing a good buck were greatly reduced since 90 percent of the deer he had killed in the saddle in the past were collected on opening day. We later figured he had about a 10 percent chance of getting a buck on the second day; if he didn't get one then, he simply didn't get one and gave up. If he'd felt more comfortable using other methods, he might have still-hunted into that gorge and killed a buck.

More so than ever before, the good bucks are fewer and harder to kill, so you've got to have more than a couple of tactics in your daypack. Flexibility is today's answer. If you're capable of using a handful of tactics with equal ability, your odds of killing a trophy buck quintuple.

Still-hunting remains the old standby and my favorite method of hunting most game species. When still-hunting, I drift through the forest or brush, scanning ahead, listening intently, searching for something out of the ordinary. I move as slowly as possible and try to sense a buck before he detects me.

Still-hunt into the wind whenever possible, of course. If it is not possible, still-hunt across the wind or, on occasion, even downwind. Strong winds aren't quite so defeating, because they scatter scent and even if a buck picks up a molecule of human scent, he probably won't be able to locate you. A disadvantage of still-hunting in strong winds is that bucks are very alert and apt to run with little provocation since they can't hear approaching danger, which makes them very nervous.

In thick timber or brush, still-hunting is a close-range affair. Be prepared to shoot quickly and at close range. More often than not, a bedded buck will see you before or at the same time you see him. As soon as he's certain he's been located, he'll jump and run in a shower of breaking branches and splintering brush.

In my experience, still-hunting in timber is a combination of tactics that may include tracking, stalking, and others. If you're

This mess is a partially butchered deer. I'm in the process of boning him out so I can pack him eight miles and three thousand feet up out of a horrendous gorge.

doing it correctly, you'll encounter deer at close range. Don't forget that since mule deer have perhaps the best hearing of any game animal on the continent (remember those big ears), plus keen smell and sight, getting close for a shot requires constant and total concentration.

One cold November day in Wyoming many years ago, I eased through a stand of lodge pole pines trying to collect a buck I had been after for a week. Deer, elk, and moose tracks were imprinted on the trails along which I stalked. I knew the big buck used a particular trail to travel to and from bedding and feeding areas.

By this time in my still-young hunting career, I was well aware that mature bucks typically bed on the downwind side of their backtrail so as to scent and spot danger following. That dawn, I had a feeling I'd learned never to discount—the feeling of action to come. I'd been still-hunting slowly along the trail for an hour, listening, scanning, even smelling, and once I distinctly smelled bull elk. I thought I heard the rutting "roar" of a mulie buck, but it was too far away to be certain. I somehow sensed something off to one side and, as I turned toward it, detected movement. Antlers flicked above a deadfall, but they belonged to a smaller buck than I wanted. I heard a grunt that was half roar from just above, and then the big buck rushed downslope toward the smaller one. The bigger buck was so angry at the young upstart, he didn't see the movement of the rifle to my shoulder, or hear the shot that broke his neck.

Waiting for mule deer, while not as popular as stand hunting for whitetails, is a tactic often used by hunters. Still, mule deer standers tend to be less sophisticated than whitetail standers.

Most mule deer hunters select stands that look good to them rather than to the deer. Instead, select a stand that will be inconspicuous to the buck, not necessarily one that's out of the wind and against a sunny rock. Typically, mule deer

Rattling for bucks does work, but it's practically unheard of for mule deer.

bucks bed in thick timber or brush and feed in open places. Trails between bedding and feeding areas are good places for an ambush or to wait as others drive deer toward you. Mule deer bucks use one to four trails to travel between feeding and bedding sites. Frequently enough to keep things interesting, a buck will leave his timbered bedding area on one trail and return to it on another. Confirm this by checking tracks; then, in the morning, wait along the trail that goes into the timber, and, in the evening, the one that leaves.

Locate your stand or "hide" downwind of the trail you're watching. In the dawn, downwind normally means downhill or downslope since the air is cold, dense, and drifting downhill. The reverse is true before sunset, however. Wind direction may abruptly reverse itself as soon as the sun sets and the air chills.

As that opening-day saddle hunter found out, ambushing along escape trails can be incredibly productive. Bucks use escape trails to run from predators, like man. Such trails will normally lead to a thick stand of trees or a rugged gorge, places a buck will feel safe. Since bucks are often intent on escaping hunters and other danger, they're not as alert for danger along their escape routes. Escape trails are useful when other hunters are stirring up the country. Wait downwind of one and out of sight.

I've found one escape trail that works in reverse. After the opening-weekend melee, deer are anxious to return to their home ranges and assume comfortable routines. I found a place where deer return from a big, steep, and safe canyon; they usually begin to return by Wednesday following opening weekend, and I've collected several good bucks there.

"Pushing" or "driving" is more commonly used in whitetail country than for mulies. It's just as effective, though, in mule deer habitat. Driving involves pushing animals from one place to anywhere one or more posted hunters can get a shot. In mule deer country, good places to post hunters include canyon heads, saddles, river-bottom goosenecks, and brush "islands" in otherwise open terrain. Driving may be effective in any type of weather. One drawback is that it may permanently frighten a wise old buck out of his home place.

Posting hunters at canyon heads works well. Standers form a half-moon crescent around the canyon head and down the sides if feasible. Then drivers, afoot or ahorse, push up the canyon toward the hunters waiting above.

Back before trophy buck hunting in northern Utah had pretty well had it, I sometimes posted myself on someone else's drive, without either their knowledge or permission. It was usually a big drive, with hunters posted at the head of the canyon and in a saddle that led into another drainage. Horseback drivers began a mile or so down the canyon and pushed up toward those waiting above. Eventually, the place sounded like a Middle East war zone, but nearly all the bucks killed were small ones (I'd often see hunters pack the deer out later in the day). I would post myself overlooking a small ravine midway up the canyon; it was so thick it was nearly invisible to anyone not specifically looking for it. A game trail ran up its bottom. Over the years, a score or so bucks retreated up the ravine, and I killed two adult bucks there.

River bottoms make good places to drive or push deer. In the West, rivers frequently turn on themselves as they twist through spectacular canyons. Peninsulas between channels of the river are often hot places to drive deer; hunters push from the base of a peninsula toward its tip, where one or more hunters wait. Deer often break from the peninsula and splash across the river.

Other types of thick river-bottom brush also provide ideal spots for driving deer. The more hunters, the better the chances that someone will make a kill. For my purposes here and for most Westerners, "brushing" is similar to driving except it's not necessary to post sitters. One person can do it, and I've killed an awful lot of deer using this method solo.

Discussed later in the book is the form of brushing called, among other things, the stop-pause-start tactic. It works well when you still-hunt up a small canyon or ravine, preferably above the brush so you can see the opposite slope. You pause across from a likely looking cover, perhaps to eat lunch, glass as you eat, then start again. If a buck is lying up in that likely looking patch of brush, he may get nervous enough to jump when you start out again, thereby giving you a shot. This simple method has collected me several real wall-hangers.

Another brushing method employed more commonly in the West that I like is what I call "platoon brushing." In Utah, where I've hunted most of my mule deer, gangs of horsebackers congregate to drive entire drainages. These platoons are often large—once, I watched twenty-six horseback hunters push up Magpie Canyon in Weber County. They simply ride through brush and flush deer onto the opposite slope or upcanyon and hopefully into other members of their group. There's lots of shooting, most of it is hurried, and too many deer are wounded and escape. Usually, no one dismounts to check for signs of wounded deer. It spoils the day for other hunters in the area, too.

The best and most effective way of brushing out bucks has been to still-hunt upcanyon through timbered or brushy north slopes. The idea is to flush the deer from the timber below and onto the open opposite slope. It used to be effective back in the '60s, but with the nocturnal habits of today's adult bucks, it doesn't usually work—except for young, naive "meat" bucks.

For me, tracking is the most satisfying way of collecting a trophy buck. It demands patience, finesse, intelligence, and single-minded determination. And faith. You have to be aware always of wind direction, buck habits, and where you put your feet. On several occasions, I spent days tracking down big bucks. The narrative of such a hunt appears later in the book, but briefly, I spent three days trailing a monster in and out of canyons, across plateaus, through timber, and across rock slides until I was miles from camp.

That trail taught me more about tracking in three days than I could have learned otherwise in three years. I found where big bucks are likely to bed (where they can watch and scent their backtrail), what they eat (in that area, mountain mahogany, bitterbrush, forbs, sagebrush, grass seedheads), when they move during hunting season (at night), and how to find a trail again after I'd lost it (by moving in ever-widening circles). Near the end, the droppings became moist, soft, and pliable—fresh. I jumped the buck from a tangle of chokecherry, and he bounded downhill and across a stream, and as he started up the opposite slope, I collected him.

The "loop method" of trailing is dealt with elsewhere in the book in considerable detail. However, I should talk about it here, too, since it is one of the basic methods of tracking mule deer and highly productive. The hunter follows the trail but makes loops on its downwind side since that is where the buck is likely to bed down.

If the loops are just right, he might catch the buck from a direction in which the animal does not expect trouble. If the hunter simply follows the trail, the buck will probably both see and scent him since the deer expects hunters and more sophisticated predators to follow his trail. Loop-method shooting is close and quick.

Rattling antlers together for whitetails has worked for centuries. Under the right conditions, it works as well for mule deer (ditto for elk and moose), though it will not necessarily bring the buck to you. The best times to make things happen by rattling are just before, during, and after the rut. In November and December, try rattling if other methods don't work. The first time I found it successful for mule deer, I tried it more or less as a lark. I found a dead buck, broke the antlers from the skull, and continued on my way. Later in the day, I located a buck's rubs and fresh tracks. I clattered the antlers together, waited some minutes, then clattered again. To make a long story shorter, a big buck as angry as I'd ever seen a deer crashed from nearby brush and bounded straight for me. I shot in self-defense, I think.

Cheri is navigating the canoe down a small western river as we hunt deer. Note the antlers on the duffel!

The most complete mule deer hunter is the guy who can use all the basic tactics when given situations call for them. Versatility makes for wide smiles for the trophy buck hunter.

LOOKING FOR DEER

I won't say exactly how long ago this happened, but back before my voice changed, I killed my first mule deer buck with a war-surplus .303 Enfield. Since that time, as mentioned earlier, I've collected more than sixty fully mature bucks. I like to think I've learned something in all those decades when I've wandered about in mule deer habitat.

First, let me cite some more of the basics. All animals rely on plants, especially herbivores like mule deer. And all plant communities are constantly in some sort of succession, or change. That shrubby hill where deer feed, for example, is only a temporary plant community; probably a hundred years from now (maybe three hundred) it may be a forest of lodge pole pine or quaking aspen. A few hundred years after that, it could be an old-growth coniferous forest. These successional stages (so called because they succeed one another toward a final, or climax, stage) are constantly changing. Once they reach the climax stage—a more-or-less stable plant community characteristic of that place— succession slows so much as to seem stable in the view of mortal and short-lived humans. Of course, this is relative because every system on the planet is changing (plants and animals and other organisms are adapting to acid rain, global warming, ATVs and other human abuse, increasing aridity, etc.), and therefore nothing is stable. Organisms that stop changing or adapting become extinct. Those that survive must adapt to the changes.

Back to deer. Most deer species are successional species; they thrive in mid-successional plant communities like shrubs or brush that are midway between open grasslands and old-growth forest (or vice versa). In much of the West, plant succession generally progresses from grasses to forbs to shrubs and tall herbs and climaxes with trees. Deer don't eat trees—

termites eat trees. Likewise, deer don't make heavy use of grasses, and in some locales grasslands may be the climax plant community. Mid-successional plant species—shrubs, brush, forbs, "weeds"—are primary deer browse. "Edge" areas are places that are in transition from one plant community to another; often found there are mountain mahogany, bitterbrush, and other plants deer love. Also important to prey species like mule deer is the fact that these edges are only a hop from cover and safety.

Now that we know where deer feed, there's another important factor in hunting adult bucks: isolation. Isolated places may or may not be remote enough to be considered true wilderness. They may simply be places that most hunters overlook, for one reason or another. If an area gets little hunting pressure and contains lots of "edge," it's a good place to look for a trophy buck. Places may get little hunting pressure simply because they don't look like deer country: The vegetation is too dense, topography isn't conducive to easy hunting, etc. No trophy buck would bed down within half a mile of a dirt road, would he?

On many parts of the continent, good places to stalk mule deer are the "edges" between logging clear-cuts or old burns and stands of timber. Both logging and fires put climax forests or grasslands back to another, earlier stage of succession and create a plant community on which deer feed. While I worked for the U.S. Forest Service years ago, more than 95 percent of the deer and elk I spotted were in these edge areas.

Once, while hunting moose in central British Columbia, we spent all of our time checking old burns. In addition to moose, we spotted scores of mule deer. Clearings in timber caused by excessive soil moisture typical of meadows or marshes may also be good places for mule deer. On that hunt, mule deer we didn't see at the burns were spotted in marshes and meadows. One dawn I stepped out of the wall tent to answer the call of nature and found myself right in the middle of a herd of mule deer. I dodged back through the tent flap, and grabbed the gun, and collected a nice buck. In the dense surrounding spruce forest, we saw no deer and few tracks. Of course, deer retreat to heavy forest for escape and often bed there, especially during storms.

Large areas of blown-down trees, places where insect infestation has killed trees, and other openings in forests are good spots to check out.

In much of the West, beavers create edge by felling trees. Beavers eat the bark of cottonwoods, aspens, and willows, and in cutting them down the animals change forests into open fields and set back succession. In the increased sunlight, successional species proliferate and produce deer food. Years ago I regularly hunted an area of eight or nine acres that beavers had cleared of trees. Not only deer but also elk and Shiras moose browsed in the place. Other animals also were common, some of them hunting the herbivores that concentrated there. I killed two good bucks in the opening— for two reasons: first, because it was again producing deer browse, thanks to the beavers, and second, because it was overlooked by other hunters.

I found a similar place in northern Utah. Beavers had built four small dams in the bottom of a ravine about half a mile from a four-wheel-drive road. They'd cleared back the pines and cottonwoods and created three acres of opening. Since the road was so close, I didn't believe any large buck would be in the canyon. Others thought the same thing.

As a last resort one season, I tried the canyon. I started down the steep slope and through the timber and brush. As I neared the bottom, I sat on a boulder to think it out. The boulder I sat on was substantial and round, good for rolling. After a minute of grunting and heaving, I loosened the boulder and sent it bounding down the slope. As it neared bottom, two forkhorns jumped and bounded across the stream. An instant later a decent buck crashed through the creek and started up the opposite slope through the aspen forest. I was surprised—what was a big buck doing so near a dirt road? Partway up the slope, the buck paused in an

This is the correct way to cross a ridge. Don't skyline, and stay low!

opening between trees. I raised the cross hairs above his backline and squeezed the trigger. The 130-grain .270 bullet shattered the heart at nearly four hundred yards, one of my longer shots. As I climbed down and then up to the buck, I checked for sign of other hunters, and there wasn't any. The place just seemed too obvious to get much hunting pressure, but it had plenty of mid-successional plant food and was a perfect hangout.

Brushy parks breaking up stands of timber, islands of aspen or scrub oak in an ocean of sagebrush or grass, or grass and chaparral communities offer good edge throughout the West. A place near Big Piney, Wyoming, consistently produced big deer for me in the past (I understand it is badly overhunted these days). The terrain was primarily sagebrush on top of the big plateaus, with stands of mixed pines, aspen, and other trees growing on the north-facing slopes of the shallow canyons. The edges between the tangles of trees and the sagebrush produced a variety of palatable deer browse, most notably serviceberry and chokecherry. Most of the deer were found within a few yards of this edge, and probably all of them fed along this edge. They holed up in the trees during daylight. The few bucks that survived (even back then) were largely nocturnal until the snows and cold hit the country, which is one of the coldest places in the United States. These aspen woods, obvious places to hunt in an otherwise barren landscape, got most of the hunting pressure; hunters drove along the opposite rim of the canyon, and when they spotted a deer in the woods, they got out and shot across the canyon. Adult bucks lived elsewhere, except at night when they browsed there.

In the Ruby Range of western Nevada, edge is limited. Stands of aspen, juniper, and other small trees and large shrubs break up the predominant sagebrush-grassland expanses. Most deer concentrate along the edges for food and nearby cover. These obvious places get most of the hunting pressure. For a buck to survive long enough to get some size, he must hide in less obvious areas.

One season, during three days of hunting and a few days of scouting before that, I'd seen plenty of does and small bucks but nothing with any heft to it. I'd scouted the obvious places and found small deer there. One evening I noticed a dense but small tangle of vegetation high on a mostly bare slope. Through binoculars I noticed that most of the vegetation was willow, and since willows are phreatophytes and grow only where water is close to or at the surface, probably there was a spring in the tangle. And willows, too, are deer food. The buck could spend his time there without straying too far, and that only at night. Dawn found me near the tangle. I tossed a few rocks into it, and a whopper buck bounded out and across the open grasslands. I missed clean with the first shot (or was it two? It's convenient to forget our misses), but settled down and killed him with the next. Judging by the concentration of droppings, beds, rubs, and cropped willow shoots, the buck had been living in the tangle for at least a week, and perhaps longer.

Deer must have plenty of edge. And big bucks are often where you least expect them. Deer season in Utah may coincide with the time when sheepherders bring their bands down to load on trucks and ship off to either winter range or the slaughterhouse. One autumn I'd been hunting Magpie Canyon doggedly. I hadn't seen a decent buck in the week I'd been pounding the brush, and back then, that was an oddity. As I eased into a favorite basin where I'd taken good bucks in earlier years, I was disgusted to see it full of noisy and smelly sheep. We called them mountain maggots for obvious reasons. I stood up and swore. At that moment a monstrous buck bounded from a tangle of maples and up the opposite and open slope. At more than three hundred

My ol' hunting pal Rick Lovell with an opening-day "meat" buck in northern

yards, my bullet entered between the shoulder blades and broke the spine. He nearly fell on two sheep standing nearby. I've always wondered if he was intentionally traveling with the sheep.

Hunters may avoid some canyons that are steep and brushy. And they're missing opportunities at trophy bucks. One such spot produced one of my best bucks. A Jeep road runs past the canyon head and along one ridge, and because the place seemed so obvious and was so thick and rugged, no one hunted it. The slopes are so steep that many rocks sit at such a precarious angle that a slight nudge will send them bounding into the depths below. In some places, brush and timber are so thick as to be nearly impenetrable; in others, sagebrush and grass break up the tangles and create unlimited edge and feed. Deer browse is abundant. Cover and food are always close at hand.

It's no trick to see forty deer a day in that canyon, and mature bucks are more common than in any of the surrounding country. During deer season I'd hurry home from Weber State College, where I was then a freshman, jump in Dad's Jeep, and drive up the canyon in time to hunt during the evening. Sometimes I'd still-hunt, or I'd climb on a rimrock and glass.

One afternoon I parked the Jeep at the head of the canyon and still-hunted down into it. When I got to the bottom, I sidehilled down the canyon. Deer were always in sight, and the big problem was not spooking them and thereby ruining any chance at a trophy buck in the canyon ahead. Halfway down, I jumped a herd of elk. They crashed through the oak scrub like a runaway semi-truck. Then I caught a movement across and well down the canyon. Because I'd forgotten my binocular, I screwed the variable scope up to 9X and looked. My jaw dropped. Even at six hundred yards, the buck was obviously bigger than anything I'd ever killed. Antler spread exceeded the ear tips by a considerable margin.

He was browsing along the trees four yards in the open. With one jump, he could disappear in heavy brush. I started the stalk, reasoning that slow, deliberate movement, like a browsing deer might make, would soothe his suspicion. If the buck couldn't scent or hear me and couldn't identify my outline as that of a human, perhaps he wouldn't spook. I more than halved the distance, trying to act like a feeding deer. I would be pushing my luck trying to stalk any closer in the open, so I wadded my coat into a fork of an aspen sapling and rested the rifle on it. I let the cross hairs settle just above the back and squeezed. The 7mm magnum bullet kicked up red dust above his back. Incredibly, he continued to stare. I lowered the cross hairs and touched off again. The buck hunched, turned, and wobbled for cover. I lowered the sight picture slightly and held ahead, and the buck fell. He had a spread of better than thirty-two inches and good mass.

Decades ago, when I hunted the mountains east of Cokeville, Wyoming, I'd see hundreds of deer a day. A poor day's hunting revealed fifty or sixty deer. There was plenty of cover—lodge pole pine forest, aspen, fir. The woods there are broken by sagebrush, grasslands, and brushy openings. Edge was plentiful.

The country is easily accessible and a road runs down nearly every ridge, so armies of residents and nonresidents pounded the deer (I made another trip there a few years ago and things haven't changed). Few bucks last beyond their first or second year, and those that do manage it seek out remote and inaccessible places hunters won't get into. Typically, these are small, steep, tangled ravines. Few hunters would consider clawing through these jungles, and deer were mostly safe in them.

One season, I'd seen more than three hundred deer in less than a week's hunting. All had been does and small bucks. On my next-to-last day of hunting, I still-hunted into a small but steep canyon, probably less than three hundred yards rim to rim. Aspen and shrubs grew in a tangle in the bottom and up the sides. I sidehilled and tossed rocks, or rolled them if I could, into the brush below with the hopes of spooking a buck up the opposite slope. Halfway down the canyon, I caught a glimpse of two immense bucks crashing over the opposite ridge. I couldn't shoot because I was tangled in the willows. Those bucks bounded full-out until they were out of sight.

The next dawn, I hunted into a similar small-canyon tangle. Its head started on a ridge and near a dirt road. The place was just as tangled with brush as the canyon I'd hunted the day before. In jackpine I jumped something with antlers. The buck hit bottom and raced up the opposite slope as I sprinted for an opening where I could shoot. The buck slowed as he clattered up a rock slide. He wasn't as good as the two I'd jumped the day before, but it was the last day. When the cross hairs settled behind his shoulder blades as he climbed, I squeezed the trigger. The buck collapsed at the shot and slid down the scree slope.

To consistently collect good mule deer bucks, learn to think like one. Recognize and be able to identify mid-successional plant species (also called "seral" species). They include both tall and short shrubs and brush, tall forbs and herbaceous plants, and saplings. If you're hunting wooded terrain, look for openings

I shinny up a poplar that overlooks brushy patches where mule deer feed in southwestern Saskatchewan.

and concentrate your efforts there. In hard-hunted country, search out places hunters miss.

As indicated earlier, hunters tend to avoid steep and brushy places and areas that simply don't look like deer habitat. These are often hot spots. No one wants to pack a buck out of a steep, deep, and brushy gorge, so they won't go there. You, on the other hand, should. Collecting a good mule deer buck these days is often at least 50 percent determination.

TROPHY BUCK ANTICS

Unfortunately, big bucks get away. But if we are wise, we learn something in our loss.

As I watched through the binocular a canyon away, the buck had minced down from a high ridge into a bare and rolling ravine where the highest cover was shin-high sagebrush. Now, I slowly scanned the edge of the ravine with the binoculars; it was unneeded, though, because if he'd been there, I'd have seen him without visual aids in that open land. He'd simply vanished.

The frost had settled and the light was going fast. I hiked back up the ridge toward the pickup. Once on the high ridge, I turned and scanned slowly with the glasses. The buck stretched like a big dog in the bottom of the ravine. It was too far to try a shot and too late to stalk him before dark. He'd been there all along, bedded in the short sagebrush. If mule deer can grin, he did it.

That buck was one of scores that have got away. They all taught me something—if only that I can be incredibly stupid at times. In decades of hunting mule deer bucks, I've dealt with highly sophisticated deer—intelligent, incredibly patient, cool, and as unpredictable as a she-grizzly in heat.

One summer long ago, I regularly fished the upper reaches of northern Utah's Causey Reservoir. I'd paddle the canoe five miles to the ends of the arms and cast flies until dark. Nearly every evening I'd see a good buck high on a steep and brushy slope broken by limestone cliffs and scree slides. He browsed on mountain mahogany and cliffrose and other plants impossible to identify at that distance. I watched him through much of August and September and into early October. The Utah deer season opened in mid-October, and I was sure I'd collect him. I even made a bet on it.

I lost. Somehow the buck sensed the advent of deer season and simply disappeared. Though I paddled the canoe up the reservoir and watched seriously with the glasses, he didn't show.

A week after deer season ended, and as I roll-cast a No. 14 Blue Dun from shore, I glanced up his slope. He was browsing as if nothing had happened. I'm not sure of the mechanisms adult bucks use to sense the oncoming deer season—whether it's memory, possibly associated with photoperiod (day length), the condition of browse vegetation, whatever—but bucks often disappear before or during hunting season, only to reappear after it's over. Many undoubtedly become totally nocturnal, and some certainly simply migrate to thick, steep, and inaccessible country.

While scouting for elk on a backpacking trek into Montana's Buffalo Plateau in the Absaroka-Beartooth Wilderness, I located a monster mule deer buck in a high basin. I was convinced he'd score high enough for the Boone and Crockett record bible. He haunted a particular ridgetop. I packed in two weeks before the opening of elk season to enjoy the Indian summer. The buck was still around, and happily, a band of bull elk lived in the timber in the basin just south of my camp.

Several days before the season opening, outfitters began packing dudes through the country. The buck disappeared. I shot a nice bull elk on opening morning, packed him more than twenty miles to the trailhead, and drove home to Utah.

The route through Yellowstone National Park was quickest and most scenic, and I took it. Near Tower Junction, actually less than ten air miles from where I'd been hunting but more than one hundred by road, I spotted the buck. Tourists photographed him as he browsed. I got the distinct impression that this was his routine. He'd simply trot a few miles into the safety of the park when hunters began showing up. No mistaking this buck, either, because the heavy and high points had a single short cheater tine dropping off the main left beam.

More odd was the Utah buck I hunted in the early '80s. I'd pitched camp on a ridge above the south fork of the narrows of the Ogden River. I had the place to myself because the canyon and surrounding terrain were very rugged—steep canyons fed into the gorge and the headwaters of the Ogden River, invisible between limestone cliffs thousands of feet below. No one in his right mind would want to pack a buck out of that place, and most hunters are sane people. Trophy mule deer hunters, however, don't always shoot with a full magazine.

I scouted the area for the better part of the week before the opening. The weather was mild during the day and cold at night and very dry. I'd seen scores of deer from camp through the glasses and spotting scope. One buck was a keeper. He hung around a peculiar orange sandstone cliff. An ancient Douglas fir tree grew at the base of the cliff, and scrub oak was thick in the vicinity.

In the black predawn of opening morning, I waited across the ravine from that cliff. I shivered in the cold as the black in the east began to change to a faint pale blue, then magenta, gold, and finally I could see. The buck didn't show up. When the sun had climbed above the ridge, I crossed the ravine to check it out. Large, fresh tracks meandered along the cliff base, and I was certain they'd been made shortly before it got light enough to see. But I couldn't find a bed. Twenty feet up, a ledge crossed the cliff face. I climbed back across the draw and looked the cliff over once more. The big fir tree hid most of the cliff base, and the ledge crossed from one side to the other. I hiked back to camp for lunch and to puzzle it out.

From the bluff below camp, I again scanned distant ridges and canyons, but paid most attention to that orange sandstone cliff. A few moments before dark, the buck was again browsing near the fir tree. One moment, nothing, and the next—poof, he had materialized out of air. I hunted around the cliff again in the dawn, but again, no luck. I stood beneath the fir and scratched my head.

I searched through the oak brush slowly and meticulously, looking for a bed hidden in an unusually thick tangle somewhere. Then I eased along the ledge and sat down next to a big hollow. I was pondering it and staring out over the ravine when a shrill, whistly snort sounded and a flash of gray rocketed over me and over the ledge. I nearly dropped the rifle. The buck landed in oak twenty feet below and crashed down the ravine. I was too surprised to get off a shot. From the bluff below camp, I hadn't been able to see the hollow, even with the spotting scope, because it was hidden behind the fir tree.

On the last hunting day, I again stalked to the cliff. I climbed on top of it and dropped stones to the ledge below, hoping to spook the buck out and get a shot. This time I had a round in the chamber and my thumb near the safety. I heard something behind me and up the slope. When I pivoted, the buck was disappearing over the ridge.

One that didn't get away hung out with a band of sheep in northern Utah. I alluded to this buck earlier in these pages. Though sheepherders then were fond of pulling the legs of gullible kids, these herders assured me the buck had hung around the sheep all summer. On the other hand, perhaps their lonely existence had taken its toll on their sanity.

Deer season was hot and dry, and I hadn't seen a good buck. I'd hunted Magpie Canyon diligently because I'd killed good bucks there before. I decided to try a basin where I'd done well in past seasons. When I got to the ridge, the basin was full of smelly, noisy sheep. I cursed—no self-respecting buck would hang out with mountain maggots. Then the immense buck crashed from cover and raced up the steep slope and right through the sheep. At my shot, he collapsed nearly on top of some sheep.

"Sure," one herder said in heavy Basque-accented English, "he been wid de sheep all de summer." I didn't necessarily bite, because there was another explanation: They'd disturbed the buck when they were pushing their bands of sheep along and he'd simply run ahead of them. After more years of hunting deer, I finally realized that adult bucks are unpredictable, if anything, but at least this one didn't get away.

Another buck hung out in a tangle of willows on a barren slope in Nevada's Ruby Mountains; I finally killed him after passing within a few yards of his haunt every day. I actually may have hit him with a rock before he flushed out along the open slope where I could get a shot. I'd tossed a handful of rocks into the tangle to flush anything that might be there, though I didn't really expect anything.

A mulie I named the Sheepherd buck will be mentioned elsewhere and in different contexts, but he was either the luckiest buck I ever hunted or the smartest. I named him after Sheepherd Canyon in Weber County, Utah. I hunted him four years—five seasons—and each year I spotted the buck at least once, and often more than that. Each season I got a chance at him, and each season he outsmarted me. Except that last time.

Over the years the buck had pulled these stunts: hidden while four horseback hunters rode within a few yards of him; run away in a band of other bucks so I couldn't get a shot; crossed ridges in the only place, because of cover, where I couldn't get a shot; circled behind me as I stalked him; and performed other feats of cunning and cool.

In the end, I killed him more out of luck than skill—that and simple pigheaded persistence. In the dawn, I spotted the buck in maple scrub a long shot across the canyon. He stared hard toward noises made by hunters far down the canyon, and since his attention was riveted on them, he missed seeing me, at least until I sat in the snow-covered sage and made ready to shoot. He stared hard in my direction, having spotted some movement, and I couldn't believe that he didn't bound into the trees. I squeezed one off, and the buck leaped straight up and landed three yards down the slope in maple shintangle. I held several inches above his back and touched off again. The buck jumped and raced off through the maple trees, but as he disappeared, I thought I saw the great rack sag slightly to one side. When I climbed into the canyon and up the opposite slope to where he had been standing when I shot, I found a few drops of dark muscle blood, which could mean about anything. The trail was easy to follow in the new snow, and I found the buck dead. The second shot had entered low in the chest and nicked the heart; the first had grazed the brisket. The quest was over, and mixed with the ecstasy were other emotions and an odd lump in my throat.

This chapter's lesson? You cannot hunt trophy mule deer bucks by the book, even by this one. Whitetail-buck smarts are pretty well accepted, but whitetails are more predictable—a big mule deer buck is apt to do anything. The whitetail is high-strung and nervous and jittery by nature, while a big mule deer buck is icy calm in comparison. When hunting cagey mule deer bucks in hunted country—and nearly all of it is these days—be ready for anything.

CANYON COMBING

The old-timers used to call me a "sidehill galoot" when I was a kid. As the theory went, I'd wear one leg shorter than the other by hunting sidehills too much, and as a sheepherder pal told me, "You'll walk in circles on the flats." Along with other deer-hunting aphorisms, they also said that "Antlers make poor soup" when I passed up too many nontrophy deer. Since those days, I've put in more than my share of hunting the sidehills, and even though one ex-wife accused me of going in circles, I still walk pretty straight down in the flatlands. And I learned from an Alaskan sourdough when I lived up on the Yukon River that if antlers are boiled, the fat can be skimmed off the top and makes a pretty good butter substitute, particularly on sourdough bread. So much for old tales.

Canyons are inextricably part of buck hunting for mule deer (with the possible exception of desert mule deer—more on this later in the book). I've killed very few bucks on the flats, and when I did, they were near canyons of some sort.

The most basic canyon-combing technique is simple "pushing." The idea is to move deer to a place where you can get a shot. Most of mule deer country is arid to the point of being technically classified as desert. Here, timber grows on the north- to east-facing slopes where less moisture is lost to evaporation by exposure to the sun. South- and west-facing slopes are more open because they're more directly exposed to the sun and lose enough moisture to evaporation that most trees grow poorly.

When "pushing" a canyon, then, the idea is to move deer out of the timber on the north-facing slope, where they bed, to the south-facing slope, where you can get a shot.

The objective is not to panic the deer so they're steaming full-out up the opposite slope, probably more than three hundred yards away across the canyon. Instead, the idea is to move them to that open, opposite slope in such a way that they're not sure why they are retreating and are still calm. As mentioned, mule deer have astonishing hearing—as witness the big ears—so they'll hear you even if you aren't intentionally making a racket. If you do it right, mule deer will move off at their own pace—which is quiet and safe and slow (so they don't miss detecting danger by moving too fast). The deer will assume they haven't yet been detected and will try to do nothing that attracts attention. They'll move slowly and be easier to hit.

Often, timber or brush stands are small enough that deer will move simply because they catch your scent. The idea here is to get

Here I'm packing out a boned buck. The best bucks are too often in gorges and other remote places, where you have to cut them up to get them out.

upwind of the brush or trees and let your scent drift into it; walk back and forth along the upwind edge of trees or brush to be certain your scent permeates the cover. After sundown and before sunup, the air is cold and drifting downhill; in these conditions, get above the trees. The reverse is true during daylight hours. It often takes a while for a buck to move because of human scent alone; be patient and keep at it. I've taken bucks in exactly this manner, and I've often tossed rocks or made other noise to speed things along.

Big bucks will lie doggo in cover until they're convinced they've been spotted. You may have to walk them up, and when they do jump, they'll waste no time leaving. Be ready.

In smaller canyons, it's often necessary to make only one push through the forested sections. It's easier to push downhill, so start at the canyon head, wind direction permitting. When you have made it to the bottom of the small canyon or ravine, cross over to the open slope, return to the canyon head, and repeat the procedure.

If the canyon is steep, timber tends to be thicker and more tangled. Here, work through the timber several times; it's too easy to miss deer with just one pass, especially adult bucks that lie tight until you step on them.

Push large canyons in sections. They're simply too big to work adequately in one piece. Work each section as a separate canyon.

I've found tracking and still-hunting to be most effective in the larger stands of timber. Concentrate your still-hunting along game trails. Move as nearly upwind as you can. Remember that adult bucks typically buttonhook and bed downwind of their backtrail. Be ready to shoot quick and close, and stay on full alert. Always keep a round in the chamber and your thumb on the safety. Don't let your mind wander.

Unfortunately, a buck is not about to walk into the wind and make it easy for you. Here, revert to the loop method of tracking discussed elsewhere in this volume, or one of its variations.

Pushing, still-hunting, and tracking are best in timber during the day, after the bucks have bedded. Ambushing, on the other hand, is best in late evening and before sunup. The idea is not to be detected, so work into position silently.

Deer feed predominantly on open slopes, so these are the places to search before sunup or after sundown. Identify feeding areas by tracks, browsed plants, droppings, and other spoor. Don't waste time waiting near little-used openings. Be sure deer are actually feeding in the place, since they can completely forsake one open slope that looks good to you and use another you haven't found.

Game trails to and from bedding and feeding areas are good bets for ambushing. Look for a concentration of tracks, new and old, on the trail. Many trails won't be used currently or are used very lightly and don't warrant the time it takes to set up an ambush. Watch trails most intently where they enter timber. In the morning, get on your ambush site before first light; in the evening, stay as late as you can see to shoot.

In more timbered habitat, old burns and clear-cuts can be productive. Much of the Northwest, including Idaho and Montana, as well as British Columbia, have abundant old burns and old logging clear-cuts where vegetation is in rapid succession and producing highly nutritious browse. Deer concentrate in these places.

Maybe the old-timers were right. Perhaps I have become a "sidehill galoot." I do feel out of sync hunting anywhere but on a canyon sidehill because 95 percent of the mule deer bucks I've collected have fallen on sidehills.

ON THE EDGE

I was young then, and he was the first buck I had a chance at whose antlers spread beyond that mythical thirty inches. The buck stood in the dusk against gray scrub oak far down the canyon. I'd seen him there the evening before, too, but he'd sensed me and disappeared into the tangle of oak.

I studied him through the glasses—the same one all right. His antlers spread well beyond the ear tips as he cautiously scanned my way. I stuffed my jacket in the fork of a sapling and lay the rifle across it. He stepped toward me, to make out the slight movement he'd apparently seen as I readied to shoot. I let the wobble settle out as the cross hairs settled on his backline and touched off, then heard the bullet hitting home. He turned on wobbly legs, and I hit him again.

Back then I had no understanding of edge or edge effect. I'd collected decent bucks in earlier years and would kill more before I learned of edge. And even then, it took my first university wildlife-management class to explain the phenomenon.

In a thimble, the edge-effect concept states that where two types of plant communities—say, pine and grasslands for illustration purposes—come together, the edge between the two communities will be better wildlife habitat than either the pine forests or the open grasslands. This is true for successional or "seral" animal species that thrive in temporary plant communities that are in succession to a higher and more stable condition called the climax community. Mule deer (as well as elk, moose, and white-tailed deer) are successional or seral species. Mountain sheep tend toward being a climax species, as do caribou, bison, and others. Since relatively stable climax plant communities are easily disturbed so that they revert to an earlier successional community, animals that rely on them most heavily are always in the most danger of local extinction. To put it another way, if the plant community is disturbed by the activities of man or by nature, seral animal species that are adaptable will fare better.

The edge effect is obvious to anyone who has spent much time hunting mule deer, though observers may not call it that. Forests seem almost lifeless, but when a hunter works into an opening, he may be amazed at the relative abundance of birds, insects, and other wildlife, including deer. Of course, big bucks bed in timber, but they are active in edge areas.

One of the best bucks I've taken was never seen more than a step or two from cover—in other words, right on the "edge." The obvious reason was safety—one bound and he was out of sight. The other reason was hunger. Successional plants like bitterbrush, mountain mahogany, cliffrose, serviceberry, and others grew at the edge, not in the forest, and the buck had to eat. In the dozen or so encounters I had him, he was always within a hop or two of heavy cover. Younger bucks, often his companions, would stray farther out into the open, but odds were they would never survive to trophy proportions, or pass on their genes for carelessness.

The day I finally bagged the buck, he stood at the edge of a heavy stand of maples in the early dawn. I'd seen him there before. This day, as in other seasons, I'd settle for no other buck. The distance was farther than I liked, but this time I did it right.

Before concentrating on the edge in a given area, be sure there's a good buck around; simply sitting on some edge isn't likely to do it. Look for big-buck sign—mentioned in detail elsewhere in the book—so you're not wasting time trying to ambush a big buck where none exists.

These days most mule deer country is heavily hunted. There's a bright spot, however. Hunts are becoming tightly controlled by state game agencies, with lotteries and other complicated bureaucratic devices that are designed to limit hunting pressure. As a result, some areas aren't hunted so heavily that no big bucks survive, and mulie bucks are even returning to crepuscular habits (moving in the low-light conditions of dawn and dusk) instead of being active only at night. At least, that's my impression and that of several other mule deer biologists. All of which makes it more likely that you may catch a buck at first or last shooting light along the edge.

I used to hunt the late part of the season in Wyoming just east of Cokeville. Back then, you could buy a tag at the local hardware store or honky-tonk. I hunted well into November, and by then it was cold, often well below zero. Except for one half-crazed mule deer hunter, no one camped in the mountains at that time of the year. I had the place to myself. The bucks knew hunter routines, and except near Jeep trails, they returned to their normal habits. Even decent bucks browsed into the open in early morning or early evening. Ambushing was a good tactic; if a hunter located a big buck by sign and knew where one was feeding, all he had to do was wait and ambush the animal as it

A buck browses frost-killed forbs at the "edge" between a pine community and a mixed-sagebrush community in southern Montana.

fed out of the timber and into the open at the edge. The really tough part was sitting still in the cold.

One afternoon, I still-hunted up a small canyon toward an opening of various kinds of brush and forbs where heavy lodge pole pine timber flowed down the ridge. I'd seen smallish bucks in the place, and the four-inch tracks of a good buck. I reasoned that if I waited long enough, the buck would eventually show. I knew that earlier, in October, the place had been combed pretty heavily by other hunters, but it had been more than a month since the good weather, and I was certain adult bucks would eventually show themselves during shooting light at the edge of the timber.

By the time I scrunched down into sagebrush across the ravine, the cooling, dense air was flowing downhill, carrying my scent away from where I hoped a trophy buck would step from the woods. I'd been arriving at the ravine at the same time for four or five days. My time was running out, and I'd made up my mind to shoot the next decent buck that showed. And besides, I was anxious to get out of the cold and sleep in a warm bed again.

As I climbed the ridge and peeked into the head of the ravine, deer were browsing in the mixed brush. One was a fairish four-by-four. I waited; he wasn't going anywhere, and I could always collect him later if a better buck didn't show up. Then a slightly larger buck stepped from the timber. A few minutes later, an even bigger buck walked from the pines and scanned the clearing. My heart rate kicked up twenty beats. A fourth and even better buck minced out of the pines. He dropped without a shudder at the shot, and the other deer in the opening vaporized back into the timber.

Artificial edge is as attractive to deer as the natural kind. I used to hunt on Herschel "Bud" Hendrickson's ranch in western Colorado along the Dolores River. The natural vegetation along the river consisted of pinyon pine, oak, juniper, and a scattering of grasses, forbs, and shrubs. One of the best places to locate deer was along the edge between the natural vegetation and one or another of Bud's alfalfa fields that spread along the creek-bottom ravines.

Bud, my hunting buddy Rick Lovell, and I drove along the alfalfa fields after dark one night. Bud was checking the devices the game department had installed to frighten the deer out of the alfalfa fields. As near as I could determine, they were firecrackers timed to go off at certain intervals. Deer grazed placidly in every alfalfa field; we spotlighted over seven hundred in two hours. Between eighty and ninety were bucks; most were yearlings, but some were small four- or five-pointers, western count. The bucks were smart enough to head for the rimrocks when they saw the spotlight. The frightening devices had no effect, unless it was to attract deer. Bud's Mesa Creek Ranch was ideal for deer—plenty of edge, alfalfa feed, and escape cover—and deer had no reason to stray.

I wanted a trophy buck, though, so I wandered some high and remote rimrocks away from the fields. Unfortunately, I didn't find the big buck. Once again, time was running out, as so often happens when hunting trophy mule deer. Rick had already bagged his buck one evening as it stepped from the pinyon and juniper and into an alfalfa field. On the last day, he and I walked along pinyon-juniper woods a few yards from its border with an alfalfa field. Less than fifty yards in, I spotted a buck lying under a juniper tree. He was dead asleep. At the shot, he dropped his head and lay still. He wasn't a trophy, but trophy hunters don't always succeed.

I'm as drawn to the edge as mule deer are; I suspect most hunters are. I dislike pitching a tent in heavy forest without an opening of some sort; likewise, I won't set up camp in a completely open prairie if there's an alternative (on pronghorn hunts, a couple of African safaris, and many sheep hunts, there wasn't). Another reason I prefer camping along the edge is simply that it looks like game country.

When I step from a heavy forest and into the open, I automatically look down for browsed brush, for round, black droppings, and for big-buck tracks. My pulse quickens as I scan the edge.

RIFLES

Legendary hunting and shooting writer Jack O'Connor's favorite gun was the Winchester Model 70 in .270 caliber. The pre-1964 Model 70 was one of the best rifles ever made. And arguably, the .270 is the best all-round cartridge of the last century. Perhaps not so arguably. Warren Page, O'Connor's counterpart at *Field & Stream*, reluctantly agreed with O'Connor after testing everything from the .220 to the .458. I say reluctantly because all the gun editors of the "big three" hunting and fishing magazines—*Outdoor Life*, *Field & Stream*, and *Sports Afield*—had a healthy disrespect for each other and often took potshots at one another from behind typewriters. Today it's tough to imagine such color and individualism coming from the sanitized large-circulation magazines, which may be one reason subscriptions and retail

Old burns like this one in British Columbia make good deer range. The forbs, shrubs, and young trees that grow in them provide excellent forage.

magazine sales have dropped off drastically in recent years and why some have taken to selling T-shirts and ball caps. (If the Ivy league MBAs on the board of Times-Mirror and other big corporations that manage dozens of magazines and any number of other media would pick up a gun once in a while, perhaps the big three could return to their former glory; culling "company men" might help, too. Forgive the editorializing.)

As an impressionable kid in the early '60s, I viewed what O'Connor wrote in *Outdoor Life* magazine as biblical. I vowed to someday own a Model 70 in .270 caliber. I made some detours before I finally got that pre-'64 Model 70, which I stocked with a Fajen fiddleback maple stock with rosewood grip and fore-end and scoped with the latest Redfield 3–9X variable. I used the gun for years, and decades later gave it to my better half, Cheri; she cut down the stock to fit her diminutive frame and refinished it, and it glows like a fine piece of Finnish furniture. I bought a Model 700 Remington in the same caliber, which I used on everything from jack rabbits to Alaskan moose to leopard with incredible success. I shot more game with that rifle than with all the other guns I've owned before or since combined. I finally left it with bighorn sheep guide Ken Olynyk as a tip; Ken recently sent me a photo of a nice California bighorn ram he'd killed with the rifle west of the Fraser River in British Columbia. The gun is still producing.

All of which means that I agree with O'Connor—the .270 is the best all-round caliber for medium-sized game, mule deer included. After I gave away my Model 700, I acquired in trade with my gun-swapping pal Rick Lovell a Remington Model Seven in 7mm-08 caliber. The rifle is a sweet sheep gun or backpack rifle because it's so light and short. I've killed a dozen or so North American and Asian sheep with the rifle. And it's excellent on mule deer, with ballistics similar enough to the .270 that no buck struck in the "lights" will know the difference.

Anything around 7mm makes a good buck rifle, though after having shot for years with the 7mm Remington Magnum, I've decided it's too heavy for deer-sized game and tends to unnecessarily savage the animal. The .280, .284, 7x67mm, 7mm-08, and, of course, the .270 would be my choices for good mule deer cartridges. The .264 magnum is still a bit too heavy. The 6mms—.243 and .244, for example—are too light, and a big buck hit poorly with one will probably escape and die elsewhere. The .30-06 is good, too.

The old favorite .30-30 isn't popular for mule deer because too many hunters are too savvy about ballistics and know that its rainbow trajectory isn't the best choice for shooting across canyons. Still, I've taken bucks and a variety of other game with my Model 94 Winchester, mostly in the flat deserts of Sonora and in the southwest United States; there, shots were normally close as I still-hunted through cholla and mesquite thickets, and the .30-30 is an excellent choice for close and quick shooting. I'm still heavily biased toward the traditional American Model 94, and in recent years I've killed two mountain lions and a black bear in trees with it; I use it exclusively when hunting treed game and frequently when I'm in the saddle because it is so short and handy. It's still the rifle of choice of the Mexican *vaqueros* of the Sierra Madre for anything from javelina to Coues whitetails to puma (cougar or mountain lion to you and me). I collected my first buck mule deer, a giant that went

269 pounds field-dressed, with a "sporterized" .303 Enfield bought in an army surplus store for $30. It fit me, and probably anyone else, so poorly that it bloodied my lip when I missed clean with the first shot. In spite of intense buck fever, I recalled my NRA rifle training and settled down and squeezed with the second shot.

That Christmas, I got a .30-06 Springfield; it, too, had been sporterized with a cheap Monte Carlo stock. The barrel had been pitted so badly by shooting old military ammo that it wouldn't put five shots into a foot-wide group at 100 yards. Still, perhaps because the buck walked into the shot, I somehow took a forkhorn that fall with the thing.

My next rifle was the 7mm Remington Magnum. It was accurate, flat-shooting, and too powerful for mule deer and pronghorn, my primary quarries in those days. Eventually, the bolt cracked and I got rid of it.

That's when I purchased my Model 70 .270. And later that Model 700 Remington .270, as mentioned earlier. I suppose I've killed forty species of game animals numbering several hundred in Africa and North America with that caliber. I've never been disappointed with it, and if it did not kill cleanly, it was my fault or the bullet's. Still, the .270 is a bit light for animals like moose (though I've killed several efficiently with it), grizzly (ditto), muskox, Cape buffalo, kudu, and sable (I've taken a handful of these with one shot apiece), unless conditions are just so and the marksman is cool under pressure.

So much for calibers, and I won't delve into ballistics, about which there's so much literature out there. All major ammunition manufacturers have statistic sheets on their ammo, and they're usually free from the factory or sales reps. Help yourself if you want numbers. The last mule deer I asked didn't even know the muzzle energy of the .30-06!

To me, rifle characteristics are more important. Is the rifle light enough that you can carry it over ridges all day? Will you settle for a composite stock, or are you like me and prefer the beauty and naturalness of wood, even with its disadvantages? Is the barrel too short or long, too light or heavy? What about the action?

The advantages of light rifles are obvious—they're easy to tote and won't fuse three vertebrae by season's end. But there are tradeoffs. Light barrels heat up rapidly and may shoot erratically, which is important on the rifle range. I had this problem with the Remington Model Seven in 7mm-08. The barrel was short and thin, and groups got erratic after three shots, which was disconcerting if I was tuning for a Siberian snow-sheep hunt in a week or two. My remedy was to shoot two shots, let the gun cool down while I shot something else, and then shoot two more. I also glass-bedded the receiver, which helped out, too. If I'm not going to walk all day, I prefer a heavier barrel, first because it doesn't heat up so much and shoot erratically, and second because I can steady it in a hurry on running game with the extra weight out front. Still, give me the short action and light weight of a 7mm-08 or .308 any day; I'll live with the disadvantages.

Yes, I know composite stocks are light, durable, and won't warp. No one cares if they're gouged or trampled by horses. Still, I am old-fashioned and I prefer wood. I get no joy out of handling or fondling a composite stock. I am planning to buy

I must have been eighteen when this was taken.

one, however, for its strengths. I'm looking at several brands in .300 magnum for a future Asian argali hunt; on hunts this expensive, reliable is more important than handsome. If you're a wood lover, choose a stock made of fine walnut or maple; otherwise, choose a functional but unappealing synthetic stock.

With the exception of my Model 94 lever-action and one experiment with a breaking-action gun, all my rifles have been bolt-action. They're reputed to be more accurate, stronger, and more trouble-free, and those are reasons enough for me. I started with a bolt-action .22 and have preferred them ever since. I have shot autoloaders but never felt comfortable with them; it was too much like shooting ducks, and in the back of my mind they seemed inadequate for big game. I could never get the hang of the few pump rifles I've shot. So I'll stick with bolt-actions.

Choose your mule deer caliber and rifle based on the hunting you do. If I'm going to stalk through timber all day in hopes of killing a buck in his bed at close range, I'll choose my short and quick Model 94 .30-30. If I'm likely to shoot a buck across a canyon, I'll stick with the Model Seven 7mm-08 with its compact, variable-power Leupold rifle scope. If it's a combination of those habitat types, I'll choose the 7mm-08—it's short and quick in the trees, and flat-shooting for cross-canyon shots. In brush, select a heavier caliber and bullet weight; I'd choose the .30-06 with 220-grain bullets. Large calibers and heavy bullets are less easily deflected by brush. The "ott-six" has a flat trajectory, too, for those longer shots. Actually, the rifle and caliber you select aren't as important as your ability to handle and shoot the rifle. I've seen some big bucks killed in their beds with the .32 Special by men who knew how to hunt and get close.

Chapter 4

How-To Section

THE COMPLETE STILL-HUNTER

To my deer hunting neighbor Ezekiel "Zeke" Gumbo, still-hunting is sitting against a tree stump and waiting for a deer to walk by. "After all," he tells me, exasperated that I don't see his logic, "I *am* still, and I *am* hunting."

Another hunting buddy thinks still-hunting is simply hunting without talking. "I'm so still," Waldo says, "you could hear a snowflake drop." Most of his still-hunting is spent dozing under a pine tree, and if he could hear himself snore, he'd realize he was anything but still.

Still another acquaintance—one who, some would argue, doesn't shoot with a full magazine—thinks still-hunting is what you're doing at the end of the day after twelve hours of traipsing over ridges and mountains. "Wal, now," I imagine Jeremiah drawling, "I'm still a-huntin'."

The only two formal definitions of still-hunting I could dig up were slightly contradictory, so for the purposes of this chapter, let's define still-hunting as moving slowly (that's a key word) through game country while keeping alert and attempting to find the quarry before it finds you. It means getting as alert as you ever get and using all senses: Watch ahead, to the side, even behind, being sure there's nothing within your radius of vision before you move on; listen for sounds that might indicate game (rustling leaves, the swish of a limb, the scrape of an antler against a branch) use your nose, too, especially around the rut when game animals have a strong odor. Still-hunting requires special shooting techniques that involve making calculated, deliberate movements and shooting without panic, even if the quarry jumps before you're ready.

Above all, stalk as silently as humanly possible, and to do that you must move slowly. "Whoa," I hear Jeremiah telling me, "that's slow huntin', not still-huntin'." Jeremiah aside, moving slowly allows you to more thoroughly scan the surroundings and to watch for twigs and branches you might step on or scrape against. To stalk quietly, discard jeans, status-symbol parkas, and other stiff fabrics; use wool, pile, or soft cotton that won't give you away at four hundred yards when a branch scrapes against it. Consider still-hunting in moccasins or use pile gaiters to cover the stiff rubber and leather of hiking boots or pacs.

Asking Westerners to give up denim jeans is about like asking a mountain lion to give up venison, but I learned the hard way not to hunt in denim. Once, I was hunting an immense mule deer buck—his foretracks were longer than four inches—in northern Sonora with a diminutive Tepecano named Pacquito. Pacquito had led me through a rugged volcanic canyon and up onto a vast lava plateau, where we found the tracks of the buck where he'd browsed through palo verde and mesquite. We followed quietly, Pacquito's eyes gleaming—he knew where the buck bedded. He squeezed my arm and put his fingers to his lips to indicate silence, then pointed above. He stalked silently and slowly, and as we rounded a clump of scrubby acacia, a thorn scraped against my jeans. I heard a commotion above, and a moment later the buck flashed across the ridge. I had a momentary glimpse of a yard-wide rack (literally) against the skyline. I felt even smaller than Pacquito's five feet when he shook his head, smacked his lips, and walked disgustedly away.

Another rule of still-hunting is that if you can hear yourself, you're too noisy. Sure, you'll make the odd noise once in a while—the grate of a pebble underfoot, the swish of brush or grass as you pass through it, the squeak of snow, but deer and other game make the same sounds. If, on the other hand, I hear myself making rhythmic small noises, no matter how natural they may sound taken individually, I know any nearby buck will be alert and tougher to approach, if he doesn't actually run for it. Unnatural noise, like branches scraping stiff fabric, the squeak of a sling swivel, or the clink of cartridges in a pocket, will give you away instantly.

When you're still-hunting with a buddy, don't talk unless you're convinced there's no game within earshot (remember, mule deer have astonishing hearing, and what you think is quiet will likely be heard clearly by a buck). If you must speak, whisper. If you must communicate when game might be near, do so with hand signals. Still-hunting alone is tough enough, but you treble the problems when you do it with someone else.

Keep to game trails whenever possible. They hold fewer twigs and branches to scrape against, step on, and break. Also, game animals expect movement along trails. When you get off trails in thick timber or brush, you'll have problems moving quietly. You'll alert game more quickly, and at greater distances, and since they don't get far off trails themselves (except when fleeing), they'll get suspicious more easily. Usually, too, deer, elk, and other game bed and feed near trails, often well-used trails. Since you can still-hunt more quietly along a game trail, pay special attention to the downwind side of the path—as cited earlier, mule deer, whitetails, and elk often bed on the downwind side of their backtrail so they can scent anything following them.

Just as you should strive to still-hunt more slowly and quietly (you can't be too quiet), increase your awareness of what's there. Don't just rely on vision—listen, smell, and even trust in hunches.

Compared to the senses of game animals, our smell and hearing are rudimentary. Our vision, on the other hand, is among the best in the animal kingdom, and if we learn what to look for, it goes a long way in making up for our shortcomings.

In open country, locating game by sight may be all that's needed. This is especially true for prairie and mountain game. At great distances, even with the aid of a spotting scope, you may not see the entire animal. Instead, look for a piece of him, like the sun glinting off an antler or a bit of horn sticking above a rock.

In brush and timber you'll rarely spot the entire animal unless he's fleeing; by then, it may be too late anyway. As you still-hunt,

Sometimes this is the best part of hunting—broiling buck chops over pine coals in a high-country camp.

search the cover for a tawny flank, the flick of a tail, any slight movement. If you see something suspicious, ready yourself; fight back the excitement rising in your throat by planning what you'll do if he jumps and how you can get closer if he doesn't. Before you do anything, wait until you know exactly what you're seeing and what you're going to do about it. Think it out carefully so there will be no mistakes or surprises, which make for misses.

After decades of still-hunting on several continents, I've at last learned what to look for, particularly in thick woods and brush. If I actually see the entire animal, it's such a rare occurrence that I'm astonished (or liable to overlook it; one time I walked to within ten yards of a dozing elephant in an open Zambezi acacia forest before I noticed him—I was startled spitless). Another time, and more typically, I was still-hunting through a pinyon-juniper forest in the rimrock country of western Colorado when I saw something a bit odd. At first glance, it seemed to be a dark woodpecker hole in a very weathered fallen tree. I looked closer and longer, because something just wasn't right. I very slowly raised the compact binoculars (close, sudden movements are apt to catch a buck's attention, even if he isn't staring in your direction). The ear flicked, and the woodpecker hole became an eye. The buck stared off into space, possibly dreaming of past loves, so I slowly lowered the binocular and very carefully raised the rifle (it seemed to take eons, though the slow, deliberate movement probably took only two minutes). Through the scope, all I could see was the buck's head and two inches of neck. As I raised the rifle, I'd already decided what I would do if the buck jumped and raced off downhill (he'd have to cross an opening where I could get a shot), so I was prepared for whatever happened. Fortunately, the buck never did sense me, and the bullet killed him in his bed. That's the way it should work.

Don't rely only on vision. Listen for small sounds. More often than not, they'll be only a chipmunk darting across dried leaves, a titmouse climbing bark, or the wind rattling twigs. But often enough, they'll indicate a mule deer buck mincing up a trail or nipping at bitterbrush twigs. I don't know how many bucks I killed because I heard them first, but it must be in the dozens.

Use your nose, too. Our scenting abilities when compared to a deer's are woefully inadequate. We could never detect another human at half a mile or follow a trail by scent, even it if belonged to my pal Jeremiah, who wears the same unwashed duds for the entire three-month hunting season. Yet occasionally, our paltry sense of smell does work. I once followed my nose to three rutting bull elk bedded in timber two hundred yards away. I killed a bull in his bed, breaking his neck, and the two others crashed off through the pine deadfalls with all the din of a twister demolishing a trailer court. Still-hunting along a Montana ridge another time, I caught the strong stink of a rutting mule deer buck. I still-hunted into the wind, occasionally losing the scent, then casting across the breeze like a German shorthair until I found it again. Then I'd mark the wind direction, pick a tree downslope in that line, and head toward it. I jumped the big mulie buck at twenty yards and killed him with a spine shot.

If you still-hunt alone—and you should, since a companion will distract you—you'll learn to pay attention to hunches. Whether this sixth sense develops through subconscious cues received from the environment or is in the realm of the paranormal is up to question. Whichever it is, I NEVER discard hunches. I've rolled out of the bedroll too many times in the predawn with the conviction I should hunt this ravine or that timber stand, only to jump and bag a buck. I've often felt that exhilarating sense of action to come just before I found a big buck or bull. There are all sorts of hunches, and if you can forget civilized practicality and pay attention to them, you'll be a more complete still-hunter.

Still-hunting through moderate to thick timber or brush requires special shooting techniques. If you're doing it right, you'll be close to the buck when you find him (hopefully, he won't yet have located you). If you move suddenly and in excitement throw the rifle to your shoulder, the animal will catch the sudden movement and crash off, giving you a difficult shot if any. Make slow, deliberate movements if the quarry isn't already running for it. Ease the gun to your shoulder, shift your body carefully, and take your time. Slow movement is less apt to attract attention. Unless the buck is running, every movement should be planned out before you do it. Calculate the shot carefully and avoid surprises, since they contribute to buck fever. Occasionally, you'll jump an animal in close, but if you've expected it and practiced some snap-shooting, you'll score.

"Hell," I imagine my neighbor Zeke saying, "you're not still-huntin' a'tall. I'm still-huntin'—haven't moved away from that stump all day. What yer a'doin' is slow huntin'." He has a point.

THE ART OF STALKING

If you hunt, you must know how to stalk. Here I used stalking in its broadest sense—that is, hunting game fairly without the use of motor vehicles or excess gadgetry (and we have too much of it to begin to list). Stalking is an act you perform alone, and if it is to be successful, you must be determined, perceptive, and precise. Most hunting tactics qualify as stalking—tracking and still-hunting, for example— and basically it involves pursuing game.

Animals that inhabit heavy forest or thick brush rely on smell and hearing to detect danger since they can't count on their eyesight to protect them in those close confines. So it's especially important to move quietly when stalking in such terrain. This involves wearing quiet clothing such as wool or pile, and soft-soled footgear. Keep the wind as nearly in your face as possible so your scent won't give you away long before you get there. Once on a set of tracks, you have the choice of three basic tactics.

The first and often the most useful is the loop method of tracking. This method is as old as human hunters and probably in the neighborhood of three million years. It works best when the wind is blowing across the trail. It involves making loops on the downwind side of the track, to which you return every fifty or hundred yards, depending on thickness of vegetation to make sure you're still going in the right direction.

This is an effective tactic for stalking big mule deer bucks in hunted country, since these animals almost invariably make a buttonhook on the downwind side of their backtrail so they can scent or see anything following them. If you pass the end of the trail, make smaller loops back toward where you last saw the track. Unless the buck made a right-angle upwind turn, he'll be somewhere between you and where you last cut the track, so move very slowly and quietly, and keep the rifle ready. This method is also effective for many forest-dwelling game animals like whitetails, elk, or moose, which often bed downwind of their backtrail.

The parallel method of tracking is best when the timber is open enough that you can see the trail several yards away as you track alongside it. Most timber-dwelling game animals, especially mule deer, expect trouble to come from their backtrail and so watch it closely. If you work parallel to the trail but twenty-five or more yards away, you'll stand a better chance of catching a

Cheri with a big-bodied and very old Utah buck. His molars were worn down to the gumline, which meant he probably would not have survived the winter. His antlers were spindly, too, indicating he was well past his prime.

buck from a place where he doesn't expect trouble. This works best when the wind is quartering from behind or across the trail.

Straight-trailing, or staying right on the tracks themselves, works if the trail is old and you're not expecting to catch up with the buck soon. When the trail becomes fresh, switch to the loop or parallel method. Straight-tracking also works for trailing a herd, because when deer bed, they're likely to spread out through the trees, causing the loop and parallel methods to lose some of their effectiveness. Deer bed along the contours of a slope since they dislike lying with their heads either up or down the slope.

Still-hunting is an especially pleasant way to stalk. You drift along slowly and quietly, stopping often to look and listen and sometimes even to smell what is there.

Shooting is often quick and close, so you must stay ready and alert. Still-hunting in timber is a tense adrenaline rush, especially if you're sure game is near. It requires plenty of patience and perseverance. Stick to game trails, since there's less brush and you'll scrape against fewer twigs and branches, and also because deer expect movement along them.

Stalk inchworm-slow. Watch where you put your feet. Scan ahead and to the sides. Look closely and carefully for a piece of the quarry—the shadow-dappled flank of a buck, the nearly imperceptible flick of an ear. Slow, deliberate movement on your part is considerably less likely to attract a buck's attention, and if it does, it's less likely to alarm him.

Most hunters think of stalking as an active, physical act. Ambushing, however, is a very nonphysical form of stalking (although to reach your ambush position, you'll normally have to stalk there). Ambushing is a productive tactic along game trails between feeding and bedding areas, especially during dawn and dusk hours. Few game animals feed in timber; they use it for hiding and cover. Most mule deer browse in openings where grasses, forbs, shrubs, and other vegetation grow. Always select an ambush position downwind of the trail, of course. During the day when air is warm, less dense, and rising, this means upslope. The opposite is true before sunrise and after sunset.

When the buck finally shows, make absolutely certain he doesn't see you. It's even more critical to keep quiet, watch wind direction, and position the shot. Finally, move so slowly there's no chance you'll make a mistake—you can't afford even a tiny one in this close.

THE STUTTER-STEP

I once wrote an article for *Field & Stream* magazine about this tactic and called it the "Start-Pause-Stop" method, which describes it pretty accurately. I got a lot of response from readers, and many of them wanted to know if it would work for whitetails and elk. The answer then and now is yes. One African professional hunter from Zimbabwe wrote to tell me he would try the method on kudu and eland on the lowveld; I never heard how it worked, but I do know that I used the method successfully on safaris from Botswana to Tanzania to Zimbabwe and in between on species from lion and Cape buffalo to bushbuck.

This technique, a form of still-hunting, involves drifting through timber very slowly while straining to sense anything within shooting distance. I listen and look for anything out of the ordinary, something that alters the grid of the scene, and more often than not it's just a downy woodpecker searching aspen bark for grubs or a red-backed vole scampering across autumn-dead maple leaves. If you don't smoke and it's moist, you might even smell a buck. A Shuswap Indian guide up in British Columbia once told me to "drift like smoke," a concise description of still-hunting.

The "stutter-step" is a form of still-hunting designed to move game in such a way that the hunter can get a shot. Its stages are more stylized and drawn out than the more or less instinctual movements of simple still-hunting.

In country that gets any kind of hunting pressure at all, mature bucks are largely nocturnal during the hunting season. Of course, there will be exceptions, and these will be mentioned elsewhere in the book, but 95 percent of the time, old and smart bucks aren't going to show themselves when it's light enough to shoot. So when there's shooting light, you're going to have to get a trophy buck to leave his bed if you are to have any chance of a shot. Along with scent-driving (discussed elsewhere), tracking (ditto), and other methods, the stutter-step can be highly effective. Over the last few years and half-a-dozen deer hunts in two states and Mexico, I found the stutter-step effective in flushing more than half of the bucks I spotted. Two of my four largest were taken using the stutter-step (one was a behemoth, a heavy-antlered buck that scored over 200 Boone & Crockett points).

Of course, you use the tactic only in a good place where a monster buck might be hiding and where you can get a shot if he jumps. The best places are ravines and small canyons, geographical features that are plentiful in most mule deer country.

I discovered the stutter-step many years ago while still-hunting up the sparsely vegetated south-facing slope of a shallow ravine through widely scattered chokecherry bushes and scrub oak. I'd skipped breakfast in my haste to get hunting before first light, and decided I needed to stop and eat lunch. I sat on a big orange sandstone boulder across the ravine from a small, thick tangle of oak scrub. Since the oak leaves had fallen, I could see into the tangle pretty well and didn't see anything suspicious. Nearly an hour later, I suppose, I fumbled around loading my daypack, loosening my belt a notch to accommodate the lunch, taking a whiz, and a few other actions. I gave one final stretch and then started up the ravine (such commotion is important in getting a buck nervous enough so he'll jump). To my surprise, a big buck crashed from the oak brush and bounded across the slope. A .270 slug in the back of the neck settled him.

Timbered canyon bottoms, ravine heads, stands of timber, and extensive "thickets" are top spots to try out the stutter-step. Another good place is near brush patches below you but on the same slope. If you choose correctly and a good buck is lying tight just where you think he is (most often they won't be there, since trophy bucks are scarcer than honest politicians), it's critical to get into a position where you can shoot when and if he jumps. It does no good to jump a buck where you won't be able to get a shot. The best places are pockets of cover surrounded by open prairie or fields across which a buck will have to flee and thus give you a shot. Nearly always, the buck will be running, so shooting has to be quick. If you're hunting flat country, you'll need at least two hunters, one to wait on the opposite side of the cover.

Though I discovered the stutter-step by accident that day in the ravine, all of the elements of the tactic were there in that situation when I carefully analyzed it later. Luckily, I stopped at a good place to eat lunch. While eating, I paused longer than the tactic normally requires. The commotion I made getting ready to start back up the ravine was the catalyst that made the buck just too nervous to sit it out any longer.

First, locate prime cover and then stop. Make some sort of minor commotion so any buck becomes aware of your presence (he probably will be anyway, regardless of how much noise you make). He has to be aware of you to get nervous, and then he must get fidgety for the method to work. Don't make so much commotion that you frighten bucks up the canyon; make just enough to alert any nearby buck (remember, deer can hear, scent, and, in this case, probably see better than you can).

Next, just wait. Don't conceal yourself, since you want the buck to know you're there. Eat your lunch out in the open, or sit on a conspicuous blowdown to do your glassing. Wait half an hour or so. This is a good time to eat lunch or read.

The final act of the stutter-step is the commotion you make as you prepare to leave. This often makes a buck too nervous to stand it any longer. He is finally convinced he should run, and when he's sure he's been located, he'll flush. And you'll shoot if it works right.

The stutter-step works best in late morning and from midafternoon until nearly dark. Mule deer sit tighter the longer they've been bedded in a particular spot, so the tactic may be an effective way to move an otherwise well-hidden buck. A buck that has just bedded isn't as sure of his bedding spot as one that has been in it for hours; he's more apt to flush and with less reason, so stutter-stepping here isn't needed.

Bucks are more likely to flush readily in early afternoon. They're often contemplating getting up anyway about that time for a stretch, to change positions, or simply to nip a nearby sprig of bitterbrush or serviceberry. This is especially true in thicker cover. A buck bedded in sparse cover is more likely to stay put until dark.

In mid- and late afternoon, bucks have been bedded for hours. They'll likely sit tighter. This is the best time for the stutter-step. Since older bucks are always unpredictable, stalk quietly until you're ready to use the tactic. Actually, any hunter should make it a practice always to move or still-hunt quietly and inconspicuously unless he has a specific reason to do otherwise.

In the evening, as light intensity decreases and feeding time approaches and bucks are more apt to get up and sneak away on their own, the stutter-step is less useful. Just the same, using it won't hurt your chances.

Since I've been talking about wise and old bucks, let me note here that young bucks from yearlings up to three-and-a-half-year-olds aren't normally nocturnal. It's easier to flush them from brush, so creating a commotion might not be needed. But do it anyway, even if nothing has shown itself. Of course, young bucks, naive in the ways of people with rifles, are easier to bag using any method one chooses. It's the old-timers that make things difficult.

The stutter-step is not really a three-act screenplay. Trophy mule deer bucks are never predictable, and won't always react in the expected manner to any tactic, let alone the stutter-step. So be flexible and think of tactics as rough suggestions to be altered at will to suit the conditions and your hunches. A buck is probably more adaptable than the hunter, so you have to become as fluid as he is. Don't discard hunches out of hand. They can be as useful as any input from eye or ear.

CENTER AREA, HOME RANGE, AND THE MULE DEER BUCK

If you can get an ORV or four-wheel-drive pickup near your intended area, you won't likely find a good buck there during hunting season. And since most deer hunters these days won't get far from their machines, they spend the majority of their time hunting where no big bucks live. So, then, hunters are largely hunting doe and small buck pastures on most mule deer range. Killing an adult buck in these places is purely accidental. If a hunter is ambitious enough to leave the machine some distance behind, all he has to do to locate a big buck's home range is find the buck's tracks (forehoofs are 3½ to 4 inches long, excluding dewclaws), scrapes, and rubs (mule deer make all three). Then he can exert all of his hunting efforts in that place with a realistic chance of success.

Big bucks spend more than 90 percent of their time in a small area. They may have as many as half-a-dozen of these areas during the course of the year as they migrate up to and then back down from summer range. These areas are called home ranges. A big buck will tolerate other deer there, even bucks of equal stature and antler size, except during the rut. Then the mature buck will exhibit what behaviorists call agonistic behavior—which means aggressive, flight-or-fight action—toward other mature bucks. Even then, however, the big buck is not defending a "territory" from other bucks. Within a home range, bucks usually have a very small locale where they bed and spend most of their time when they are not feeding or rutting. Some outdoor writers and even wildlife managers call this the "core area," a catchy term. Since this term has been overused and misused to define several different concepts, I coined the term "center area" back when I was conducting elk research.

Home-range sizes vary from less than half a mile on one side to more than two miles in diameter, depending on available food, cover, water, and, in the rut, does. The better the habitat with more of these basics, the smaller the home range. The smaller the home range, the less the buck has to move around and expose himself. The best bucks tend to have the smallest home ranges and are very secure there.

In my experience, bucks use the same home range in more or less the same season year after year. In the summer he'll be pretty close to the same place he was last year; likewise for autumn hunting seasons, the rut, the post-rut, and winter range. What does this mean? One obvious answer is that if you muffed a shot at a big buck in a remote gorge last season, you'll have a chance at him again this year if the backpack doesn't weigh too much and the mountain lions or winter or dogs or highways haven't already got him.

An example I used in a magazine article some years ago was a buck I traced through the '70s. He appeared on the same small slope just across from my favorite camp on the eve of each opening day. The slope had plenty of good food—chokecherry, sagebrush, serviceberry, mountain mahogany, forbs—and escape and bedding cover were just around the curve of the slope. I first saw him when he was 2½ years old. Then, he had a tiny four by five rack. Unless you were meat hunting, he was no keeper. He had one abnormal point off the main left antler beam. The following season he was back with the same points in the same arrangement. He was noticeably larger through the body and the antlers were bigger, though still not in the trophy class. I ignored him. He was back again the following year, heavier and with antlers most deer hunters would not pass up. And the season after, he had a cheater tine about four inches long and antlers almost no deer hunter wouldn't take. I had a tough time holding off, especially since he was bigger than the buck I ended up with the season before.

The last time I spotted him was again on the eve of opening day. He was an exceptional buck then, and my mouth watered. I didn't see him again that season. And I was almost glad. Almost. It would have been too much like shooting an old pal.

I did, however, crawl into his center area to see if I could get a shot and, more importantly, to examine in detail his sign or spoor. Before I entered the thick, blown-down tangle of chokecherry, big-tooth maple, willows, and Douglas fir, I noted fresh, big tracks on that open slope where he fed. But he was eating only at night. I crawled along a game trail into the tangle and noted the rubs, old ones dried and forgotten and new ones oozing with sap. He preferred to rub willows and fir saplings three to four inches in diameter, perhaps because the fir sap clung to the big antlers and the dark willow bark gave a nice color to the hardened bone (or just as likely for reasons known only to himself). The big, outward-pointing tracks packed the heavy loam down wherever there was bare soil. Several fresh beds were hidden through the tangle, and each was about four feet long. I'd found where the buck lived—his living room, so to speak, his center area. I knew he was there someplace, perhaps even watching me, but I didn't find him. My scent perhaps had permeated the area, or maybe he'd seen me, because after several days of sneaking into the tangle, I found no more fresh sign.

I was luckier on another occasion. I'd located this buck during preseason scouting, had sneaked into his center area the week before the opening so that if I did frighten him away, he would have time to settle down and return. I knew what the place looked like, and had even drawn a rough map to try to figure the most likely bedding places. I'd noted where a seep came out from under a boulder and where big buck tracks were sunk in the mud where he drank each morning or afternoon. I found his favorite rub saplings and where he'd scraped. I'd already figured out where he'd browsed, which, not surprisingly, he did only at night. I found the main trail between the feeding slope and the center area; I would watch this at first and last light with the hope of catching him moving along it. In short, I knew about his routines, and if I was lucky, he had no idea I was plotting against him. That was my big advantage.

In the dawn of opening morning, I stalked to the edge of the small ravine and looked in. He wasn't there, but then I didn't really expect to see him. He hadn't gotten big by showing himself during hunting seasons. I still-hunted very slowly down the trail and into his center area. I stopped to let the light come and untangle the shadows; it was simply too dark to shoot in the gloom of the brush. When it was light enough to see the fresh tracks in the soil of the trail, I followed very, very slowly. Those who chase game from machines have no idea how slowly. I passed a thoroughly barked sapling, one that had been rubbed within the last day. Strips of bark littered the ground. I crawled underneath the spreading fir branches, pared away aspen saplings so I could ease through, and slowly worked into a sitting position. It was still shadowy and too easy to miss something, so I slowly scanned the tangled brush ahead and off to the sides. Ten minutes, and nothing. Twenty. Thirty, and my neck was getting stiff. And suddenly he was there in the gloom, nibbling at fungi on the rotting bark of a blowdown. He stood thirty yards away and yet was nearly impossible to see in the deep shadows and brush. If he hadn't moved to reach a bit of fungi on a branch, I wouldn't have seen him. I pressed the trigger of the .270 as his muscles bunched to jump.

In his years the big buck had never been disturbed in that tangled thicket and had no reason to believe he ever would be. And that's one advantage of hunting into a big buck's center area; few hunters even know they exist, and fewer still have the patience and ability to stalk into one.

Even though most bucks don't expect trouble in the center area, a hunter who has wormed his way into one when the buck is home is near to an animal with exceptional hearing, smell, and good sight. Shooting is normally close and often quick. Be ready. Wear "quiet" clothes and soft-soled moccasins or sneakers.

As a rule, preseason scouting involves seeing bucks. Scouting for a buck's home range, however, is more efficient because you don't rely on trying to sight a big buck that is more or less nocturnal and will probably spot you first and run into the next drainage. Look for tracks first, then rubs, beds, droppings, trails, browsed feed plants, escape cover, and even scrapes. Do it during the day when you are less likely to disturb the buck, since he's deep within his center area. Try not to get into thick places that look like they might house the big buck's living room, or center area.

Try to pick out peculiarities of a big buck's trail and hoofprint. Usually, careful examination of a fresh track on soft soil will show details revealing that each buck's track is slightly different. True,

Heavily rubbed willows in an adult buck's center area. A week later I killed a buck within fifty yards of this spot.

the differences may be subtle and you may need a magnifying glass to see them, but others might be obvious. Bucks live in tough country and the hoofs of many have chips, scrapes, or other small deformities that show up in the prints. Others have more obvious problems caused by frostbite, cougars, falls, or other accidents that show up in the gait of the buck. It's best to identify the track of a particular buck so that you can note it again elsewhere while you attempt to find out where the buck lives, waters, eats, and moves. Find the geographic limits of the track, and those will be the limits of the buck's home range. Once you feel pretty secure about that home range, try to figure out where its center area might be.

A good place to start is in the thickest, steepest tangle of brush you can find. If a big buck's sign isn't thick around that tangle, look for another one. Look not only for a concentration of tracks but also for beds (they're about four feet long and cleared of small pebbles and branches), rubs, scrapes, and droppings. Be especially cautious, and once you've located the center area, get out as soon as possible and don't go back until hunting season. It's best not to frighten the buck; though nine times out of ten he will return when things quiet down, there's always that tenth time. And even if he returns, he'll be wary.

I don't always recommend finding the center area before you are ready to shoot, simply because it is risky. Unless you really want to stack the odds in your favor and are willing to gamble for those stakes, settle for identifying the home range and be content with the knowledge that the center area is somewhere within it. Then, you can wrap up preseason scouting by finding tracks here and there, looking for cropped food plants and aging them (more about this elsewhere), identifying feeding and bedding trails, and locating scattered rubs and scrapes outside the center area but within the home range. When examining rubs, be aware that bigger bucks beat up on bigger saplings. Mature bucks tend to batter saplings around four inches in diameter, while smaller bucks use smaller saplings. Of course, all this sign will be much more concentrated in the center area, but generally I recommend staying away from it until you have a rifle or bow in your hands.

Bucks will rub anytime after the shedding of velvet, but they rub most frequently before and during the early part of the rut. Fresh rubs, of course, with the sapling still oozing sap, indicate that a buck passed there not long ago.

Possibly the first time the concept of center area truly sank in (I may have been reading about something like it in obscure biological journals) was the day I blundered into a classical place in northern Utah. I'd climbed onto a high plateau and then descended the north slope of a steep and deep canyon and entered a stand of centuries-old Douglas fir trees. There I found a deeply scarred game trail and followed it, admiring the gargantuan trees that had been growing in the deep loam since before the Spaniards had invaded Mexico. I love huge, old-growth trees, especially conifers, and in Utah where the industrious Mormons made heavy use of all available resources, old-growth timber is rarer than zebras in Nome. Unconsciously, I continued following the path of least resistance, the game trail. Eventually, it split into smaller trails, and I followed the one that had the freshest deer tracks. When I stooped to examine the tracks, they were larger than anything I'd seen in some time. And they were fresh—the edges hadn't dried and crumbled inward, and the dawn's frost had not softened their outlines. On I followed, and on.

The trail led through and underneath an intertwined tangle of willows, through a growth of aspen saplings nearly as intertwined, across a small brook (that's Eastern talk for "creek"), and into thick, young firs. I paused and noted a rub, and then, as I scanned slowly through the shadowy gloom, found another and another, and an old bed, then one not so old. I eased a cartridge into the chamber and screwed the variable-power scope down to 2X. Sap oozed from one of the battered fir trees. A musky scent hung heavily in the damp, still air. Despite my naivete, I'd managed somehow to move fairly quietly, because I wasn't really thinking about it. I scanned ahead, then took another step, and the buck stood behind a screen of bare willow branches. As he bounded over a blowdown, the slug caught him at the root of the tail and he dropped as if blasted by the hand of God. The buck was a good one.

Dragging a "meat" buck out in the subzero temperatures of a Wyoming late season.

Later I thoroughly examined the area. In about twelve hundred square feet (an area similar to my main trophy room), I found nineteen rubs old and new, three of what I would later come to identify as scrapes, eight beds, twenty-one piles of droppings, tracks as old as two months (they'd been made in thick mud during the last heavy rain two months earlier), and bits of deer hair.

By late October, northern and central mule deer begin to rub more vigorously. You'll see the majority of these rubs in the center area, of course, since bucks spend most of their time there, but they'll also become more common outside it. However, unless it's unseasonably cold or stormy, don't waste time looking for bucks outside the center area; remember, they're mostly nocturnal in hunted country. Concentrate on rubs in center areas, especially near a trail. In my observations, bucks will often get up in the middle of the day just to beat up on some sapling.

Old timber bucks often locate center areas near canyon heads where they can quietly slip into the next drainage if noisy hunters approach. If you suspect this is the case, post a hunter near the upslope side of the center area in a place where he'll have a shot should you spook the buck, intentionally or otherwise.

I learned this seemingly obvious lesson the hard way. I'd been hunting up a long, steep ravine in hopes of finding a big buck I'd seen earlier. When I was still a too-long rifle shot away from a thick tangle of maples at the head of the ravine, two giant bucks burst through it and raced across the open saddle and into Cottonwood Canyon. Both were monsters, but one was the big one I'd seen earlier and even more stupendous than I'd thought. I was awed by the high, heavy, widespreading antlers silhouetted against the blue autumn sky as they disappeared into the next canyon. If I'd been wise, I'd have still-hunted the buck's center area first, and from the top. But then, live and learn.

I've learned a great deal from such blunders, of which I've made more than my share. But now I have a pretty good idea where deer lay up and where their center area is located. Often it's near a place where a few bounds will take a buck out of sight, and more often than not, it's in very thick brush at a canyon head or ridgetop.

I hunt with a companion near a buck's center area only when things get desperate and time is short, often at the tail end of the season. Two people in the thick tangle of a center area just don't work—the buck goes out the opposite end before anyone can possibly see him. However, if you have a companion or two, one of you should enter the center area and move very slowly, and perhaps he might get the shot; if not, one or more hunters posted along likely escape routes should get a shot. More often than not, there'll be one or more trails the buck makes moderate use of at night, and these are good places for the ambush. The buck, if he's there and he doesn't take another route, will be jetting through; trophy dear intensely dislike exposing themselves during daylight, so keep a round in the chamber and your thumb on the safety and don't daydream.

During late seasons, the rut, or sometimes in lightly hunted places, you might catch the buck along a feeding trail in the dawn as he returns to the center area or in the last light as he moves onto the trail. Again, in moderately to heavily hunted places, adult bucks almost never show themselves during shooting light. If time isn't a factor, wait early and late along such trails. I've killed a number of adult bucks this way, though none in recent years; wise, old animals are adapting to the habits of deer hunters, further illustrating Darwin's showpiece theory of natural selection.

While scouting for a buck's home range, look for food plants. As mentioned, bucks feed on a variety of short brush— bitterbrush, sagebrush, mountain and curleaf mahogany, and rabbitbrush—as well as forbs and grasses. In mid-June of the year this is written, I watched two 3½-year-old bucks feeding in a meadow near my house. In fifteen minutes, I saw one eat dyer's wode (a European weed used to make fabric dyes), mule's ear, serviceberry, chokecherry, scrub oak, big-tooth maple, sagebrush, herbaceous sage, goat's beard, lupine, checker mallow, three genera of grasses (*Agropyron*, *Bromus*, and *Poa*), wild geranium, skyrockets, and several plants I couldn't identify with any assurance from thirty yards away, even with binoculars. Of course, food differs with the locality—a Mexican desert mule deer feeds on completely different vegetation than a Montana buck. In your hunting area, it's not necessary to know what the food plants are called, but it is important to recognize that they are something mule deer eat. The most obvious way to get familiar with food plants is to look for browsed vegetation and then corroborate your findings by watching deer feed; this may take time, but it's pleasant time. Since does and small bucks eat the same things big bucks eat, you need not watch only for nocturnal adult bucks. Perhaps make sketches of plants deer eat so you don't forget, or do what one young hunter I met did—press the plants in a book.

It's useful to age browsed food plants. Once, I located the home range of a nice buck a few weeks before the season. It was in a short, small canyon that had all the right things—water, escape cover, abundant food, and a tangle of deciduous saplings for the center area. The buck had rubbed maple and aspen saplings as large as seven or eight inches in diameter; the tracks measured a hair over four inches in length, and he'd cropped curleaf mahogany, bitterbrush, and a few forbs in his feeding area

Crooked Lake, British Columbia base camp. This was my first out-of-state hunting trip, and I chased goats, moose, bears, and mule deer here. I was seventeen and had saved for a year to make this solo trip.

and along the trail back into cover. I felt optimistic indeed as I anticipated opening day.

After I set up camp on the eve of the opening, I checked the feeding area. The cuts on the food plants where the buck had nipped his morsels were brown and oxidized, meaning they were old. I couldn't find any fresh ones, either. For whatever reasons, the buck had left—possibly frightened off by elk hunters earlier.

That same season I located another buck's home range fifteen miles east. In much of the intermountain region of Utah, Colorado, Wyoming, Nevada, Idaho, and Montana, bucks have a strong preference for a broad-leaved evergreen shrub called chaparral by the locals and manzanita by others. Aside from coniferous trees, it's the only green plant in the late or mid-autumn. This afternoon, armed with binoculars and a spotting scope, I glassed distant high ridges for patches of that telltale green. Specifically, I looked for that green as far away from roads or trails as I could find it. If I could locate big stands of timber or thick brush nearby, the place had possibilities. And if I could find water in a canyon bottom nearby or in a spring or seep indicated by dense, deciduous vegetation, the place had everything.

The next day I shouldered my backpack and trekked in and out of canyons and over ridge after ridge until I got to the right canyon that evening. After erecting my tiny three-pound tent, I rushed off to look for sign, and I found it before dark in the form of big tracks, rubs, and a well-used trail. I also found freshly cropped mahogany and chaparral and chokecherry, and a trail led from that feeding area across an open sage-covered slope, through a stand of scrub oak, and into a tangle of blowdowns and timber, the buck's center area.

I felt awfully good as I sat by the campfire that evening and watched the brown rice steam and listened to the teapot whistle. A big buck lived within a mile of where I sat at that moment. I'd take it slowly. I was in no hurry. I had a good idea where the buck spent the days, and I was confident. Two days later, I spotted the buck disappearing into the timber just at the first hint of daylight. Even in the poor light, he looked huge through the binocular. I still was in no hurry—I was having an excellent time doing what I'd rather do than anything else in the world, so I didn't push it. I figured that if I watched intensely in the last light of evening or in the first touch of dawn, I just might catch him either leaving or entering the center area. Ambushing under such conditions would be much simpler than crawling into the tangled center area with hopes of catching him dozing.

It didn't work out that way. I was forced to go in after him. A wet snow the night before would quiet the awkward movement I would make as I eased into the tangle. Almost always (I really want to say always, but the American penchant for qualifying concrete statements helps keep me from getting pinned down), the odds favor the buck in his center area. The only thing in favor of the hunter is that the buck doesn't expect trouble in his living room, so his guard is down somewhat (which is, I suppose, why SWAT teams kick in doors in the middle of the night).

As I literally crawled through the snow and mud, the breeze drifted downhill in the cold air. I strained to see through the predawn gloom of the trees. The air would warm later and then drift uphill, so I was hunting the lower part of the center area while the wind was moving downhill and away from the buck, if he was home. I'd grid my way back and forth across what I was sure was the center area and work uphill with the idea of still-hunting through by the time the air warmed and began drifting uphill. I paused often to scan everything I could see, hoping to spot a bit of hide, a flick of an ear, an antler tine. I crawled past a fresh rub, shredded bark littering the snow. I thought I could almost scent the buck's musky odor but wasn't quite sure. I slipped the bolt back to make sure I had one up the throat. Inside the tangle I could stand and walk, and I took a step, looked carefully, took another, and another. Something moved in my peripheral vision, and then again. A spruce sapling whipped forward and then back just down the slope. Then I spotted the buck's antlers as he gored the sapling. I was in his line of vision, but since he was busy with the sapling and felt secure in the tangle, he didn't spot me. When he hooked the sapling again, I brought up the rifle. He sensed something and stared in my direction. Too late. The 130-grain .270 bullet caught the base of his neck.

Often enough, a buck may abandon his home range for more remote digs when hunters pour into the country. And just as often, he'll return when things cool off, often after the weekend melee. One year I found a nice buck's home range and scouted it thoroughly. I was certain I knew nearly everything about it. I checked for fresh buck sign each weekend for the month preceding the deer hunt. On opening day, he'd vanished. I gridded through the center area, then wandered around the rest of the home range. Nothing. Still, I couldn't quite believe he'd left so suddenly, and it took two more days of fruitless searching to convince myself that he'd gone. Finally, I hunted elsewhere.

In overpopulated northern Utah (more than 85 percent of the state's human population is located along a 100-mile strip called the Wasatch Front), I've competed with other redshirts for more years than I care to admit to. Most hunting occurs on opening

This kind of brush is typical of a big buck's center area, but don't do it this way! Denim jeans make too much noise when they scrape against brush. Instead, wear wool pants.

weekend. Thereafter, as pressure lessens, deer reestablish their old routines. When I checked that buck's home range again the day before the season ended, he was back. I killed him in his bed under the umbrella canopy of an old Douglas fir in the center area.

Do not waste valuable time wandering around mule deer habitat. You have roughly the same chance of scoring on a monster mule deer buck as of getting struck by lightning in your bathroom. Instead, get remote and search for tracks, rubs, and other sign that indicates a big buck's home range. Then try to locate his center area. You'll have to hunt more quietly and carefully than ever, but if you do and you bag a big mule deer in his bed at close range, you will have done the hardest thing in North American hunting. So celebrate!

ON THE RIGHT TRAIL

In the dusk, I sat on the same boulder I'd parked on all week, watching a faint deer trail in the bottom of a tiny ravine. In a few minutes it would again be too dark to shoot, and then I'd again climb onto the flat and return to camp.

A big buck was using the little trail regularly, and I found his tracks each dawn. He fed on an open slope on forbs, bitterbrush, and mahogany in the dark, then returned to a tangle of scrub too thick and noisy for a man to get through without spooking the buck out the other side. My only chance would be to ambush him as he left his hideout a bit early in the evening, or returned a moment too late in the dawn. So far, it hadn't worked.

It was almost too dark to shoot. I looked through the riflescope to check how the cross hairs stood out against the pale sagebrush, and sensed something just at the edge of vision. I put the rifle down and looked carefully. Nothing. Did I want to spot a buck so badly my mind had begun to play jokes? I stared hard at where the faint trail disappeared into the brushy thicket. There—something, back in the shadows. But what was it?

A buck stepped out of the tangle, stared down the trail, and then walked down it in my direction. He was leaving the center area (at the time, I was not yet familiar with this concept) early to feed—precisely what I'd hoped for. I settled the cross hairs, nearly too faint to see in the gathering dark and shadows of the ravine, on the shoulder as he quartered head-on. I lost the buck in the flash of the muzzle blast, and when my vision readjusted, I couldn't find him. He hadn't run out of the ravine or crashed back into that tangle—I'd have heard that. I slid down the slope. The buck lay in the shadows just off the trail, and his antlers were the stuff of fantasy. I hurriedly field-dressed him in the dark and then whistled my way to camp in the starlight.

As mentioned earlier and as I will mention again, the myriad hunters afield these days force big bucks to become nocturnal to survive long enough to get big. Like the buck above, there's always the chance of catching one as he leaves the bedding area in the evening to feed in the open, or as he returns in the dawn. Here, the hunter needs time—if it works on the first try, you should visit Las Vegas. Of course, if a hunter will settle for a meat buck, these feeding-bedding trails are even more productive.

Make sure a buck is using the trail before you waste days waiting. If large tracks show regularly, it's a good spot for an ambush. Fresh droppings, newly cropped food plants, and other buck sign near or on the trail will increase your confidence.

Get on your stand long before the light begins to fade in the evening, in case the buck might hear your approach. And do it silently. If you aren't quite as silent as you should be, getting there early gives the buck time to forget about any small noise you might have made. Likewise, in the dawn, get to your stand long before the light begins to come in the east, and be especially more silent since the buck (you hope) is still out feeding and highly alert. Don't waste time sitting during midday unless other hunters are working toward you and may jump something out of its bed. During midday I normally still-hunt likely looking cover, carefully work a suspected center area, glass distant ridges for good-looking deer areas, or return to camp for lunch.

I return to my spot to wait in midafternoon, usually before 3 P.M. It's usually prudent to sit in a different spot in the

An adult buck in his center area.

afternoon and evening than in the morning, since the afternoon air is warm and drifting uphill, the reverse of dawn conditions. Also, bucks may use different trails to leave cover to get to the feeding area than they do to return to cover. Check tracks for confirmation one way or the other. I used to spend a few days each early autumn attempting to photograph a gang of bucks in southern Montana. Three of them were pals and would feed out of the timber in the evening along one trail and return on another trail several hundred yards farther down the ridge. Those bucks very likely became nocturnal at the onset of hunting season.

Trails crossing ridges, or otherwise leading from one drainage to another, are very often good spots to ambush a buck. These include trails through a saddle to another canyon or ravine, trails out of canyon heads, and ridgeline trails. Trails through timber, especially along a bench, are also good spots.

Crossing trails are often used for escape (more about that later) when bucks are pressured, and they may be used to reach and leave feeding and bedding areas. Usually, though, they are avenues for a deer to get from one canyon to another.

Early in my hunting career, I heard that saddles were good places to ambush bucks. I waited along a trail through a saddle for several evenings after high-school classes. Deer tracks were plentiful in the dust. After a few days, I was ready for any action that came my way. One dusk, cold and hungry, I was ready to head back down the mountain when a deer materialized, and then another and two more. One was a small three-pointer, western count. I suddenly caught an intense case of buck ague. I yanked one off and missed. I shot again, then again, and just as suddenly, the deer were gone. I'd blown my big chance. I'd read somewhere always to check for blood, so I walked down to the trail. Where it dropped off the ridge and down the slope, I found still-drying spatters in the dust. I stumbled over the buck in the dark farther down the trail.

Trails between two patches or stands of timber and escape trails produce when conditions are right. More often than not, escape trails lead to thick brush or timber or to an inaccessible gorge or other place a buck can hide out. Deer may lose themselves by escaping along natural trails through saddles or canyon heads.

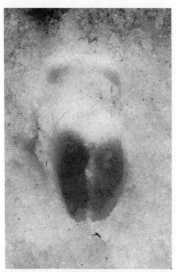

Wise old bucks don't always take the shortest route between A and B. Over the course of their lives, mule deer are widely and heavily hunted. Big bucks are experienced in the ways of hunting and hunters. They're likely to realize that if someone is pushing them out of cover, other hunters may be on the other side. I'm certain that big bucks I have hunted were more capable of reasoning than hunters and biologists give deer credit for; I'm equally sure bucks are adaptable. An old buck does what the hunter least expects, including selecting an obscure route to a distant refuge.

Buck track in snow. Note the dewclaws at rear of the main track. The main print measures 3½ inches in length.

Years ago, back when I regularly hunted in northern Utah, I often hit a certain saddle on opening morning. As regular as the autumnal equinox, one group of hunters made a big drive through the timber at the head of a canyon to force deer through the saddle above to a place where standers were posted. Most of the standers were meat hunters and happy with any legal deer. The hunters had performed the same ritual for years and knew that the saddle was a natural crossing place as well as an escape trail.

More than a dozen hunters always started pushing at the low end of the timber in the canyon bottom. They worked the big timber in a crescent, the ends of which were upslope on either side of the canyon. Some deer always slipped through the drivers. But more of them panicked their way toward the saddle and into the ambuscade. The canyon sounded like a war zone for a few minutes each opening Saturday.

Unknown to that mob, I also participated in the drive. A small, deep, and thick ravine entered the timber at right angles to the escape trail through the saddle. A trail ran up its bottom and was invisible in the tangle unless you were on it. The slopes above it were thick with chokecherry and aspen tangles. I'd get to the ravine before the riders started their drive into the timber. I collected several good bucks there, bigger than anything the standers ever shot. One cold opening dawn, I muffed a chance at a true mossy-horn. The buck trotted up the ravine before skidding to a stop, sensing something out of place. He was screened behind brush, and I could see massive antlers jerk this way and that as the buck tried to figure it out. He then bounded straight uphill through aspens, and I couldn't get a shot. Hunters along the trail in the saddle above didn't get big bucks, because only the young and foolish ones retreated in the direction they'd been pushed. Experienced bucks either wouldn't be in the timber to begin with at that time of year or were aware of other escape routes.

The best trail ambushing occurs along migration routes leading from higher country toward lower winter range. At the right time, they'll give you the best trophy mule deer hunting imaginable. With luck and the right weather, a hunter can look over literally scores of bucks and pick and choose. I've caught this buck migration twice, and I dream of doing it again.

A recent, heavy snow or a storm front with plummeting barometric pressure, which many animals sense, may trigger a massive downward migration, especially late in the season. To have much of a chance to enjoy these spectacles, try for late-season permits. Late hunts are more and more rare these days, what with the decreasing mule deer densities and the scarcity of adult bucks, but some still exist as of this writing. In the past, late hunts, often into December and even early January in the intermountain region, weren't so hard to find. If you're preparing for such a hunt, do the homework: Talk to local ranchers and game managers, study topo maps to determine drainage and ridge directions, question local hunters. Mule deer prefer to migrate down bare, windy ridges where there's less snow to fight through, unless the wind is too severe, as it can be on ridgetops. They also migrate down broad, open canyons and along plateaus. Look for tracks and animals themselves to determine the best places.

My most memorable late-season hunt back when I was a youngster was in the high plateaus and open country west of Big Piney, Wyoming, one of the coldest spots in the continental U.S. I'd been hunting the plateaus and lightly brushed breaks, and I'd seen does and small bucks, but nothing worth spending my tag on; after all, it cost me $25! One afternoon it began clouding up. An hour later, a warm wind blew in from the south (in Big Piney in December, anything above zero is warm!), a sure sign of an approaching storm front. Just before dark, deer began moving down the ridges toward the Green River bottoms in the east. I didn't get a chance at a buck.

That night, the storm dropped twenty inches of snow on the plateaus and more in the mountains farther west. Deer were moving down every ridge and across each plateau. The mesas and breaks had filled with deer almost overnight. Most followed well-used trails along the ridges or mesa edges where wind had blown away some of the snow. I remember counting two hundred deer before giving it up that morning. Some were good bucks on distant ridges. I stalked several, but by the time I got there they were halfway to the river. Stalking may not be the best option when hunting migrating deer.

I found a contorted pine overlooking a packed-down deer trail and built a fire from the dead branches I could break from the tree. The cold, dense wind blew down the ridge, carrying my scent and the smoke away from the deer approaching from above. Several times an hour deer trudged down the trail forty yards below. A medium-sized five by five walked by, but I let him pass because I'd seen much bigger bucks on distant ridges. By evening, more than one hundred deer had slogged along the trail below my stand.

As I stamped my feet in the below-zero temperature before starting back toward the truck, a good buck walked over the ridge and down the trail. He was so intent on making the bottoms before nightfall that he didn't notice me behind the stunted pine. He wasn't as big as some I'd seen in the distance, but he'd do. At the blast, he pitched forward into the powdery snow and lay still.

I've been lucky enough to catch only one other such migration, and had even better results. I'll always dream of lucking into another.

Trails aren't the only spots for good ambushes. Bedding areas and feeding sites are often as good, under the right conditions. If you know how.

I've heard more stories than I care to recount about hunters finding a buck's bed, waiting for him to return, and then shooting him when he does. I'm skeptical. True, a buck will frequently bed in the same general area, usually the center area, but it's exceptional that he'll sleep in the same bed day after day. Nevertheless, find where a buck regularly beds and you stand a decent chance of collecting him.

Normally (and again being redundant), bucks bed in thick timber or brush during hunting seasons. A typical spot I've hunted in the past is an open, west-facing slope buried inside a big stand of spruce and fir timber in Utah's Wasatch Mountains. Deer usually bed near the top of the open slope, where they're just a step away from the cover of the big trees. Merely by standing up, they can browse on all sorts of prime plants. If I hunt the place, I wait just inside the edge of the timber, or stalk through the timber and into the opening in the morning or evening.

Favorite feeding spots are good places for ambushes. ID the area by tracks and other sign and by plants deer prefer, whether they are bitterbrush, the mahoganies, sagebrush, cliffrose, forbs, or mesquite beans and manzanita. Waiting at a favorite buck "pasture" will eventually pay off if you're patient, you have sufficient time, and other hunters aren't mucking up the place.

My favorite element of ambushing along trails is that it's a pleasant way to spend time. You'll very likely spot other wildlife, whether it's a white-footed mouse or red-backed vole or a bighorn ram or a cougar. Ambushing is a lazy man's way to hunt. Fat, old financiers stand nearly as good a chance as a decathlete of waylaying a good buck.

ALL-WEATHER BUCKS

A given mule deer may experience weather ranging from droughts and 110 degrees to minus 40 and blizzards, all within a calendar year. So the animals must be highly adaptable. And they are. Because they live in such widely varying habitats, they must change habits drastically to meet changing conditions, and hunters must do the same. Let's start with winter-type weather.

If an autumn storm has dumped significant snow in deer country, deer move down, predictably enough. As mentioned in another chapter, if a hunter can catch this weather-caused downward migration, he can also catch the best trophy buck hunting imaginable. Since fewer late hunting seasons are held these days, it seems unlikely that I'll ever get in on this kind of action again.

Deer react to single-digit and below temperatures in specific ways. They will often be out and feeding, since cold temperatures make additional demands on their metabolism—it takes more calories just to maintain body temperature. An exception is when the energy cost of looking for food exceeds that of lying doggo. And with the decreased quality of winter vegetation (plants don't grow during winter and therefore produce fewer nutrients), deer may feed throughout the day when at other seasons they would

Buck on a well-used trail between feeding and bedding areas. Such trails are ambush hot spots.

lay up in cover. This phenomenon is even more exaggerated when the bedding areas they are using are close to feeding sites. Wind throws a virus into their internal computer, however; even a slight wind in cold temperatures causes mulies to head for protective timber. Hypothetically, the wind saps more heat energy than the deer can compensate for in calories they'd gain feeding. Generally, the colder it is, the more actively deer feed, but the breezier the conditions, the less time they expend feeding. In extreme cold, deer may not move at all.

During late autumn and winter cold, deer may not begin feeding until late morning, when the sun begins to warm their habitat. They may then feed until a bit after sundown (see data elsewhere in this book). I've seen this numerous times during November and December hunting seasons in the middle and northern parts of mule deer habitat. During hunting seasons in November, December, and, in the old days (and currently in Mexico), January, the most productive methods of hunting in cold weather are simple glassing and still-hunting during daylight hours. Back when late seasons were relatively common, some of my favorite spots were the plateaus and mountains west of Big Piney and La Barge, Wyoming. You could pick up a deer tag at any hotel, sporting-goods store, or honky-tonk (a couple of us freshmen even screwed up our nerve enough to pick them up at the Dixie Hotel, a reputed cathouse). A nonresident tag cost $25 then.

Since this place is one of the coldest in the lower forty-eight, I wouldn't leave my hotel room until after sunup, or arrive on the plateaus until midmorning. It didn't matter. When it was cold—and I remember one day hunting at 41 degrees below zero—deer were out all day. When it was windy—and it often was on those high plateaus—deer bedded in the aspens in the ravine bottoms out of the wind. It was simple to walk up the ravines opposite the brushy north-facing slopes and pot a deer, even if they were bedded. I didn't like the wind any better than the deer did, and I never stayed out in it too long.

I'm convinced deer can sense an approaching storm by the dropping barometric pressure. I've noticed the same thing with elk (in the course of research financed by the National Science Foundation, the Utah Cooperative Wildlife Research Unit, and Utah State University). Both species feed hectically before a storm hits, possibly to compensate for time that may be lost sitting out the storm, which may last days. If it's late in the season, you might catch even trophy bucks out and about browsing during the day; still, they know it's hunting season and won't expose themselves any more than need be. In these conditions, I've found that the best places to seek trophy bucks are in hidden meadows or on open slopes surrounded by timber or heavy brush.

When a storm approaches, the most productive tactics include glassing from ridges across canyons to those protected openings just mentioned, or still-hunting along high ridges, watching closely for openings on distant ridges, then making a long stalk. If you're familiar with a buck's home range, waiting along feeding and bedding trails can also be highly rewarding. I've collected good bucks under these conditions, both by glassing and stalking and by ambushing along trails. During the storm, mule deer lay up in heavy cover (more about this later). After the storm, they may go on a feeding binge. They might be everywhere, and even trophy bucks may be feeding during midday—especially if it's cold and clear.

Deer seek protection in heavy cover during hard rain or snow. Unless you're willing to stalk into this cover and move very, very slowly and carefully, stay in camp. During a storm, deer prefer the umbrella canopy of stands of conifers—cone-bearing trees like spruce, fir, and pine. Good umbrella-type protection of, say, a big Douglas fir ensures that a buck will remain practically dry even in a blizzard, and be protected from the wind.

If you're the kind who hates sitting around camp and doesn't mind rain or melting snow dripping down your neck and can stand wet feet all day, heavy rain or snow can offer exceptional hunting. Wet conditions in the forest make for silent stalking. The heavy moisture muffles your sounds, softens dry leaves, makes soil sodden and silent, and saturates dry twigs and branches. If a hunter is careful, he can move more quietly than at any other time. Added to this, he knows where the deer are— bedded in heavy cover. Even though it is wet and quiet, wear clothing such as wool (though it'll get wet, it stays warm, more or less, and nothing is quieter) and soft, pliable, silent footgear. Avoid noisy rain gear, even though it will be more comfortable; even wet, this stuff is noisy when a branch scrapes against it.

When a storm drags on and on, deer eventually ignore it and go on about their feeding business. Since feeding is the most important activity to maintain body heat and metabolism at a critical time of year, it's their Number 1 priority. Eventually they'll move to open slopes where most browse plants grow. In wet forests of the Northwest U.S. and British Columbia, deer feed in trees on what the Indians there call "caribou moss," fungi and other lichens. When a storm continues for days, deer feed heavily for long periods, making up for feeding time missed while sitting out the first part of the storm. I've seen precisely the same thing

Still-hunting bucks in the fog can be fantastic.

with elk in western states and with moose, caribou, and Dall, bighorn, and Siberian snow sheep.

Another consideration is that because of reduced light intensity during heavy overcast associated with storms, deer may feed later in the day or start earlier in the afternoon because light intensity then is similar to that during crepuscular hours (dawn and dusk) when deer normally feed most of the year. Which leads to another observation: On cloudy days, at least in the mid-intermountain area, deer feed later in the morning and begin feeding earlier in the afternoon than they would on a clear day, even in the relatively mild conditions of autumn.

Aside from caveats already noted about breeze and wind, windy conditions are good times to hunt. Deer simply can't hear you or any other predator as well, and so you might get closer. On the other hand, since mule deer rely heavily on hearing to detect danger, they're extremely nervous when they can't hear it approaching. They're apt to jump and run for it at the slightest provocation. They'll try to bed in protected places out of the wind and will carefully watch their backtrail. Windy conditions are good times to hunt patches of brush or timber so thick you would not otherwise work them. Since you can't hear much except whipping branches and howling gusts, don't worry about hearing a buck. Instead, do what a buck will do, rely on vision, and move slowly enough to give yourself time to carefully scan ahead and to the sides. Move your head slowly when scanning. A wise old buck's scenting doesn't work too well in the wind, either, since variable gusts scatter scent far and wide. But don't mistake this as a reason not to try to move into the prevailing wind.

For now, let's skip spring and summer weather, times of no significance to most buck stalkers, and fast-forward to late summer and autumn. Conclusions made earlier about clouds and rain still apply. Light snow has about the same general effect as heavy snow, though the results are reduced. With snow and cooler temperatures, deer may feed more commonly during daylight hours. Thanks to the increased human activity of hunting season, though, it's unlikely that big bucks will show themselves even with cool weather and early snow.

I've had awfully good luck buck-stalking in the fog. Fog seems to give mule deer confidence, so they may move about in the open. Still-hunting is the best tactic, since stalking is quieter and bucks' vision is reduced in the murk. If you're doing it right, which means slow and quiet, you'll often see the buck before he spots you, and this is the idea. And you'll be closer. I've killed bucks less than thirty yards away by simply still-hunting in the open. I've taken two in the timber much closer than that. Once, in British Columbia while moose hunting, I stumbled onto a good mule deer in thick spruce forest at twenty yards. He didn't see me until just before I touched the trigger. Another advantage of hunting in foggy overcast is that light intensity is reduced and deer react as if it is dawn or dusk, normal deer movement times. During fog, with water dripping off the tent fly, you can either stay inside next to the cookstove with a hot cup of coffee and dry feet, or get out, get wet, and possibly shoot a buck. I prefer the latter, and because I do, several more racks hang on my walls than I otherwise would have had.

OK, we've dealt with cold, storms, fog, and wind, so what about calm and clear weather? Conditions of light intensity, temperature, humidity, and browse being equal, mule deer will be more active in clear weather, when they can rely more heavily on eyesight, than in overcast, murky, or stormy conditions. Mulies depend almost as much on sight as they do on hearing and scenting, and nearly as much as pronghorn antelope or mountain sheep do. This may seem to contradict earlier claims, but mule deer move during reduced light conditions because they feel more comfortable then. During clear and calm weather, however, much deer movement occurs during the dark hours, and since they've fed all night, they lay up earlier in the morning.

Moonlit nights don't help the hunter, other factors remaining equal. In western mule deer country, it's a commonly held belief that moonlit nights make buck hunting tougher than it already is. The reasoning goes that deer bed down before first light because they've been out all night. I used to believe it, and I still may at times. Mule deer see so well at night that they don't need moonlight to keep them up and feeding. I vacillate between the belief that moonlight makes hunting harder and the idea that it has little effect. Over several years, I've kept notes on the number of deer seen feeding during daylight on full-moon, half-moon, quarter-moon, and moonless nights. If the weather was clear, there seemed to be little difference; I did not find that deer bedded earlier in the morning, but this was counterbalanced by their getting up to feed a bit earlier in the afternoon or evening. Lately, however, without taking precise notes, I have noticed that it's tougher to see antlers after nights with a full or nearly full moon.

Mark Twain once jested about New England weather and said that he'd ". . . counted 136 kinds of weather inside of four-and-twenty hours." Though most mule deer country is not quite that extreme, much of it experiences huge changes of weather over the calendar year and even within hunting seasons.

We haven't yet discussed hot weather. I've done much buck hunting in Utah during the general season that began in mid-October. Then, more often than not, it's hot and dry and stalking through maple and oak leaves is like stomping through an echo chamber full of potato chips. On the other hand, I was never surprised to see blizzards and subfreezing temperatures. Western hunting weather is nearly as unpredictable as Twain's New England in the spring.

In hot and dry conditions, mule deer predictably lay up during the day and move when it's late, dark, and cooler. They'll bed in dense, cool cover on the moister and shadier north- and east-facing exposures. Since less moisture is lost to evaporation there, both cover and food plants grow better. When it's very dry, deer frequently move down to lower altitudes where there's open water and creekside food grows more abundantly. A seep or small spring in heavy cover is a good place to find deer, especially if good browse is nearby.

Adult bucks are in their prime from late summer to just before the start of the rut in early November. It's not uncommon to collect a prime-time mature buck with more than 2½ inches of tallow over the loins or rump. Fat men suffer more in the heat than thin ones do, and so big and fat bucks get hotter than thin youngsters. Big bucks won't move during the day unless they're forced to, and they seek the coolest places they can find in the densest cover so they are not forced to. On one occasion, I found a buck lying in an old elk wallow in the timber. Unfortunately, I hadn't expected it and the buck bounded away unscathed.

If you're out during the wilting and parched conditions of some early hunts, seek out likely looking heavy cover on north- or east-facing slopes. Then locate beds and bedding sites. Bucks may bed on relatively open and breezy ridges, especially if the insects are bad, but only in remote or unhunted country. They also often bed in inaccessible gorges near streams, but here, too, they prefer the timber. On this temporary, seasonal

Big Piney, Wyoming, deer country. The temperature is –38 degrees Fahrenheit and the deer trails are heading for the Green River low country.

home range (refer to home-range and center-area concepts discussed earlier), look for the buck in his center area, characterized by rubs, beds, droppings, and tracks. In all probability, you'll find a well-used trail from the center area to a local feeding slope. Bucks tend to feed in openings, since that's where preferred browse plants grow.

When it's hot and dry and bucks are bedded in timber, either still-hunt slowly into the trees or ambush just downwind of their main trail. When still-hunting in cover, be especially alert and focus on the downwind side of the trail since wise old bucks bed there. Another alternative is driving or pushing through the timber. I dislike this method because it's too disruptive and may permanently or temporarily drive deer out of the home range. Sometimes driving simply won't work well because of too-steep slopes, too-large stands of brush or trees, or other considerations. Still, time may be short and "pushing" the timber may be your only hope. Understand that a big mule deer buck is as cagey as any whitetail with twice the experience, and much more unpredictable. Take any and all precautions you can possibly think of.

In southern Arizona and Sonora, Mexico, mule deer regularly survive intense heat and aridity. The sometimes searing, parched desert conditions have made mule deer tolerant of such elements. Since they're used to the desert, they're not so influenced by heat as their northern cousins. Too, desert mule deer seasons tend to be held later, when it's not so hot or dry. Desert seasons may begin in October, which is plenty hot in Sonora, and run through January, a time of pleasant days and very cool nights. While I was hunting once in Sonora, it snowed three inches, an event so rare the locals migrated into the foothills just to touch the stuff. Many children were seeing snow for the first time in their lives, but the snow melted by midday.

Even though vegetation, including food plants, is drastically different in the desert and deer habits are dictated to a large degree by climate, bucks behave pretty much the same in Sonora as they do in Montana. They just do it later—say, two months later. Desert deer typically rut heavily in the middle of January (as opposed to a general mid-November to mid-December rut in the intermountain region), and they'll keep antlers into April before shedding them. Once, on the Kofa in southwestern Arizona, I saw two medium-sized bucks with antlers in late April. Old-timers in Arizona say that some mulies will keep antlers into May. In Utah and Wyoming, places I'm most familiar with, mule deer usually shed antlers in February. I've seen only a few bucks with big antlers much into March.

The short of all this is, you can't be a consistently successful trophy mule deer hunter without understanding the importance of climate and weather in determining mule deer behavior.

A SHELTERED LIFE

For as long as they have lived on this planet, men and mule deer have sought cover from two things: weather and enemies. I've wandered through caverns on four continents where humans have found cover, as evidenced by layers of soot and millennia-old rock art. In parts of Africa and southern Asia, men still bar their doors at night against man-eating lions, tigers, and leopards (see, for example, my book, *Safari: A Dangerous Affair*, from Safari Press).

In our high-tech society, protection from animal predators (never mind human predators) is no longer a concern. And most of us have a roof over our heads when the weather turns foul. Mule deer, however, seek shelter from both the elements and predators, which during deer season means you. When you hunt big bucks, rely on instinct and think like a big buck.

When a squall blasts through the country, mule deer head for the trees, and when it's hot, they abandon open country and find shade. If it's too windy above timberline, in basins or on open slopes, they'll descend and seek shelter in a dense stand of lodge pole pine or Douglas fir.

Often, a small patch of trees provides sufficient cover from a storm or hot sun. Since wolves are seldom a problem for mule deer on most of their range these days, bucks in remote country seek cover mainly to get out of the weather. Mountain lions or cougars are efficient predators of mule deer, and cover often is not a guarantee that a big cat will not be able to sneak up on a buck. However, some cover is thick and noisy enough that it can be sufficient protection from lions. But a small patch of brush may not be sufficient cover for protection against you, the ultimate predator.

I've hunted wild country in the northern part of mule deer range and have jumped bucks from tiny patches of wind-tortured fir or pine called "shintangle," well above timberline, where the buck had to cross completely open terrain and offered an easy shot. I've also flushed them from small tangles of willow on open slopes where the nearest escape cover was five hundred yards almost straight down.

I've already written about that buck in Nevada's Ruby Range that lived in a living-room-sized tangle of willow on a completely open slope. He hadn't budged in the days I'd walked by the brush, and one day I almost idly tossed a few rocks into it. To my surprise, a big buck crashed from the tangle and across the open slope, and I collected him, after a miss or two. There's a fair chance I actually hit the buck with one of those rocks.

If it's windy, bucks seek heavier cover. Don't bother with small patches of brush on open slopes or ridges; instead, still-hunt into the timber. The wind ripping through the branches of the big trees will mask most noises you make. A disadvantage is that wise old bucks are likely to be spooky; since they know they can't hear approaching danger, they'll run at the slightest provocation.

In heavy weather bucks also head for forests, where they prefer the umbrella canopy of coniferous trees. Dampness, especially snow, makes it easier for you to stalk quietly through the woods. Deer are normally calmer in wet weather than during a strong blow, another plus for stalking. I've found that storms often offer the only chance to stalk a timbered mountain undetected.

The fruits of hunting late in heavy snow.

Most mule deer country we hunt these days isn't wilderness; we compete with other hunters and bucks are wary and tend to bed in nearly impenetrable cover. This cover may be a vast forest into which a buck needs only to retreat farther if he's disturbed. Escape cover, as opposed to cover used only as protection from weather, is so thick it's difficult for a predator to move through it without being detected.

As mentioned earlier, if hunting season is going full-bore, it's a safe wager that you won't find adult bucks in open places. Most beeline for the thickest timber and brush they can find, and won't move across an opening during daylight. Some good bucks will bed at the edge between a meadow and heavy forest, where they can feed or watch for danger approaching. If a hunter shows, bucks simply disappear into cover, the hunter none the wiser. Again, escape cover is normally both dense and large. It does bucks little good to hide in a thick but small patch of brush surrounded by open country since that's a logical place for a hunter to search.

Of course, the trick to stalking in cover is to prevent the buck from knowing you are there. This means hunting into the wind, or as nearly as you can do so. It also means moving slowly and quietly. And I'll say it again: Wear "quiet" clothing, stuff made from wool (my favorite), pile, or supple cotton, and soft footwear like moccasins or sneakers. So what if you get wet? Camp and dry clothes will be there at the end of the day. Keep to game trails where possible because there will be fewer branches to scrape against, step on, and run into, and deer expect movement along game trails. Some of these trails are not much more than tunnels under brush where you'll be forced to crawl. Keep an eye out ahead and to the sides, searching for a bedded and unsuspecting buck. You'll seldom spot the entire animal, so search for a piece of him, like the dark forehead or an antler tine or ear.

I've spent entire days stalking through dense stands of fir or aspen only a mile across. I knew bucks were in the tangle because of abundant tracks, rubs, beds, and droppings. As long as I was certain at least one mature buck was in the jungle, I had faith enough to still-hunt the area with extreme care. If you've found solid evidence of a trophy buck, persist in that place.

Mule deer don't browse in old-growth forest or dense tangles of brush; they eat developmental vegetation growing in more or less open places, so look for forbs, bushy plants, and other vegetation that tends to disappear in the forest. Though an adult buck won't browse in daylight in hunted country, search for buck spoor on open slopes or flats where he feeds at night. Again, a good buck's foretrack measures about four inches in length, and his stride is noticeably longer than a small buck's. Adult bucks rub larger saplings, be they fir, pine, or aspen; younger bucks may only rub thumb-thick saplings or branches. Destroyed saplings thicker than three inches in diameter were probably bashed by bigger bucks. Correlate the rub with tracks for confirmation; we're dealing with unpredictable nature here, and you'll always find exceptions.

Even though I may take a day to still-hunt only a mile through escape cover, I'll emerge scraped, bruised, and as tired as if I'd trekked twenty miles up and down mountains. Still-hunting through thick cover requires so much concentration, in fact, that once you hit the bedroll that night, you won't budge until morning. But it's an absorbing way to hunt, and you'll learn more about stalking, tracking, sign, and buck behavior in two days than you will in ten seasons of just beating the brush. And if you're careful and controlled and don't get impatient, still-hunting through cover is the most consistent way to take good bucks in these days when all big bucks are too familiar with the ways of man, the predator.

I once watched a small group of Bayei tribesmen prepare their shelters for the coming night on an island in the Okavango Delta of Botswana. Two prides of lions patrolled the vicinity, and the Okavango was thick with leopards. The natives closed the thorn-fence openings, then piled vicious thorn branches in front of the doors to their huts. Inside, they kept spears and pangas (broad-bladed knives) handy. As we watched, I thought I could smell the acrid stink of fear. That night, I fully understood why a wise mule deer buck hides in the thickest cover he can find during hunting season.

BIG-BUCK COVER

While pursuing an advanced degree in wildlife biology years ago, I learned that along with food and water, cover is a basic requirement of all animals. Most animals, if they are sought by any kind of predator, use cover for escape as well as protection from weather. Each type of cover is used at different times.

Protective cover tends to be the vegetation that best keeps the rain, snow, or wind off. Small patches of timber or brush or perhaps only two to four trees can serve the purpose, but here the buck isn't looking for concealment from predators, especially the ultimate beast with the high-powered rifle, telescopic scope, and all the other gadgets he comes up with to get away from it all. If a buck knows a lion is around, he can easily outrun it; it is the one he doesn't know about that's dangerous. I've often seen bucks bed down in small patches of shintangle or chokecherry surrounded by open country, and when I jumped one, it was no great feat to collect him as he raced across the open. When it's windy, bucks normally vacate smaller brush patches on open slopes or ridges. On windy days, still-hunt through timber or other protected places like ravine bottoms. In rain or snow, bucks favor thick trees, especially conifers with their umbrella canopy.

Escape cover is the densest and largest stand of trees or brush a buck can find, and he's usually in it because it's hunting season. It's called escape cover because he's there to escape hunters, and bucks are safe there because few hunters can move through it without being detected. Adult mulie bucks have adapted very quickly over the last few score years. For example, they've learned not to pause on top of a ridge to look back during hunting season— or at any other time, for that matter. Those that did so were killed and thus couldn't pass on their stupidity genes; those that didn't live to breed and produce more intelligent offspring, and therefore all mule deer are becoming more adept at dealing with humans.

I once spent two days stalking through a big stand of fir in Utah. As in all such stands in the area, the trees grew on the north- or east-facing slopes for reasons already discussed. I stalked slowly, examining spoor as carefully as I knew how. I was in no hurry, and didn't want to risk spooking the buck into the next county.

Late in the dawn of the third day, I found still-warm droppings steaming lightly in the early chill. Obviously, the buck had just left them. I took up the trail, easy to follow in the needle-covered loam, and measured progress by the inch. I'd take a step or two, pause, and scan the woods meticulously as far as I could see, searching through fir boughs, and under blowdowns. I kept track of wind direction, from time to time dropping a pinch of caribou moss or a handful of fir needles to see how they drifted in the breeze. There wasn't much breeze that day, and I concentrated fully on moving silently and searching ahead with my eyes. I saw first a tip of an antler keeping time to an unknown rhythm. That rhythm was the buck's heartbeat and the chewing of its cud. The antlers stuck up from behind a massive blown-down fir trunk. I had no shot, so I eased around a big standing fir, watching very carefully where I put my feet and avoiding any twig that might catch on clothing. I spotted his neck and eased the gun up. A single shot killed him at a measured sixteen feet.

Still-hunting and stalking through escape or other cover is more absorbing than any other type of hunting, and often it's the only hunt on the mountain.

MULE DEER HIGH

On that fateful day when I was thirteen, I started hunting mule deer in the traditional way—in accessible country on the lower part of deer range, say, 4,000 to 7,000 feet in elevation. Mostly, I hunted within half a day's walk of some sort of road. Utah's Department of Fish & Game, as it was called in those days, selected

Late-season still-life.

a few isolated small mountain ranges for early season hunts. The first season was so successful I bought tags in other states (then, you didn't have to suffer through complicated drawings; you just crossed the state line and plunked down your $35 at a gas station) and wandered from one high mountain to another.

On those hunts, I found that big mule deer stay up in the peaks, weather permitting, until the beginning of the rut in November. There's a lot of high country in the West, but few hunters will expend the effort to get up there because it requires a backpack and a considerable chunk of time. I felt like Colter, the mountain man, who in 1807 "discovered" the Jackson's Hole country (never mind that American Indians were already there)—I had it all to myself. Even on my last high-mountain hunt a few years ago, I was alone up there.

In remote basins where big mule deer bucks aren't badgered much by hunters, they may browse during daylight hours. This meant I wouldn't have to resort to complicated tactics just to see a buck, let alone shoot one.

One of the simplest tactics is to locate a buck in the morning when he's out feeding, wait a few hours for him to bed, then plan a stalk. Trophy bucks typically bed in open basins where the most obvious approach is from below. But during the day, the air warms, becomes less dense, and rises toward the buck, which will scent any danger beneath him. Wise bucks also bed where they can watch a sizable chunk of basin or ridge. Since their vision is nearly as keen as that of a pronghorn antelope, it's tough to stalk from below because you'll be seen as well as scented. Occasionally, you'll be able to stalk across the slope at about the same altitude as the buck, but only if there's sufficient cover, and here cover probably means boulders. More frequently, you'll need to circle above the buck, taking care to stay out of sight in the process. This might involve climbing into the next drainage and then stalking down on him. That way, the wind is in your face, at least during the day, and the buck is likely facing downhill.

In high timberline basins, rocks tumble at the slightest encouragement, so the buck might ignore small noises you might make while stalking. If you make consistent noises, however, he'll get suspicious. When you stalk downward, the odds for success are better, but you've got ice water in your veins if you don't get at least a touch of buck fever.

Back in the 1960s, before I'd become an irretrievable high-country junkie, I made a stalk on a big buck I'd located in an elevated basin southeast of Afton, Wyoming. I retreated into an adjoining drainage and, using hands, ascended the sidehill onto a bare, blade-thin divide of unstable, jagged boulders. I sat up there chewing a strip of jerky and staring out across an endless alpine piece of the West, with nothing nearer than I to heaven but a distant golden eagle. I wondered if John Colter felt the same way as he worked his way through the Yellowstone country nearly two centuries earlier.

The buck was six hundred yards below, but if I eased down a rocky chute—where I'd be in plain view if he looked over his shoulder—and then down a short cliff, I'd be out of sight in a tiny glacial basin. If I got across that into a jumble of bulldozer-sized boulders, I'd be within range of the trophy buck. That's about how it worked out, except that as I made the final approach, the sun dipped behind the ridge and the air cooled suddenly and began drifting toward the buck. He caught my scent and jumped up. I shot as he bounded across the slope. Even as I touched off, I knew my hit was too far back, but the slug nicked the lungs and the buck dropped two hundred yards down the slope.

I camped in that spectacular basin for two more nights and feasted on buck chops grilled over shintangle coals. Not even Colter could have been closer to heaven. Since that time, I've often used the stalk-from-above tactic for high-country bucks as well as elk, and for mountain sheep on two continents. It works.

High-country bucks sometimes bed in the timber at the throat of basins or the bottoms of bare ridges. They browse out into the open late in the day, and move back into cover in the morning. If you're pressed for time, or impatient, as I too often get, track the buck to his bed in the trees. Up high, bucks find less need to bed downwind of their backtrail but instead bed anywhere that seems comfortable. This isn't always easy to figure out in the rocky terrain. Their lack of caution results from one thing—predators

A nice buck and his protégé bedded in the timber.

are as scarce as a generous billionaire up there in high heaven. As you follow the trail, try to anticipate what a buck will do. Ask yourself where you would bed if you were a wise buck; this often works surprisingly well. Stalk upwind of where you suspect he is, and keep the gun in your hands and ready, not hanging from a shoulder by its sling. Your thumb should be on the safety. If the buck wasn't where you anticipated, return to the tracks and follow farther.

Up high, much of the soil is too rocky for tracking, so ambushing may be the best tactic. If the buck was undisturbed when he went into the trees in the morning, he'll feed out that same way, probably before it gets dark. Position yourself across the slope from where the buck disappeared into timber so he won't scent you when the air drifts downhill in the cool evening. I get as far as possible from where the buck went into the trees, but not so far that I won't feel sure of hitting him, in case the wind is erratic.

One season, I located a good buck feeding near timberline in a basin that was part of northern Utah's Wellsville Mountains (the steepest mountain range in the country according to the

U.S. Forest Service). I climbed up in the dark. As the sun colored the highest peaks a rich salmon, the buck raised his head from a wind-tortured clump of fir. As I spotted him, he disappeared into trees at the bottom of the basin. I gave him time to settle in and doze off before I eased across the slope to a sunny niche in the rocks. I dozed off, too. I waited until almost dark and kept an eye on the trail he had followed into the woods. Finally, the buck minced out of the timber. As with most good stalks, the shot was all anticlimax.

Although preseason scouting is a good way to locate bucks, you'll find they move around because of the changing availability and palatability of browse plants, especially after the first heavy frosts. Hard frosts change the chemistry of plants and fallen leaves, making some tastier, others inedible. If a buck you've found while scouting is gone, check the next basin, and the one after that. Once you're high enough, moving laterally along a mountain range isn't that tough. If you're like me, you'll get high from both the scenery and the hunting, and even a buckless day up there can be better than lots of shooting down below. You might even quit thinking of yourself and pity those poor wretches down in the lowlands who haven't yet experienced a mule deer high.

Back in high school, when I sluffed school to hunt deer, my mother used to say that I might as well enjoy it because with my habits, I wasn't likely to get any closer to heaven than a mountain. I haven't changed much.

BUCKS IN THE TREES

My pard nearly choked on the apple he was wolfing down. A huge buck had just bounded out of a creek bottom and stood staring a hundred yards away. After a few moments, he trotted across the meadow and dirt road in front of us and down into the aspens. We'd both killed lesser bucks earlier, so we couldn't shoot.

That was back in the early '70s, and he was the last buck I've seen acting so foolish during the hunting season. Today, adult bucks simply do not show themselves in the open while redshirts are afield; if they do, they die. Today, bucks get old enough to become a trophy only by becoming survival experts. Simply, this means hiding, staying out of sight, becoming invisible.

When I started hunting in the '60s, I took a trophy buck every year. Most had antler spreads in excess of thirty inches, then the standard for a trophy buck. I remember actually passing up thirty-inchers because the antlers were too thin, uneven, or for some other reason I wouldn't even consider these days. Back then, hunting was simpler. I'd seldom venture into the timber. It was just too difficult, even if bucks were in there. If they were, they could stay, because there were other bucks in places much easier to hunt.

But times change. Big bucks became scarce, yet it was years before I forced myself into the thick timber. That first time, I spotted a big buck browsing at the edge of timber just at dark. In the dim light, I couldn't shoot. But he was the best buck I'd seen in years. That night I rolled up in the sleeping bag and his rack bounded through my dreams.

In the dawn, I found his big tracks where I'd seen him the night before and followed. The snow and subfreezing temperatures froze my jeans from the knee down. The frozen cuffs scraped each other like fingernails on a blackboard. I was still relatively new to hunting, though I'd been wildly successful bagging good bucks in "easy" places out of pure persistence and endurance. I didn't yet understand just how keen a mule deer's senses really were. The thought of wearing "quiet" wool pants didn't cross my mind, and besides, they itched.

I trailed down through the timber as the tracks twisted this way and then another. Occasionally, I forced my way through willows or aspen saplings. I found his bed. Droppings were still soft—hadn't yet frozen in the cold. I guessed he hadn't left the bed longer ago than an hour or so. The trail led across the slope; through ravines, where he browsed; and into a patch of willows, where he battered one barkless with his antlers. Brown willow bark lay on the snow. Then he'd walked on, meandering at times, moving with purpose at other times.

It was cold. I jammed my hands in my pockets and let the rifle hang from the shoulder sling. I hopped a small stream, and the willows bordering it scraped against my frozen pant cuffs. And there in the shadows of the timber, the buck stood staring hard in my direction. He was gone in one motion. My hands were still in my pockets.

It took more than one blown stalk for me to learn the significance of that encounter. I'd spent too many years hunting in the open with great success to change old habits immediately.

Next season I went back to hunting the same old way and the same places—the rolling sagebrush and chokecherry-covered hills and open canyons and plateaus. In the open country you could take your time, find a rest, and pot a buck in the distance. It had worked for years. I managed to spot a few small bucks in

You're lucky to see them stop and stare like this in the timber.

the open. I did locate big tracks, and it dawned on me that they had been made out there in the open places in darkness when hunters weren't a threat.

But I didn't see a good buck. Where had they gone? The bulb flashed on: in the timber, of course.

Full of enthusiasm, I stalked into the trees, still-hunting down the same trail I'd used the year before while trailing that big buck. In the shadowy gloom, big tracks angled down the slope. A big set moved along the game trail, and another crossed it. I stalked quietly on the fir-needle duff, carrying the rifle at the ready, my thumb on the safety. He stood wraithlike in the deep shadow, his nose working to scent whatever it was that made him nervous. The buck dropped at the shot. I gloated just a bit—not at the magnificent five by five set of antlers but rather at finally understanding where the big bucks lived during deer season.

But now I had to start over. I had to learn new skills and devise new tactics. So what if my rifle held a three-inch group at 300 yards? Splitting crabapples at 350 yards wouldn't get me a buck here. Instead, I learned to move quietly and pay strict attention to the direction of the breeze. I relied more and more on my eyes to untangle the shadows and find a patch of hide or note the difference between an antler tine and a chokecherry twig. I learned to evaluate and age tracks. I learned to age beds, scrapes, rubs, and droppings, to tell how long ago a buck passed. I learned the true meaning of "slow." I developed patience I never knew I had. Now it wasn't impossible to slowly stalk through a stand of timber or heavy brush, often spending an entire day doing it. Covering vast expanses of country had paid off in the old days, but no longer.

Still-hunting after big mule deer in the timber makes you a complete hunter. It's not good enough to rely on marksmanship, silence, tracking, or anything else. To be consistent in the timber, where the deer are these days, a hunter must do it all and do it well. A lapse in any area may lose you a buck.

In the old days, I hunted the morning and evening, times when deer moved about, and pretty much wasted the rest of the day in camp. Hunting in timber meant I could hunt all day long, even while deer were bedded. One afternoon I followed a large set of tracks through a dense stand of fir. Deer tracks crossed this way and that, and it was hard to keep from getting confused and following the wrong trail. I concentrated harder than I ever had—and nearly stepped on the snoozing buck. He jumped at four yards, scaring me half out of what remained of my frazzled wits. Had I been fully aware, and not focused just on the tracks, I could have collected the big buck.

Tracking is good, but still-hunting is just as effective. It works best when you're familiar with a stand of trees or patch of cover. Most places have good spots for bedding, heavily used game trails, and thick places out of the weather. By knowing where these places are, a hunter raises his chances of killing a buck.

One place I used to hunt regularly (though not for the last decade or more since it's been overrun by ORVs) was on a high plateau in northern Utah. Even then the country was too accessible and overhunted. A big stand of Douglas fir ran down the north-facing slope of a big canyon. A ravine angled down through the trees. One slope of this ravine faced west. The steepness of the slope was such that the soil eroded easily and was too shallow for the roots of big trees. Here in the sunlight good deer browse grew thickly, especially mahogany, forbs, cliffrose, and other plants that in graduate school we biologists called deer "ice cream". Big trees lined the rest of the steep ravine. If at ease, big bucks bedded underneath the trees, where it was a step to safety in one direction and a step to the ice-cream parlor in the other. I frequently still-hunted through the timber toward the ravine. I collected one very good buck there, and missed two other chances.

To still-hunt in the timber, you must have a good understanding of the importance of wind direction. It's nice to keep the wind in your face, and it's even better if the buck you're trailing is cooperative enough that he moves into it, more or less. It seldom happens that way. When the buck or the wind isn't cooperating, try to anticipate what he'll do. If you're familiar with the location of trails, bedding areas, food, and the normal wind direction at various times of day (yes, it does change; more about this later), it's much easier to correctly anticipate a buck's location.

OK, this is complicated. You have to understand not only the buck's behavior but also the lay of the land. Yet this is the best of all deer hunting. Hunting one small place year after year and learning all there is to know about it, yet disturbing it so little that the bucks won't leave, is the epitome of buck stalking.

Because of lack of time or commitment, most hunters working a stand of timber for the first time will never really learn about the cover. Still, you can try. For example, if you can find big buck tracks that aren't too petrified, and even though the buck is uncooperative and moving with the wind, you've still got a chance.

One season, I followed big tracks through fresh snow. The breeze quartered from behind and over my left shoulder. By this time in my hunting career, I knew that bucks buttonhook downwind of their backtrail to scent following danger. I was fairly certain this buck would act no differently—that he'd bed on the downwind side of the backtrail so he could scent and see any predator following. The best chance I had was looping downwind, and in this case downslope, of the trail, returning to it every hundred yards or so to affirm that I was still moving in the right direction. Using this millennia-old tactic, the hunter spends more time downwind and off the trail and is less likely to be detected by the buck. Morning had passed, and I guessed it was after lunchtime, judging by the sounds of my stomach.

I'd paused at the bottom of a loop, probably fifty yards below the buck's trail, when I felt that old and familiar sense of action-to-come. I'd been around long enough not to discount it. I stood, my thumb on the safety and the rifle held across my chest. I scanned slowly for perhaps twenty minutes, then took another step. Something moved slightly behind a tangle of branches ahead. Nearby twigs suddenly congealed into antler tines. The "twigs" moved slightly, but there was no wind. I slowly eased the rifle to my shoulder and slipped off the safety. I waited, hoping the buck would step clear of the branches. I could see that he was uneasy from the way he twitched an ear and arched his neck to stare. He hadn't located me, since I was downwind of his backtrail and of his bed. Still uneasy, he silently stepped clear ahead, his nose working frantically and his ears twitching this way and that, until the neck was clear of the brush.

He was a fat and prime buck, with six points on each side of heavy, high antlers. His molars were worn nearly to the gumline, which meant he'd have survived at most one more winter, and probably not that. He'd lived so long by keeping to the trees.

Waiting along a trail is another productive tactic when hunting in the trees. I prefer to still-hunt or trail because I like the activity, and standing or waiting anywhere is usually sheer torture for me. However, one season I hunted with a lady friend. I knew of heavily used trails through the trees and settled her along one of them. I left to still-hunt through the stand of timber and perhaps push a buck her way. I heard her shoot an hour later, and when I climbed back up the slope, she stood proudly by a yearling buck. The buck had trotted down the trail and she'd killed it cleanly. She wasn't even disappointed when, a

Hunting the high country of eastern Nevada's Ruby Range.

moment after her shot, a mature buck had bounded up the trail and nearly trampled her.

Many large stands of timber or brush—forests, if you will— contain open areas within them. These places usually grow deer browse, so some deer can live in these woods without ever leaving them. Normally, the openings are on steep, west-facing slopes with soil so shallow that big trees can't grow on them. They may also have been cleared of trees by beavers, fire, or other disturbances. These openings are top places for an ambush, but you must stalk there very cautiously.

The best such location I've hunted is in southern Montana near the north boundary of Yellowstone National Park. It's on a low mountain with pine and spruce growing on the north and east slopes, lodge pole pine on the south- and west-facing slopes, where it's warm and dry. On top, sagebrush flats drop into a steep ravine, which is dry except during spring runoff. The ravine is thick with good deer browse. It slopes gently to the east before disappearing into the timber. The entire opening is about three football fields in diameter. It's an exceptional place to find big bucks in the early autumn. I've hunted with a camera there several times, but not with a gun.

Working the timber has re-enthused me for hunting trophy bucks. After watching hunting deteriorate throughout mule deer range, I've suddenly got a chance at the big heads again.

RUT HUNTING 101

Ignore desert mule deer for a moment. In more northern latitudes, mature bucks begin rutting about mid-November and may continue into mid-December, depending on factors such as temperature, availability of "hot" or estrous does, and the general weather. As a generality, mule deer rut a little earlier if it is cold, and a storm front in early November can kick off rutting activity even in mature bucks. As a rule, the rut peaks during the last half of November. It's pretty well finished by the third week of December, in my observations, though some of the subadult bucks

Here I'm splitting kindling at a dramatic Idaho camp.

may be running around as if they're rutting. By this time, virtually all does have been bred, and those that missed getting served by a stud buck during their first estrus (time of receptivity to breeding) have had time to become impregnated their second time around. Like young bull elk, which get pretty rutty about a month later than the mature males that father most calves in a properly balanced herd, young mule deer bucks are still acting rutty into January or even later. Back to desert mule deer momentarily: For them, set the whole clock back six weeks; the rut in Sonora peaks about mid-January, from my experience.

The biggest piece of misinformation on hunting during the rut is that big bucks become addled when chasing cute does. Let's debunk that one; during the rut, mature bucks in hunted country stay as secretive and nocturnal as at any other time. Immature bucks, those under 4½ years of age, do become foolish, a bit like high-school jocks or college fraternity boys. Mature bucks do, however, hang around the does and will show up as individual does come into estrus. According to my research, mid- and northern-latitude does first come into heat early to mid-November.

Adult bucks seem to breed most frequently at night, which doesn't help the hunter any. They will breed during the day if 1) the doe is in heat then, 2) hunting pressure is light, and 3) younger bucks are present. The best way to collect a mature buck during the rut is by keeping close tabs on doe herds. They tend to stay in the same, often limited geographic locality. If coyotes move in, they'll move out. I know more than a dozen places within ten miles of my house where does live consistently, year in and year out. I used to hunt one or another area during the old muzzleloader season, which covered the beginning of the rut. I was confident that if a good buck was in the vicinity, eventually he'd show in one of these doe pastures. Here, time is the main consideration.

I've also noticed that mature bucks often shift their center area closer to doe pastures during the rut. Search for thick timber or brush in ravines or canyon heads first, then enter them very cautiously (you don't want to force the buck to relocate) and look for big tracks, scrapes, rubs, and beds. A rutting mulie buck has a musky, pungent odor that most hunters will recognize once they've scented it. In the center area, wear those "quiet" clothes and track or still-hunt very carefully, with the gun at the ready about like a grouse hunter approaching a shorthair on point. Don't worry if the buck isn't in; he's likely off checking another doe pasture or bedded in a similar tangle near one. All mature bucks wander during the rut, depending on the availability and proximity of does. Some bucks wander surprising distances.

Rattling is frequently productive during the rut. I'm still surprised that the technique works so well at times. I'm also surprised that so few hunters use it. I've never talked to or read of a hunter who used rattling to collect a mule deer buck, and I've never seen the method mentioned in scientific literature. It doesn't work as well on mulies as it does for whitetails, and it's not as predictable as a variety of other mule deer hunting methods. The best time for rattling is just before or early in the rut, and the best place is in or very near the buck's center area.

I've been nearly trampled by bucks on two rattling occasions, and have bagged others at very close range. On three occasions, mature bucks actually "roared" at me, they were so angry, and at close range it's intimidating—even though I did have the rifle. If you see a buck as he "roars," you'll notice the bristling fur and aggressive attitude, and that's even more frightening. Once, in Yellowstone, I got between bucks just as they were about to begin fighting. I was trying to get some dramatic photos. I went up a lodge pole pine so quickly that a branch snapped my camera strap and the camera dropped in the mud. The breeze drifted from the biggest buck directly at me, and at ten yards he smelled horribly.

I've had luck rattling near doe groups, too. At least twice, bucks plunged into the open from the timber the first time I touched the antlers together. These were immature bucks. The big boys were probably hanging in the center area, but perhaps there simply were no big bucks in the area; after all, they are becoming more and more rare.

Even younger bucks tend to approach rattling with care; they certainly do not want to bust in on an old master that may thrash him seriously. This lessens the possibility of a lethal battle, though members of the deer family, Cervidae, do kill each other more often than we think. (For example, as a graduate student I once necropsied a dead moose that the local fish and game authorities were sure had been poached; after all, they could see two bullet holes in the chest cavity. But the bullet holes turned out to be puncture wounds made by antler tines that had broken off in the chest cavity.) It's to a species' evolutionary advantage not to kill each other off in battles, so most have devised means to avert battles. With mule deer bucks of nearly equal size, most confrontations take place early in the autumn before the rut, when they aren't so testosterone-driven. They size each other up and decide who is toughest in fairly placid sparring matches, to avert disastrous battles later on. After a shoving match in October, one buck decides he is no match for the old master and never again challenges that buck. He simply goes elsewhere for his loving or waits for another year.

If you're hunting only for a trophy buck, make sure one lives in the area. Look for sign. You'll find it if a big buck lives anywhere nearby, since he'll be traveling widely as he searches for estrous does.

Again, don't plan on trophy bucks getting stupid during the rut. In truth, collecting one during the rut is tough if you're pressed for time. They move around more, so it's harder to pinpoint their location at a given moment. If time is the major consideration, still-hunt, track, or rattle—active tactics that make things happen. If you have plenty of time, wait around a doe pasture. Eventually, the dominant buck will show up.

SCRATCH AND SNIFF

Conway Twitty growled from a tinny jukebox, an ancient potbelly crackled, and tobacco smoke was layered blue in the neon of a south Montana honky-tonk. I was just back from two weeks of chasing a big whitetail buck around the Stillwater foothills. Down the bar beneath two sooty deer heads, a hunting guide and his Pennsylvania dude commiserated over their failure to collect a good mule deer. Misery loves company, so I butted in.

"You're lucky," the guide said after pleasantries. "At least with whitetails, you can hunt the scrapes." To further yank the hackamore, he added, "It's a sure thing." Outside, snow sifted out of a leaden sky while I fumbled for a clever retort. All I said was, "You can do the same with mule deer, you know."

The Pennsylvania dude hooted so loudly he nearly fell off the bar stool. The guide choked on his beer and finally snorted, "A hundred says you can't show me a mulie scrape." I took the bet—without mentioning that I'd studied mule deer biology for over a decade.

The next morning the guide led Pennsylvania and me to a canyon with a resident herd of does and said, "Go to work."

The rut was heating up in mid-November. Upcanyon, conifers clustered in the ravines. We trekked up the ridge in an inch of new powder, then dropped into the timber pockets. In the second one, I found the fresh track of a mature mule deer buck—it

Bucks sometimes get this high.

measured four inches in length, excluding dewclaws—and we followed the trail. The buck had just returned from the open slope where the does were feeding; apparently he'd "tested" for hot does during the night. We followed, keeping downwind of the trail. Pennsylvania kept his thumb on the safety, and since he was behind me, his newfound enthusiasm made me nervous.

In the next stand of pines, we found muddy oblongs in the snow; fresh urine, just starting to freeze, puddled in them, and big tracks pockmarked the mud. I stood back for effect and pointed with a flourish. "There!" I said. Then I waxed biological on some of the defining functions of mule deer scrapes—how they're made to advertise the buck's scent through the urine, feces, and gland secretion; how they're periodically freshened; how they're used more often as the rut approaches. The guide, with minor protestations, fished out a hundred-dollar bill.

When we trailed farther, we found a cluster of seven scrapes in a thirty- by forty-yard tangle of timber. The place smelled like an overused Port-a-Potti; I'd never seen such a concentration of mule deer scrapes. "This is the place for an ambush. It's a sure thing," I deadpanned. Then I went back to chase the big Stillwater whitetail.

I'm not suggesting that every mule deer hunter should adopt whitetail scrape-hunting techniques wholesale. First, there are distinct differences between the scrape sign made by the two species. A whitetail buck lays out scrape lines, often arranged in a cross or "X" formation. To get his message across when does are scarce, he makes his scrape lines longer. Still, most scrapes along either line are inactive—they're seldom visited or freshened. But normally, a group of active scrapes lies somewhere off the main line. As the rut intensifies, scraping diminishes because the does are coming into estrus and bucks are busy searching for and servicing them instead of advertising. Ditto for mule deer. In the case of that big Stillwater whitetail, the scrape lines were over a mile long because there weren't many does in the area. And although I found a fairly fresh cluster of scrapes, he never returned to them while I waited in ambush. Chances were he would return to freshen them only as the rut waned, because he was spending most of his time looking for does.

Mule deer, on the other hand, don't scrape nearly as often or as predictably as whitetails. It's my suspicion that some bucks never scrape in their entire lives. And when they do, the scrapes are tougher to find. A mule deer buck, probably because he often lives in steep, uneven terrain, has a small, localized scrape area, or cluster. He makes this cluster where he spends 90 percent of his time, the center area. Think of the center area as the buck's living room. It's typically in a thick tangle of brush near the feeding area, escape cover, and does. It is the prime spot for ambushing a buck.

Whether they're made by whitetails or mule deer, scrapes are a buck's advertising posts. To does, they say, "I'll make a great father; here's my portfolio." Does judge a buck's health and vigor by scenting urine and glandular secretions. So if more than one mature buck inhabits an area, a doe approaching estrus will search for the one with a scent that indicates virility, health, and vigor.

Mulie and whitetail scrapes are similar in appearance, but a mule deer's are slightly larger, and longer than they are wide (eighteen inches is an average length, but I've seen them up to thirty inches). Occasionally, mule deer wallow in their scrapes; I've found tracks, leg impressions, and hair left in urine- and ejaculate-muddied wallows. This is rare, however. Bucks of both species urinate on lower-leg hair tufts before stamping the ground, and both species may masturbate (by brief penis palpitation) into the scrape; mule deer defecate into scrapes more often than whitetails. The thing to remember is that fresh, well-used scrapes stink—you can smell them more than a hundred yards away.

Scraping for both species increases as the rut approaches, then drops off sharply (for mule deer, anyway) during the peak of rutting activity. Mule deer bucks may begin scraping shortly after shedding velvet in late August, although near my home in northern Utah I don't generally find the first scrape until late September or into October. The best time to hunt the scrapes is in early November, just before intense rutting. During the rut's peak, bucks are too busy chasing does to worry about writing phone numbers on walls. Scrape activity increases once again as the rut wanes, because fewer does are hot and the buck has more time and need for advertising. As a second choice, I'd hunt the scrapes again about the middle of December.

On whitetail scrape lines, there's a cluster of active scrapes that will look muddy or recently dried (perhaps with a salt crust where urine has evaporated); they'll have tracks in the mud and they'll stink (old scrapes have little odor).

To find mule deer scrapes, look first for tangles of brush or timber near doe herds, open feeding areas, and escape cover. Then search thoroughly for tracks, rubs, browsed plants, droppings. Once you find a concentration of sign, a scrape or cluster of them may be near.

If you collected a buck near scrapes the previous season, return to the same area. The buck was there for a reason—good feed or cover, isolation, plenty of does—and odds are fair that another buck will have moved in. And if you blew a chance at a good buck last season, it's nearly certain the same buck will return before the rut. The active scrape cluster will likely be in the same place, too.

As I drove home from my final—and unsuccessful— attempt to kill that big Stillwater whitetail, I noticed the guide's pickup in front of that same honky-tonk. A nice buck lay in the bed. They'd ambushed him in that cluster of scrapes as he came to freshen his advertisement. The guide had positioned the buck's rack over the tailgate so no one could miss it. He knew how to advertise, too.

CLATTERING FOR BUCKS

Here's another little-used but sometimes effective tactic for big mule deer bucks: rattling! Yes, I've heard the scoffs and hoots of derision before, even from fellow biologists who should be open-minded about such things. Hunters are less polite. Since I am a peaceable fellow, I seldom mention this seemingly sacrilegious technique, just to avoid the hassle.

As I was conducting my research on elk behavior as a graduate student at Utah State University, I noticed that bulls sparred frequently just before the rut. At first I just kept data, as any good biologist is supposed to do, but I was also a hunter. I brought some small, raghorn elk antlers into the field and tried to rattle in a bull. I was in Yellowstone at the time, and within a week I rattled in more than a dozen bulls. It was mid-September, and bulls were getting rutty and testing each other and themselves by putting antlers together and engaging in shoving matches called sparring. Sparring drops off when the rut peaks on September 21 (on average, according to years of data I've collected) because thereafter, testosterone and aggression levels are so high that sparring often turns into full-fledged battles.

Years later, I watched two whitetail bucks sparring in Montana bottomlands. Then I noticed a third buck trotting through thick willows toward the contestants. I actually jumped in surprise.

This nice rack and pack full of boned venison weighs in at close to sixty pounds. Camp is eight miles of canyons, ridges, and brush away. But this is what you have to do to collect the big ones.

"Why not?" I asked myself. I had no answer. By the way, that mule deer ran off both whitetails.

Until then, I'd never even considered rattling for mule deer. I'd never seen anything mentioned in biological literature about rattling, and I'd read magazine pieces in which hunting experts said it couldn't be done. If hunters could rattle in whitetails, why not mule deer?

Most antlered animals put their antlers together and shove. Mostly, this is simple sparring and aggression levels are low. It is an activity used to test each other and establish dominance before the rut, when battles can become serious and potentially lethal. It also strengthens neck muscles, increases coordination, and releases increasing libido and aggression as the rut approaches. Males of the Cervidae—the deer family—do fight. Mule deer seem to fight less than whitetails, though my data on this isn't conclusive (I have, however, seen more whitetail battles per hour of observation than I have mule deer fights). Moose and elk also seem to fight more often than do mule deer. While I've been exposed to several times more mule deer than whitetails, I have witnessed only a few full-fledged mule deer fights. I have good notes on nine battles: Three lasted more than three minutes, and in one of these a buck lost an eye; three other battles were fatal. I've witnessed over seven hundred mule deer sparring matches, so judging from these stats alone, mule deer spar far more frequently than they actually engage in true battles.

When clattering antlers together to bring in or locate mule deer bucks, you're trying to get a buck to want to spar with you. Bucks spar most frequently just before the rut. Even big stud bucks will spar then if other nearly equal bucks are present. Small bucks may briefly engage antlers with a stud buck, but they soon disengage and scamper off, almost as if to say, "See, I knew I could!"

Thrashing (smashing and scraping brush with an antler) works as well as clattering or rattling. It seems more effective during the rut than rattling, because stud bucks by then have already evaluated the competition and have no need for more sparring to decide who's the dominant buck on the mountain. If mature bucks put antlers together during the rut, it's to fight, not play.

The pre-rut, September through early November, is not a time to rattle too intensely. When bucks bang antlers at these times, they're sparring, not fighting. So do not clatter too vigorously, with hard and quick smashing; this indicates a real fight to a buck and he may conclude that something stinks down the draw and head the other way.

Rattle nice and easy. Put the antler tips together lightly, and don't do it too often. Here's my general rattling procedure:

1. Put antler tips together and rattle very lightly (about loud enough for you to hear it at forty yards); you don't want to risk spooking off a nearby buck by doing it too loudly.
2. Rattle in clusters of about five clashes, using the same level of intensity in each cluster. Pause after each cluster for four to ten minutes.
3. Increase the loudness with each successive cluster of clattering. This will allow the sound to reach bucks bedded down farther away. Do not increase the frequency of rattling.
4. Forty minutes of clattering in one locale is plenty of time. If a buck doesn't show, move on. If, on the other hand, you have a contrary hunch, follow it.
5. Move into the wind when changing rattling locations. The distance I move depends on how far I think the sound of my antler rattling carried, and this depends on wind direction and intensity, the terrain, the thickness of timber or brush, sounds of running water (which, of course, mute or confuse other sounds), and other factors.

Play it by ear to a certain extent. All good hunters and biologists should always enter the field ready to learn. I always start teaching class each new semester by writing the following proverb on the blackboard: "A wise man changes his mind many times, a fool never." Each time I rattle for bucks, I learn something new, no matter how insignificant it seems.

A buck in the pines.

Of course, antler rattling for smaller bucks during the pre-rut is easiest, since they're less experienced than older bucks that have heard real bucks rattle for years. Also, veteran bucks tend to be nocturnal, and less apt to leave a bed even if the rattling sounds convincing, especially in open terrain.

Adult bucks can be rattled in, but I've done it only in a buck's center area. Again, allow me to emphasize that you can't be too quiet, scentless, or otherwise undetectable. To rattle in an adult buck's center area, you have to get into it without his knowing you're there. Always assume the buck is home. Stay fully aware of wind direction at all times, keep it in your face, and rattle downwind from the spot in which you think the buck might be hiding. Move slowly; ease branches aside, crawl under intertwined branches, watch where you put your hands and feet. Sneak along an established game trail if you can find one, since there will be fewer branches to step on, break, and clatter against.

Here's a successful rattling episode in an adult buck's center area: Earlier in the day I'd found shed antlers (normally, sheds are too dry to use for rattling). I had still-hunted my way into what turned out to be a center area in a big stand of Douglas fir. As an afterthought, I clattered the sheds together lightly. Almost immediately, I heard a definite roar, and my thumb jumped to the safety. Almost immediately thereafter, the buck crashed out of tangled willows and nearly trampled me. It happened so quickly I didn't get the rifle to my shoulder. The buck whirled in thick brush just down the slope—he still hadn't located me—and roared again. As I slowly raised the rifle, he caught my scent and vanished. Previously, I'd rattled in several small bucks, but nothing with any heft to it.

I was ready the next time. I'd located and crept into a mature buck's center area. I lightly touched the antler tips together, and then again. I heard something move in a thicket just upslope, and then a nice buck stepped out into an opening between aspen trees. He was still mostly hidden by fir boughs, but from the size of his legs and rump, which I could just see, he was a keeper. I eased the rifle to my shoulder and offed the safety. He moved a few inches, exposing the shoulder, and I squeezed the trigger. He turned out to be a hefty adult with nice five by five antlers.

"Thrashing" antlers against brush works as well as rattling in many cases. I've collected both large and "meat" bucks this way. As far as I can determine, the same basic ideas that work with rattling hold true for thrashing. In both methods, use "fresh" antlers; their sound carries farther and they sound more authentic. I have reservations about synthetic antlers, but perhaps this is only because I am a traditionalist.

Rattling during the rut is a completely new show. Then, adult bucks typically cover an area several times larger than their home range (and remember, the center area is only a small part of the home range) searching for hot does. Does congregate where there's good and easily accessible food and cover. Rattling works very well for smaller bucks, but seldom large ones, near doe herds. For whatever reason, thrashing brush seems to work better with adult bucks. I particularly recall one recent muzzleloading season as the rut was just warming up. I thrashed brush near a big ravine where does typically fed and bedded. The rattling frightened two nearby does, and they bounded down into the bottom and up the opposite slope, where they turned and stared. A moment later, I heard something crash through brush upslope, and a decent buck trotted into view. He was too far for the .54 Hawken replica, so I thrashed the brush again, trying to keep any movement out of his line of vision, but did it softly. The buck looked in my direction, then minced into a tangle of aspens in a ravine that led down toward where I was hidden. Five minutes later, I thrashed the brush again, vigorously at first, then more lightly. The buck trotted onto an open slope sixty yards off and stared. The gun misfired. I fiddled with the nipple, fitted another cap on it, and still the buck stood and

Here I'm reading tracks. Snow makes it a whole lot easier.

stared. The gun misfired again, and the buck trotted into the timber and then over a ridge and that was the last I saw of him. The lesson? Keep your powder dry. The second lesson? Doe feeding and bedding areas are good places to thrash during the rut.

By the time the rut has waned, in mid-December or so in central and northern mule deer latitudes, bucks begin sparring again. This is truer for young bucks, but it also holds for adult bucks, especially if pesky youngsters are around trying to build up their nerve to lock antlers with the old master. After the rut, young bucks engaging the stud buck are in no real danger unless they don't disengage and scamper off at the right time, which they invariably do. In my research projects, I found the increase in sparring activity after the rut to be even more dramatic in both elk and moose.

If December hunts are still in progress, rattling works well. It's not as effective for adult bucks simply because they're worn out from the rutting and won't have anything to do with unneeded physical activity. Young bucks, however, are throbbing with hormones and haven't begun to feel the demands of winter, so they're good targets for rattling or thrashing. If snow is deep and the weather demanding in December, as it often is, deer show much less interest in rattling or thrashing; they're spending valuable energy finding food and simply surviving.

In rattling or thrashing, hideout placement is critical. Always rattle downwind from where you suspect the buck will approach or is hiding. Rattling seems to work better just after a cold front or snow squall has passed through the country, for whatever reason. Don't overdo the rattling; too little is better than too much.

While rattling may not be the ultimate answer for mule deer hunters, it's another tactic to increase flexibility. I rely more heavily on the old standbys, still-hunting, tracking, and even ambushing. But from time to time, rattling has fooled bucks I otherwise would not have gotten. Possibly with more refinement, rattling for mule deer may be as effective as it is for white-tailed deer. The trouble is that there are few late seasons and almost no one uses the method and so no one will refine it. Until someone has success enough to further develop rattling, it will stay as it is—another esoteric trick used by oddball hunters and biologists.

THE RUT STUFF

Outside the tent flap, snow raced horizontally in a forty-knot nor'wester, visibility was thirty yards, and the thermometer stood at 17 degrees. The horses jostled each other for cover under a big fir tree.

"Hell, kid," one of the old-timers said, "you'll freeze out there." I crowded closer to the cookstove in the big wall tent.

"Ya'd have to step on a buck 'fore ya'd see 'im," another put it. Bit by bit, they were successfully talking this naive and enthusiastic high-school kid out of hunting. But I'd come to hunt, not sit around a tent sipping cocoa. In a moment of resolve, I pulled on my coat, wrapped a woolen scarf around my neck, yanked a cap down over my ears, and plunged out into the blizzard. I'd have been lost in minutes on top of the plateau, so I dropped down into the timber.

Within two hundred yards the wind had lessened in the protection of the big fir and spruce trees, yet it still howled through their tops, drowning out any sound I'd make. Fresh deer tracks wandered through the timber. I picked what I thought was a good set and followed. It wasn't half an hour before I found myself standing over a good buck I'd dropped as he followed a hot doe. That long-ago experience illustrates a mule deer hunting basic: The best hunting conditions are cold and snowy, and not just an isolated storm warning of winter but the real deal. It helps that such weather often coincides with late seasons and the mule deer rut, which extends into mid-December, but the rut alone can't account for my late-season successes.

For one thing, animals are more obvious against snow-covered terrain (so are you, unless you wear snow camo), which makes long-range glassing a top strategy. Aspens, oaks, and other deciduous trees have lost their leaves, making it easier to spot deer in thickets impossible to see into earlier in the season.

I trailed this buck all the previous day through blizzards and subzero temperatures. Persistence pays off.

Cold weather also sends deer on the prowl during daylight hours by putting a higher metabolic demand on them. Deer must work harder to stay warm, even while they're resting, which in turn forces them out and about to forage. Sagebrush is major wintertime food, but bitterbrush, mountain or curleaf mahogany, and serviceberry are ice cream to mule deer. Add a touch of rut-induced restlessness, and there's a fair chance a buckless canyon yesterday will hold a trophy set of antlers tomorrow.

Finally, there's the obvious: Finding and interpreting buck sign are so much simpler in snow. Tracks are a cinch to spot, follow, and judge, and it's easier to find beds, scrapes, droppings, and rubs, all of which indicate the density of deer in an area.

But snow is more than a visual aid. Heavy snows in the high country can trigger dramatic downward migrations. I've mentioned elsewhere about catching one of these migrations west of Big Piney in Wyoming and another in northern Utah; I killed big bucks in each case.

If you've viewed cold and nasty weather as a hunting liability rather than a bonus, consider this: Late-season hunting puts you out in the timber during the rut. And cold, stormy weather intensifies rutting activity.

Most certainly, not all bucks become addled sex fiends during the rut. Subadult bucks often do, but not the older trophies. But the big boys will eventually show up around doe herds, and the larger the herd, the better, because big groups are more likely to have more does in or approaching estrus. Consequently, the stud buck of the valley will spend proportionally more of his time near bigger doe herds, making him more vulnerable to you, the late-season hunter.

A mature buck travels more during the rut, and this, too, increases your chance of spotting him. Much of his travel will be outside his home range in terrain he is unfamiliar with. The more unfamiliar his terrain, the more likely he will be to make a mistake, and the more mistakes he makes (such as crossing open areas during daylight), the more chances you'll get. The buck is traveling to "test" does to find those approaching breeding condition. If he finds one, he stays with her until the right moment. Since does often come into estrus during the day, the buck must be available to breed her or some young upstart will handle the job. Day and night during the rut, bucks key on does. If you've got the time, you should, too.

But not everyone has the luxury of waiting out breeding biology. If you've got a narrow window of opportunity—maybe you have to get back to the old salt mine—try ambushing a buck along one of his scouting or rutting trails. Locate the trail first, by finding new and old tracks. During the rut, adult bucks often forsake main trails and follow their own specialized trails as they test doe herds in various parts of their home range, and often outside it. If there's snow—and it's likely late in the season— you've got an excellent chance of finding his rutting trail (remember track size). The trail usually starts in the center area, moves to one doe herd, then to another and another, and eventually returns to the center area.

If you're less concerned with collecting wall furnishings than filling the freezer (antlers make poor soup), the late season is no less productive. Bucks under about 4½ years of age can be plain foolish during the rut, and they are probably the source of the old myth that mule deer bucks are stupid when they have sex on the brain. But young ones will run helter-skelter, pestering does and irritating the local stud buck. Normally, if you see a younger buck covering (breeding) a doe, bet there are no adult bucks around, something trophy hunters should keep in mind. Doe bleats work with these love-struck youngsters, and on several occasions I've attracted them with a deer distress bleat. These are tactics for immature bucks—don't expect an adult to fall for them.

Hunters have rattled in whitetails for centuries, of course, but the tactic has seldom been used on mule deer. If you've read earlier chapters, you know this is a mistake, because under the right conditions it's highly effective. Try rattling in November and again in late December, after the rut has worn itself out.

Use the right stuff for late rattling. Fresh antlers have a louder and more realistic tone; avoid antlers that are even a little weathered and worn. Rattling details are presented in an earlier chapter. If no buck shows up, make a slow circle into the wind, especially if there is brush upwind; a buck may be too timid to show himself and you may have to bump him out. Of course, he won't be the stud buck. If he were, he'd jump out breathing fire and ready for battle.

Which, in a way, exemplifies the human late-season hunting attitude. You're a fire-breather yourself to jump out into blizzards and subzero temperatures to stalk the elusive mulie.

TRACKS, STRIDES, AND THE MULE DEER PSYCHE

To be a good hunter for any species, you must fully understand your quarry. The best way to do this is not by passively watching them, as you might expect, but by tracking them to see what they do when undisturbed. If a trophy mule deer buck is the quarry, a hunter must learn to identify his tracks and strides.

Fat, adult bucks seldom move quickly unless alarmed. Even if fully alerted, adult bucks will not run if they can avoid it, because running creates its own noise, which in turn blocks out other sounds that could tip a buck off to danger. A running buck is paying more attention to his fleeing and less to his surroundings, and thus becomes more vulnerable, and he's aware of this. So, he simply does not run unless there's no way to avoid it. Moving slowly saves energy, in addition to allowing the buck to remain more alert.

In a buck's walking stride, the hind feet are placed almost precisely in the forehoof prints. An adult buck's walking stride on flat ground averages twenty-four to twenty-six inches, but this varies with the individual animal, just as it does in humans (a man 6'2" has a longer stride than one only 5'8"). If a buck's trail meanders through brush, he is feeding. Note what he's feeding on, how he goes about it, and what part of the plant he eats. If the walking trail is meandering without evidence of feeding, the buck is looking for a bed. Quite possibly he is near and watching his backtrail, if he has already bedded down. Not infrequently, a buck may meander seemingly aimlessly for some time before bedding.

If the walking trail is more or less straight with little meandering, the buck is on the move. Follow these tracks more quickly. Keep aware of wind direction and your own noises, though these are less critical here because the buck is apt to be some distance off.

The trotting stride is used frequently, especially by smaller bucks. Younger bucks may trot as often as they walk, and the trot doesn't use much energy. For years I measured deer strides when easy opportunities presented themselves. Last Sunday as I write this, at the end of February, an adult buck trotted across the road in western Wyoming while I was out on a drive. I whipped out a tape measure I keep in the pickup and measured his strides. They were typical and averaged thirty-six inches. Over the years, the stride of mature bucks on flat ground averaged thirty-five to thirty-eight inches, with the range of trotting adult bucks being thirty-three to forty inches.

The gallop uses more energy and is faster. When an adult buck gallops, he's frightened. Typically, the right forehoof strikes the ground first, and the left forehoof strikes a short distance ahead of that print. As the hind legs are propelled forward, the right hoof contacts the ground first, followed by the left. In the trail of a galloping buck, the pair of prints in front are those of the hind feet, with the left usually just ahead of the right. An adult buck can't gallop for long because it takes too much effort (a fat financier won't even attempt to run from danger). An adult buck will revert to the slower and quieter trot as soon as possible, will stop and rest in heavy cover to watch his backtrail, then will walk off.

Bounding (often called the stot) consumes more energy than galloping. If an adult buck bounds, he's really scared, but he'll do it for only a short time.

Over the past three years, I've measured the stride of more than a dozen bucks, and the stride length of bounding adult bucks on level ground ranges from twenty-three to twenty-nine feet.

An adult buck bedded down in heavy timber in his center area. It takes concentration and patience to get this close.

Of course, stride lengths shorten going uphill, especially through snow or obstacles. The mule deer's stiff-legged bound appears clumsy, but it efficiently gets a buck through rough, tangled, or rocky country in a hurry and leaves any coyote in the dust.

I started hunting mule deer back in the 1960s. Then, no one I had ever heard or read about tracked mule deer. Things are about the same. Most hunters assume that tracking mule deer is like learning ancient languages—it's too much work. But in this day of dwindling game populations largely due to habitat loss, and fewer hunting opportunities for a variety of reasons, learning to track effectively maximizes the few chances we do get to hunt adult bucks.

An adult buck's track is wider in proportion and in actual measurement than those of small bucks and does, of course. It's also wide at the tip and more rounded. In rocky country, pretty common in mule deer habitat, an ancient buck's track may be so rounded at the tip it looks like a smaller version of a Hereford steer's print.

One track I measured thoroughly belonged to a gargantuan buck I killed in the '80s. The forehoof measured 4¼ inches long and 3 inches wide, excluding dewclaws. Normally, adult buck forehoofs range from 3½ to 4 inches long. The stride of adult bucks is longer than that of subadults, and physically large bucks have longer strides than smaller adults. Big bucks frequently shuffle when they walk, and often the hoof tips point outward slightly.

Aging a trail is complicated. Experience is the best and only teacher. When I set up camp in buck country, I make sure to track up the terrain around the tent in various types of soil and in various exposures, then note how the tracks change over hours and even days. In the old days I had a skinning knife with a deer-foot handle; I used this handle to make tracks in a patch of snow under a fir, in loam out in the sagebrush, and in mud near a seep, then watch the changes over time. That exercise and other experience taught me the most about aging a buck's trail and consequently about tracking. Weather, soil types, humidity, temperature, wind intensity and direction, and other factors play key roles in how fast a track ages. Practice is the best way to get good at it.

When you track or trail, you are at any given moment at a place where a deer passed an hour or perhaps two days ago. You're behind him—the direction from which he most expects danger—and most adult bucks bed downwind of their backtrail to check on danger following.

Here's an example of typical adult buck behavior: One October day in Utah I was dawdling along, simply enjoying the Indian summer sun's rays slanting through openings in the spruce, when I flushed a buck. I wasn't even remotely ready to shoot, so the buck bounded off through the timber unscathed. Contrary to a myth popular at the time, one I hope that we have by now debunked, the buck didn't pause to look back. I took up the trail. The buck had bedded beneath the shady canopy of an old fir tree nine yards downwind of his backtrail where he could watch a small ravine he'd crossed. I followed, and at first the buck bounded through big timber deadfalls, sometimes clearing seven feet in height, at other places dodging beneath fallen trees. Within two hundred yards the buck slowed to an energy-conserving trot. He'd circle any openings, always keeping to the timber and out of sight. He'd pause on the far side of an opening to see if I was following. I suspect he heard me before actually seeing me; when he sensed me in some way, he trotted off again. I got wise and began skirting downwind of the small openings. I also started stalking more slowly and quietly. I caught the buck standing in the shadows, watching his backtrail across an opening and listening intently. I shot as he bounded off, splintering a fir sapling. With better or luckier shooting, I'd have collected the buck.

Mostly (I'd like to say always, but it just doesn't work that way), adult bucks buttonhook and bed downwind of their backtrail—for several reasons discussed in detail in earlier chapters. Remember that bucks meander before bedding down, so if the trail you're following meanders, become especially alert and careful, focus your attention downwind of the trail and as far ahead as you can see, and check the wind continuously. A meandering trail is no guarantee a big buck is bedded nearby; he may search for just the right bed for some time before actually bedding. Still, he's probably close. I try to follow some yards off the trail and downwind, returning to it every forty or fifty yards or so, depending on thickness of the vegetation. If I pass the end of the trail, I'm pretty certain the buck is bedded nearby and that I probably passed him, so I stalk cautiously back. I suppose I have killed more than a dozen trophy bucks in this manner over the last two decades.

This tactic, described in detail earlier, is called the loop method of tracking. I became aware of its anthropologic significance in a study of northern Canadian Indians who used it regularly for moose hunting. Since that time, I have seen it used not only in Canada but also by the Kung and Bayei people in Botswana, the Warusha in Tanzania, and groups in Siberia, Mexico, Zimbabwe, and Namibia. This should attest to its significance.

A recent buck on which I used the loop method was spooked by other hunters up the canyon. I watched through binoculars as he trotted through aspen and fir timber across the canyon, then over a ridge. Fortunately, the snow was heavy and fresh and made for good and rapid tracking. I climbed down into the canyon bottom and up the other slope, and picked up the buck's trail on top of the ridge. He was moving more or less downwind, which meant I would have to get far off the trail to prevent being scented. Within a few hundred yards, fortunately, he turned west down into the next drainage. Now the wind was blowing directly across the backtrail. I followed, moving about ten yards or less downwind of the trail. At this point the trail was simple to see from that distance, but then it entered tangles of aspen saplings and chokecherry and began to twist and jink. Things were sticky. He was looking to bed down, and all I could do was stay downwind of the trail and hope I'd spot him (and have time to shoot) before he spotted me. It didn't happen that way. The trail entered thicker brush and then timber, and again I began looping downwind of the trail. I was

This buck dozes in an opening deep within a big stand of lodge pole pine.

careful because the tracks were huge, and I could half-close my eyes and again see the big rack across that canyon. I was returning to the trail for confirmation that I was still hunting in the right direction when I caught a movement out of the corner of my eye. The buck stood from a tangle of chokecherry and stared back hard over his rump. I had the safety off, the .270 to my shoulder, and the cross hairs on his rump, but I didn't want to chance the shot through the tangle. I raised the cross hairs to the base of his neck, and then with one bound he disappeared. I recall standing there with the rifle still at my shoulder and staring through the scope in disbelief. I could have kicked myself, hard—I should have taken the rump shot because at that range the 175-grain bullet would have broken the hip or spine and dropped him. (However, things didn't turn out so badly; I killed that buck the next season.)

They don't always get away. One dawn I found a big track made the night before, probably just before the hard freeze of dawn. I took up the trail, the tracks frozen into the black loam as if in cement. After sunup two hours later, the trail began to melt and soften, and the tracks looked as fresh in the soil and spruce-needle duff as if the buck had just passed. Another two hours later, the trail wandered down the canyon and then onto a slope, where the buck had browsed on serviceberry and bitterbrush. I knew that with the morning sun three fingers above the ridge, the buck was already bedded down. I followed across the open slope, over a ridge, and down into thick timber on the north-facing slope. Soon the tracks began to meander again, but this time he was not feeding. The shadows were solid in the timber, and what little breeze there was drifted uphill in the warming day. I knew he'd bed upwind and upslope of his backtrail, so I moved along parallel to his trail but uphill, where if I lost sight of the track I could ease downhill a bit to find it again, then loop back up the slope and downwind. On the fifth loop, I spotted his antlers above a blowdown fir tree. I eased the rifle up carefully, slowly and silently thumbed off the safety, then crept down the slope until I could see the buck's neck. One shot settled him at eleven yards.

Snow always makes for easier tracking and spotting. I cut a track in the gray half-light of a wintry morning and followed, looping downwind, then returning to the trail for confirmation. After an hour or so of this, I spotted the buck across the ravine in a thick tangle of oak scrub. His dark body was obvious against the snow. The day before, there was no snow and he'd have been completely hidden in the tangle. But as he stared, I picked a path for the bullet through the tangle of branches and touched off. He jumped up and lunged downslope before piling up under a tree.

If you're good enough and tracking conditions are ideal, you'll find that no two sets of tracks are identical—just as human fingerprints aren't the same. If you're hunting a particular large buck, identify if possible the particular characteristics of his track, to keep from getting on the wrong trail. Chips, gouges, or scratches in his hoofs and irregularities in stride can all be used in identification. Then, all you have to do is follow.

One hot, dry season I found a big deer track. I followed it across an open slope and could look at the tracks in detail. About a quarter-inch of one forehoof had been flattened at the tip. I followed the trail across a slope of red clay and saw the track in the concrete-hard clay. The last time that clay was rain-soft enough to take and hold a print was weeks earlier, so I knew the trail was old. But I had ID-ed the track.

Later, I again found those tracks in the dust. The next day the skies clouded and rain fell through the night. Despite the water dripping onto my sleeping bag, my luck had changed. Now any tracks would be fresh, and in the dawn, as the rain stopped, I knew I'd have luck.

I found the chipped hoofprint late in the morning, and it had been made within a few hours, just after the rain stopped (there were no raindrop prints in the track). The trail meandered through forbs where the buck had browsed, then beelined for a tangle of timber across the canyon. I followed, but lost the track in a jumble of other deer trails. I continued in the direction he'd been going and at last found that same track. The trail led through oak brush and then into timber. He was looking for a bed, and I knew that at that moment he was already bedded down. I stalked downwind of the trail, sure that he'd have buttonhooked downwind of his backtrail and that would be where I'd find him. And it was. He jumped at fifteen yards, and I got a hurried shot that double-lunged him. I got that buck with an exceptionally even and heavy trophy because I recognized his track.

When you follow a buck, you are trying to catch up to him. You don't do this by straight-trailing, as I have shown in the above anecdote. You kill the buck by anticipating what he will do when you get to the end of the trail, not simply by following blindly. And you anticipate by watching what the trail is doing. A trail is more than merely a path to a deer; it is an indicator of the buck's state of mind, the weather, and a predictor.

THE PSYCHOLOGY OF TRAILING

I'd been watching the buck through the glasses from a ridge a mile away. He minced down the timbered slope and onto a brushy hill, moving with purpose in the dawn, his neck rut-swollen. Then he disappeared.

I slipped the binocs into my coat and stalked toward where I'd last seen the buck. By the time I cut his track, the sun had colored the peaks of the Wasatch Range a bright vermilion. The buck's trail was superimposed on smaller tracks, and he seemed to be following them. "Must be a hot doe," I said aloud. I followed.

The buck caught the doe three-quarters of a mile down the ravine. Their tracks milled about in the brush and snow, then the doe led off again downward with the buck following. If she was in estrus, as I was sure she was, the buck would stay with

Dragging out a "meat" buck. Snow makes this easier, too.

her until he'd firmly planted his seed; then he'd wander off. Hours later I found where they'd begun to meander as they searched for beds. They'd been quartering into the upcanyon breeze, so they wouldn't smell me.

The trail led out of the ravine and onto the ridge, through tangled maple scrub, and back toward where I'd first seen the buck. They'd bedded briefly on a bluff, then moved on again. They'd caught my scent, I could tell, and I cursed fluently as I scanned the ridge above. The big buck and doe climbed the opposite slope well out of rifle range.

The animals had whipped me by circling downwind of their trail, maybe the most common trick hunted ungulates use. I was young then, but already I'd been beaten by that same tactic two seasons earlier. And it wouldn't be the last time the deer would win by getting downwind. But I learned something that day: There is more to trailing or tracking than good or bad luck, and you can't just get on a trail and follow.

"Looping" is such an important trailing technique that I haven't been able to avoid mentioning it in some detail in other chapters. I must cite it again here because it can't be separated from other hunting methods. You simply determine the quarry's direction, then loop downwind of the trail, returning to it every so often to be sure you're still going right. This works well because many hunted ungulates bed downwind of their backtrail to scent anything following them. Chances are the buck or bull will be watching the trail itself and won't expect you to be where you are.

Looping works for species other than deer. One of my early uses of the tactic was in the Absaroka country of Montana. A group of bull elk had bedded in the timber above a small creek, and I jumped them. Big animals rushed in every direction—down into the creek bottoms and up the drainage through the timber. Since they were now on the alert, there'd be little use following the tracks. I climbed up the barren, wind-blasted ridge and circled the stand of lodge pole pine timber. I circled that stand of trees. No tracks left it, at least on the upper side, so I believed at least some of the bulls were still below in the trees. I stalked down into the timber, keeping downwind of where I thought and hoped they would be. When I cut the tracks, they told me that several of the bulls were meandering into the bottoms as they searched for a place to bed. Again I looped downwind of the trail. I was as alert as I ever get, because the bulls had calmed and bulls aren't as spooky as old and wise mule deer bucks. The elk would soon bed (in truth, since I was on their backtrail and reading sign that had been made some time earlier, the bulls were probably already bedded).

At the bottom of one loop, I spotted a slight movement in the trees below. The branches of a blowdown pine slowly took the form of elk legs. An ear twitched behind a curtain of pine needles, and I made out antler tines through the riflescope. As the bull stepped out from behind the cover, trying to locate whatever made him suspicious, my bullet broke his neck. Though elk aren't as cagey as adult mule deer, the looping tactic works with them, too, as well as for whitetails, kudu, bushbuck, Cape buffalo, and other species.

If the tracks are old, you're looping for nothing. And since looping requires kilos of concentration, you're exhausting yourself for no reason. It's better to make certain the trail is fresh enough to warrant looping.

I learned this—as I do all important lessons—the hard way. I once trailed a big track of a moose along a wilderness Alaskan river. The bull meandered in and out of the flood channels, through willow flats, and along open beaches. I expected to get a shot at any moment. Geese winged south in the blue September sky above the tracks, which seemed fresh.

The trail climbed onto a bluff and continued along the river. In the sand there, the tracks were nondescript depressions and impossible to decipher, except for direction. I jumped a cow from the willows and checked her tracks. I could see every detail. The trail I'd been following was days old. The prints had looked fresh in the damp mud and soil along the river, but they weren't.

Recent weather can help you age tracks. If raindrops spatter in the track, it was made before or during the last rain, logically enough. If there aren't any rain imprints in the track, it was made since the last rain. Frost action in moist soils quickly obliterates tracks, distorting and erasing them. All but the driest soil is affected by frost action.

In very dry soil, wind plays a big part in your ability to age tracks. Here, make tracks of your own and watch how they change over time.

I spent three fruitless days in the Sierra Viejo of Sonora trying to get close enough to photograph a big desert ram. Late one dawn, as I stalked slowly up a damp arroyo bottom, I found large, fresh ram tracks. The trail climbed out of the arroyo, angling up the slope toward a ridge high above. Near the ridgeline the winds kicked in. The track led onto the fine soil of the ridgetop and became only depressions. They looked eons old, and I recalled how I'd thought old tracks looked very fresh in mud or damp soil.

Disgusted at myself for making the same dumb mistake, I turned for camp. The big ram jumped up from behind an ocotillo and disappeared around the curve of the slope. The tracks in the bottom and in the sand were fresh. They looked old on the ridgetop because the wind destroyed their outlines in the fine sand.

In some terrain, following a buck's track is impossible. Still, you can at least determine a buck's presence by its sign or spoor. Browsed or grazed vegetation, droppings, wallows, beds, and rubs are typical buck sign. An observant hunter can locate where a buck beds, feeds, and moves about, and then put himself in the right place at the right moment.

The following anecdote isn't unusual: I'd been hunting in a rocky part of the Uncompahgre of western Colorado. The country was mostly rimrock, and the only actual tracks I spotted were in stream-bottom sand and gravel and in a few pockets of soil on brushy slopes. It was nearly impossible to cut a track and follow to its conclusion. On one brushy, rock-covered slope, I found where shrubs had been cropped by a buck. I knew it was a buck because in soil between two pinyon pines I located a single forehoof print that measured four inches long when I placed a 7mm-08 cartridge case beside it. The shrub cuts seemed fresh, though a bit browner from oxidation than a fresh cut I made myself with my knife. I guessed they'd been browsed that morning. I circled around the slope and then up onto the mesa top and found a rub on a pine sapling. Sticky sap oozed from it, so I figured it, too, was fresh. I found another rub and then a bed, both considerably older than the other sign. So, I reasoned, a good buck hangs out here, and this must be a good place for an ambush. I collected a big-bodied but average-antlered buck there the next dawn.

I've taken Coues whitetails in Sonora and Arizona in more or less the same manner, as well as Dall and snow sheep, several African antelope, and other species. Find sign, then hunt the place.

In terrain that takes and holds tracks, it helps to know about animal behavior. As mentioned elsewhere, a buck heading in a straight line is going someplace in a hurry. If he is trotting or running, or even walking in a specific direction, and continues on for a good distance, have your trekking boots on. He may travel for several canyons.

Mule deer bucks, however, often return to their home range as soon as things cool down. When the hunting hordes thin, bucks make their way back home.

When a buck's trail seems to wander about aimlessly, he's at ease. Usually, he's browsing—look for cropped shrubs, forbs, and tall grasses. Or he may be searching for a safe spot to bed down. If there's no evidence of browsing, the buck may well be bedded down very near, so shift into silent and alert gear.

In Africa, animal sign is called spoor. My interest in reading spoor was heightened because it increased my abilities and success as a hunter. Now I often go onto winter range just to trail a buck or to read the spoor to determine what animals were doing. It's as absorbing and fascinating as hunting.

MACHOS ON THE FLATS

Sarge was an ancient and eccentric ex-cavalry man who lived in a stone house he'd built from river rock in the southern Arizona foothills. Like all eccentrics, Sarge was misunderstood, which in modern society means mistrusted. It took a full month of fast talking to wear down my parents to the point where they'd allow me to go hunting with him that first time, on Christmas break. After that, the hunt was always the same. We'd lead the packstring out of his ocotillo-stalk corral, across the sierra, and south into the desert. When his horse and mules stepped across a barbed-wire fence that usually lay on the ground, we were in Mexico.

Tepecano Indians call large desert mule deer bucks *machos*. "Them *machos* stick to the flats," Sarge would shout over his shoulder as he plodded ahead on his old buckskin mare. "Don't need no water, neither."

That terse comment summarized desert mule deer hunting in a cartridge case: Look in the flat mesquite, paloverde, and deserts of succulent cactus. In some places the deer drink free water only

This buck probably weighed 400 pounds on the hoof, and is the best buck I took in the '90s. The thinnest place between burr and brow tines is 7 inches.

during the wet season (a relative term in the parched Sonora Desert). Otherwise they get moisture from the vegetation they browse, from naturally removing moisture from feces before defecation, or from battering open cacti to get at the fleshy pulp. This allows desert mule deer to live in the hottest and driest places on the continent, occupying a niche with few competitors. Potential rivals for food—the graceful Coues deer—hold to the foothills and mountains, as do desert bighorn sheep. Even mountain lions, called pumas or *tigres* south of the border, seldom wander out into the flat and hot deserts.

That first season, I was a veteran of exactly one whitetail hunt, and had shot my Coues buck—a respectable one—in the high, piney Huachuca Mountains. So I was pretty uncomfortable riding out into the flat desert so far that even distant mountain ranges disappeared in the desert heat haze. We set up camp at a nearly dry *tinaja*, because the pack and saddle animals needed water. I was so dry I thought they'd drink it up before I would get any. We often rode twenty miles out of camp before hunting on foot.

Sarge looked first for a big track, about the same size as their more northerly cousins. Just how we followed depended on wind direction. If it blew into our faces, we straight-trailed. We moved more carefully as the trail became fresh, keeping our eyes peeled and thumbs on the hammer of the Model 94s. Since shots were in close more often than not, we tested wind direction every few minutes, usually by dropping fine dust.

If the buck moved across the wind, we kept to the downwind side of the trail, periodically returning to it for confirmation that we were still going right. If we passed the end of the trail, we looped back toward where we'd last seen the track. Unless the buck had made an upwind turn, he was somewhere between us and the last spot we'd seen his tracks.

If a *macho* headed downwind, we'd try to anticipate where he was going, then make a big loop well away (more than four hundred yards) from the trail in that direction. If we didn't cut tracks, we gridded back toward where we'd last seen them—a sometimes tough task. But simply following tracks downwind was a guaranteed way to lose the buck.

The desert mule deer's favorite foods grow most profusely along dry arroyos. If we could see above the bluffs and into the brush, Sarge and I still-hunted in the silent, sandy bottoms. Over the years, we collected at least half-a-dozen *machos* this way. They were usually bedded in the mesquite, and because we were in the arroyo bottoms, they were at our eye level.

If the arroyo bluffs were too high for us to see over, we still-hunted on top of them, moving slowly from thicket to thicket. I collected my very first mule deer by sneaking through brush in just that way. As I peeked through a tangle of paloverde, I astonished myself by spotting an immense buck bedded beneath a mesquite on the other side of the wash. One shot from the .30-30 Sarge had loaned me killed the buck.

I'm not sure whether we killed more deer by still-hunting or tracking, but I do know that most of the good bucks we killed were taken by one of those two methods.

We also ambushed in the flat desert thickets. We'd look for cacti—saguaro, barrel, or organ-pipe—that had been battered open by mule deer antlers. Certain areas grew more of these succulent cacti, because of soil nutrients or organic material in the earth, and bucks congregated there. We'd wait downwind in the dawn or late afternoon and hope to catch a buck coming into the cacti.

Ambushing worked well during the rut, which ran from as early as mid-December until mid- or late January. Does tend to select and stay in places with good feed and cover, and eventually a big buck will show up around a doe herd. Any good *macho* always joins the ladies. When we found heavy deer sign, we were careful; if we spooked the does, we could forget about them for the rest of the season.

Still-hunting or ambushing in feeding areas also produced bucks. In various seasons, mule deer are fond of mesquite, paloverde, palo fierro, bur sage, manzanita, and other shrubs and forbs, dead or alive.

Glassing for bucks seldom worked out on the flats—for obvious reasons. But in a particular flat valley with a single volcanic hill, we glassed to fine effect. The hill was only a hundred feet high, but that was high enough to see over the cacti

British Columbia moose and deer camp. The dawn after this shot was taken, I killed a buck as I stepped from the tent to heed the call of nature.

and mesquite. And we spotted bucks from its top. Then came the tough part—stalking through the brush on the flats to get within range. Usually, we'd estimate the distance to the buck, then pick out landmarks on the way, like a saguaro with a peculiar arm, a dead mesquite, whatever, so we'd know where we were and whether we were getting closer. We'd try to figure wind direction near the buck by glassing for perched birds (they face into the wind), bent grasses, or drifting dust.

Sarge and I killed a number of bucks in those years down in Sonora. I don't remember a single one with a spread of less than thirty inches, and the largest went forty with beams as thick as my preteen forearms. I've hunted desert mule deer since, but I learned everything I needed to know in those early years.

THOSE SPOOKY BUCKS

Back when I was conducting elk research at Utah State University, I spotted more than a few big mule deer bucks in northern Utah, Yellowstone, and southern Montana. I hypothesized that there were two kinds of bucks, behaviorally—those relying on running for escape and those relying on hiding.

In the intervening years, and wherever possible, I questioned successful big-buck hunters to determine just how each buck was taken. It seems, both from my own hunting experiences and from notes I have from other hunters, that fewer and fewer bucks are located because they're running away. Now, most hide to avoid detection by hunters. I'm convinced that adult mule deer bucks in moderately to heavily hunted terrain are exclusively hiders; that is, they'll stay hidden until they're absolutely certain they've been detected. With today's flat-shooting rifles, superior rifle scopes, excellent cartridges and bullets, and other gadgetry, putting distance between himself and a human predator is no guarantee of a buck's safety. Those bucks that run for it at the first sight or smell of danger are the ones that get shot first and can no longer pass on their genes. Those that stay put and don't run live to breed and pass on qualities that allow them to survive. Of course, this is a slight oversimplification of Darwinism, but it's apt. Further supporting the idea is the fact that when I first learned to hunt mule deer back in the '60s, nearly every big buck was a "runner."

The natural inclination of mule deer, those that haven't been hunted extensively, is to run from potential predators (you). With their unusual stiff-legged bound and endurance, they can put a lot of rough country between themselves and a predator in a hurry. Over tens of thousands of years, this was effective. Then men with rifles made their appearance, and such escape tactics were no longer as effective. The "runners" got shot off. Dig out old hunting magazines, and most of them will tell you mule deer always pause at the top of a ridge to look back, and this is the best time to shoot. Those articles were right—it was natural back then for a buck to check his backtrail to see if the predator was still a danger; if it was, he'd run more, and if not, he wouldn't have to waste more energy fleeing at top speed. As mentioned, more and more of those that did look back were shot off. Those that didn't run for it and instead remained hidden survived to pass on their genes for caginess.

Undoubtedly, some bucks simply adapted with an experience or two, perhaps when a 170-grain slug singed the hide on his neck as he stared at a hunter on the next ridge. Before the mule deer had time to adapt to the threat of the long-range rifle, he'd gained the reputation as the white-tailed deer's slow cousin. Why don't whitetails act this way? Simply because they live in thicker country and pausing to look back would offer no advantage; they rely more on scent and hearing and often do pause, but far enough off in the forest that they aren't seen by hunters as they do so.

Mule deer bucks in remote areas or refuges like national parks, where they aren't shot at by men with long-range rifles, still do pause. Here, pausing to look back is probably the best way to deal with short-winded cougars or longer-winded coyotes. I've lately seen mule deer pausing to watch their backtrail in parts of British Columbia, Yellowstone, and the odd Montana wilderness area.

Hunting the "runners" in such areas is mostly a matter of getting out early when bucks are feeding (unhunted bucks continue to feed at dawn and dusk and are less nocturnal in habit). Brushing the bucks in these remote places is a trip back to the day when mule deer were regarded as the whitetail's slightly addled relative.

In still-hunting, the runners are much easier than the hiders. It's much simpler to become a good marksman than it is to learn the tricks and tactics necessary to bag the hiders. Perhaps the simplest method is to sidehill up a canyon slope with the idea of flushing deer onto the opposite slope, where you can get a shot. When I started hunting mule deer, this was about the only method I used. I'd still-hunt up a big ravine or canyon on a side slope, hoping to flush bucks out of the brush below and up the opposite slope. Just as often, bucks flushed from brush on the opposite slope. In either case, I'd get a shot. Shots were often long, from two hundred out to four hundred yards or so (claims to the contrary, a 400-yard shot is exceptional; the next time someone says he made a 600-yard shot, ask if he measured it). I'd attempt to find a solid rest—the fork in an aspen sapling or my daypack over a rock or stump—before pressing the trigger. Often, I'd have time for several shots if I muffed the first.

In 1986 I killed my last runner. That buck was a monster and scored 200 points green. He was the heaviest deer I'd ever killed or seen killed; having weighed big bucks in the past, I suspect he weighed nearly 350 pounds field-dressed. I had tracked the buck for three days and jumped him from downslope below me. He crashed into the bottoms and then up the opposite slope of a canyon more than three hundred yards distant. When I saw how big he was, I missed clean with the first shot. I settled down on the second and forced myself into that impersonal and mechanical state you enter when you are doing it right. I heard the bullet slap, and the buck lowered his head and kicked like a rodeo bronc just out of the chute. I knew I already had him, but I took no chances and held over and ahead and dropped him as he trotted across the slope. He was my last runner, and I suspect he will remain that way. It had been many years between my previous runner and that kill.

Few of us are fortunate enough to hunt in true wilderness. In hunted country, most adult bucks are hiders. I don't waste time waiting for big bucks to feed into the open during daylight hours, and seldom wait even at dawn or dusk. You'll see smaller deer this way, and if you're hunting meat, this is a good tactic. But trophy bucks stay hidden when they're hunted.

Hiders behave more like whitetails, hunted elk in timber, or even black bears in some places. They stay close to or in heavy brush or timber. Mule deer vision is perhaps as keen as that of mountain sheep or even pronghorn antelope, and they rely on it, even in heavy timber. I suspect they hear better than any other game animal—as witness the big ears—and they rely on what they hear. They also seem to scent like a bloodhound—all of which tells us that hunting them is an extremely tough undertaking. Stalking requires the silence of a cougar, the patience of a polar bear waiting at a seal's breathing hole in the ice, and the reflexes and coordination of Wyatt Earp. Remember, too, that hiders will not flush until they are certain they've been detected; they know most hunters will walk right on by if they remain still. The best method to collect a hider is to track.

After a month of scouting, I'd located an adult buck's home range, a plateau thick with cliffrose, sagebrush, mahogany, wild rose, and various forbs. In spite of watching at dawn and dusk, I hadn't spotted him—no surprise, since adult bucks are normally nocturnal during hunting seasons. I suppose my preseason scouting had been disturbing enough to keep him lying low. The tracks told me he fed only at night on the plateau top, returning well before light to the thick timber on the northeast-facing slope of a big, deep canyon. Early opening morning, I found his fresh tracks and followed them off the plateau, down a well-used deer trail, and into old-growth fir and spruce. The tracks moved downwind, so I couldn't stay on the trail or he'd scent me before I could get close enough for a shot. So I modified the loop technique and swung below the trail and more or less downwind. I relied on the deer staying to the trail until he decided to bed down, which, judging from my preseason scouting, he'd always done. From downwind and twenty or thirty yards below the trail, I could look uphill and see the disturbance made by years of deer feet on the trail. I kept the rifle at ready with a round in the chamber, my thumb on the safety, and the variable scope on 2X. I figured the buck would bed downwind of the trail and at approximately the same distance from it as I was moving, so I watched ahead and a little downhill. I hunted slowly and silently, detouring around any object that might make a noise, so I could have time enough to thoroughly scan the tangles ahead.

Two hundred yards into the timber, I saw something ahead that didn't fit. I couldn't quite figure it out, but a small and odd shadow showed under some fir branches. The deep shadows and gloom of the forest didn't help me unravel the puzzle. At thirty feet, the small shadow shifted slightly, or so I thought. It did it again, and the gun jumped to my shoulder as if it had a will of its own. At the same instant the buck was off and over a blowdown, and as he came down on the other side I squeezed off a shot. It was as much like wingshooting as big-game hunting gets. The buck was a good one with a spread of just under thirty inches and hefty beams.

Hiders also do their thing on open slopes, and behave about the same way there: They won't move until they're certain you've seen them.

I spent four years hunting a big old boy called the Sheepherd Buck, after the canyon where he lived. He had a variety of tricks, and always seemed to come out on top. One run-in with him well illustrates a hider's behavior. I'd spotted the buck across a big canyon too far away for a shot. He'd bedded in a clump of scrubby big-tooth maple. Half a mile down the canyon, four horseback hunters were riding right at him. My palms got sweaty and I steadied myself; after all those years, these yahoos were about to kill "my" buck. I thought briefly of yelling or shooting over the buck's head to scare him off. I didn't. It probably wouldn't have worked anyway. The riders came on. My heart thumped loudly as they neared the bedded buck. At fifty yards the buck stretched his neck forward and lay his head in a clump of twigs.

Two riders moved just above that clump of scrub and two just below. The buck didn't budge, and the hunters didn't see him, though from my vantage point it seemed impossible that they wouldn't. If the buck let those hunters get so close without moving, I reasoned, he'd do the same thing for me, and I knew where he was. But the moment I stood up across the canyon, the buck stood, too. Somehow, even at that distance, he knew I'd detected him. He trotted up the slope and over the ridge, keeping to thick brush the whole time. Years later, I did collect the Sheepherd Buck.

Sometimes bucks bed in places that don't seem to have enough cover to hide a rockchuck. Rick Lovell and I were hunting sage grouse on a northern Utah plateau, pushing through wind-tortured, ankle-high sagebrush toward a clump of shintangle fir on the edge of the canyon. We expected that maybe some grouse had hidden there to get out of the wind. Shotguns ready, we had approached to within thirty feet when a buck bounded up and raced off. We both had shotguns to our shoulders before we realized what had happened.

In western Wyoming, I twice made stalks on pronghorns, only to jump mule deer out of a treeless ravine. On both occasions, the frightened mule deer chased off the antelope before I could shoot. Once, I was squirming through the sagebrush on my belly when I came face to face with a mulie buck. I was so astonished, I literally jumped off the ground. In retrospect, I suppose I was still surprised because in days of glassing I hadn't seen a mule deer, and I figured mule deer country was a small range of mountains twenty miles north.

But even hiders can be vulnerable. The more hunters in a place, the higher the odds that someone will stumble onto one and shoot it. It's logical, then, to say that in heavily hunted country you'll find fewer big bucks. Scout thoroughly for big-buck sign before wasting much time on a place. Adult buck sign is discussed elsewhere in the book, so I won't tell about it again. However, don't scout too far in advance of the season. Changes in season, weather, and temperatures alter the availability or

Mule deer migration trail in Wyoming. I've documented bucks that have migrated more than fifty miles. Other biologists say they've seen deer move over ninety miles from summer to winter range.

desirability of browse plants, and bucks move on. Bucks at home on a particular range in early October may well have left by the end of the month.

As cited earlier, adult mule deer have changed behaviorally since the appearance of the rifle, most noticeably within the past few decades. Mature bucks hide in response to hunter pressure, and few run until they're sure they've been found. I once watched hunters work up a canyon from the Dolores River bottoms in western Colorado. They were driving or pushing, but they were also pretty naive. They hadn't posted anyone above to intercept the deer they were scaring up the canyon. I sat on a rimrock overlooking the scene, watching small bucks and does bound up the little canyon. As a portly hunter passed a clump of tall sagebrush just below me, I spotted a movement in the tangle. I brought up the binocs and spotted a good buck standing on the other side of the tall brush. He moved around it to keep the brush between himself and the hunter. The hunter passed on by and the buck stood and watched until another hunter wandered toward the brush. The buck climbed around to the offside of the brush and again let the hunter pass. He then lay down in the middle of the brush. I let the buck go on his way to father more genius-level mule deer.

SCENT-DRIVING

Hunters are well aware of alerting game by their scent. We take great pains to prevent our smell from getting to the buck before we do, because if the quarry scents us before we're ready to shoot, it's over. We attempt to track into the wind or as near to it as possible. When we still-hunt, it's into or at least across the wind. We position stands downwind of where we expect the buck to appear. But to make the trick of scent-driving work, forget that chiseled-in-stone rule that you should never hunt downwind.

Here, we let the game catch our scent. Indeed, we do everything possible to make that happen. We let the human stink drift to the quarry with the idea of pushing, or driving, it to a place where we or a partner can get a shot. This tactic works consistently for all types of big game.

In much of western deer country, high-elevation basins are common enough. They're ideal spots to use scent-driving. Much of the West is also pretty arid, and timber grows on the north- and east-facing slopes that get less direct exposure to sunlight, lose less moisture to evaporation, and grow denser vegetation. High basins typically have timber in the bottom or up the throat. Post the "sitters" on stands around the semicircle of the basin above the trees. Bucks will move out of the timber, frequently along well-used game trails. Those on stand should wait where they have a view of these trails. During the day, air heats, becomes less dense, and moves uphill and into the faces of the sitters. Though deer can be pushed with a single driver, it's better with more than one. It's also less work for each individual driver. In a big stand of timber, the more hunters the better. A lone driver can improve his effectiveness by hanging bits of well-seasoned clothing along the downwind side of the timber on a broad front; that way, his scent is carried throughout the trees.

On one of my solo hunts (I seldom hunted any other way) I somehow got into a group of hunters. I'd gone to high school with one of the guys, and after listening to their laments about the lack of deer, I suggested a way that at least some of them might get some shooting at bucks. I posted all four guys on the upper side of a basin a hundred or so yards above the timber. I circled well down the ridge and below that stand of fir and spruce. I left my sweaty stocking cap on a branch at one corner of the bottom end of the timber, crossed the wind and the bottom side of the trees, and left a mitten on another branch. As I made my way to the far side of the base of the timber, I left more clothing, urinated high on a bush in two places so the wind would carry its scent into the trees, and finally left bits of tack from my saddle mare—a sweaty saddle blanket and the saddle itself—and tied the mare on the far side of the trees. Shortly thereafter, I heard a shot above and figured it was a young buck since adults are seldom so quickly or easily moved with scent. Then I gridded back and forth across the wind as I moved higher and nearer the hunters posted above. Another shot, then another and another. By the time I'd reached the guys above, three had killed small bucks and one had missed a big one.

Since that country wasn't too heavily hunted, it was not so difficult to move the bucks. In more heavily hunted locales, I doubt the adult buck would have moved unless he was nearly stepped on. In heavily pressured terrain, the driver(s) should move slowly through the timber and make his lateral passes across the stands of trees closer together so he's less likely to miss a tight-sitting buck.

The same tactic works on flat ground. Here, sitters should wait closer to trails leaving the timber and keep a close watch on them. The more sitters the better, since they won't be able to see as far as those posted on the barren slopes of a mountain basin.

Again, canyons in the West are typically timbered on the east- and north-facing slopes. When scent-driving a canyon, post sitters on the slopes or at the canyon head. In a very large canyon, or with few sitters, have them move along the canyon sides several hundred yards ahead of the driver in the bottoms. Though air generally drifts uphill or upcanyon during the day, this is not always true, due to local anomalies of terrain or wind conditions, cooling air associated with a cold front, or for other reasons. If the wind has reversed itself and is blowing down the canyon, simply reverse the procedure and hunt downcanyon.

In wide canyon bottoms, grid back and forth so you don't miss pushing any deer. They may flee up one of the canyon slopes, where either a driver or a sitter (used here in the loose sense of the word) might get a shot. As a rule, the thicker the timber or deciduous brush (like willow, chokecherry, cottonwood, or maple) the more deer will hide in it. Don't avoid especially thick brush.

If you're scent-driving a canyon where the timber is on the north- or east-facing slope, post sitters near trails leading to that timber, but position them so they can shoot across the canyon to the open south- or west-facing slope. Most canyons also have side canyons or ravines radiating out from the main cut; these are good places to wait, especially if there's cover and a game trail up the bottom.

Scent-driving is more difficult if you're alone, of course, but it can be done, especially in smaller stands of brush or trees. Here, move slowly across the upwind side of the trees, allowing enough time to let scent permeate the trees. If practical, leave bits of clothing along the upwind side of the cover. If you have to relieve yourself, do it here. Then circle quietly and quickly to the downwind side or end of the trees where you expect game is hiding. Since scent takes a while to saturate the cover, it gives you time to get to the downwind side before bucks start retreating from your odor. Be sure to move as quietly as you can. If bucks hear you splintering your way through brush and rolling rocks, they won't be predictably driven, and if you're going it solo, you must be able to predict accurately.

If you're scent-driving alone, you must be quicker, quieter, and more aware. I find that hunting downwind through brush in a canyon bottom, then climbing one of the open slopes to scan the opposite slope, works best. Then I move back into the bottoms and again climb the opposite slope to scan. I always pause long enough in the bottoms so my scent will alert anything for at least a few hundred yards ahead. The length of this pause is determined by conditions in the bottoms: Thicker trees, stronger winds, and dry conditions require an increased waiting time. I repeat this procedure until I eventually top out of the canyon. At the canyon head I'm especially alert. Canyon heads act as a sort of dam for bucks moving ahead of you. The animals know that if they leave the brush or timber and race across the ridge in the open, they become vulnerable. Adult bucks hate crossing open areas during daylight in hunting season, and they'll hole up in the brush as long as possible.

Even in terrain types other than those discussed here, the idea is always the same: Position yourself where wind direction will drift your scent to places where you think game is hiding, then place yourself or companions where you think bucks might retreat.

FLOATING FOR BUCKS

The biggest challenge in trophy mule deer hunting is locating an area with good numbers of big bucks and few hunters. I

Snowed in!

suppose the challenge is the same for all big game. As more hunters flood into western mule deer habitat, of course, fewer big bucks survive. Those that do are survival experts.

River bottoms are thought of as the domain of the white-tailed deer, but this terrain often harbors good mule deer, particularly if hunting pressure is heavy higher up, as it is likely to be. Deer trying to escape the upcountry drone of ATVs, pickups, and trailer parks often sneak into thick river bottoms.

The only way to hunt enough river bottoms to give you a serious chance at a good mulie buck is to float. Western rivers differ greatly, from big, slow, and surging rivers like the Green to clear, small streams to murky, dirty rivers like the Dolores in western Colorado. The good news is that tactics are pretty much the same regardless of which river you float.

Few rivers follow a straight course. Most turn and twist and form peninsulas between bends. These peninsulas are productive places to drive or push with a companion or three. As with other kinds of driving, it's more productive with more hunters, though perhaps less satisfying. As you float, the drivers are let off at the base of a peninsula; the shooter floats downstream to its tip and picks a spot where he'll see the tip and the channels on either side. Normally, drivers work across the base of the peninsula, up the river's edge a few yards, and then back across the peninsula, gridding back and forth in tight switchbacks so they don't miss bucks sitting tight in the thick brush. The longer the hunting season has been going and the more hunters combing the canyons above, the tighter adult bucks will sit.

If you're doing it solo, make one or three quick passes across the peninsula base and then quickly float down to the tip and watch. Initially, a rush of young bucks and does may try to vacate the area. If you move fast enough, you'll be at the peninsula tip in position for a shot when they do, and if you're after meat, you'll probably score. (I regularly used this method for moose, and an acquaintance uses it for whitetails.) If I'm float-hunting alone, I'll then quietly work my way back along the shoreline to the base of the peninsula, and make two quick passes across the base to unnerve any buck still sitting tight. I then rush back to the river and quietly but quickly hurry back up the shoreline to the peninsula tip, where I can watch both sides in the event a buck attempts to cross the river. It may take time for a buck to move out, and he may wait until he thinks the danger has passed or is downriver. I suspect an adult buck will move out of the tangle if he believes you're still at the peninsula base, and to fool him, you've got to make your way silently back to the tip. Fortunately, rushing water sometimes masks any sounds you make.

Some small canyons or ravines are accessible only from a river. Chances are good that if you can't drive to them in a motor vehicle, they won't be hunted. These places may be hot buck localities. Of course, working them is more effective with a companion or two. One hunter can sidehill while the other pushes up the bottom. If you're alone, push up the bottom and climb sidehills frequently enough to catch bucks moving ahead; this works best in combination with scent-driving, discussed in an earlier chapter. Be aware that normally, hunting up a canyon during the day means hunting downwind.

On larger rivers, islands are good places to find bucks. This is especially true on larger islands—say, in excess of two acres. These are rare in mule deer country. I love to solo-hunt islands. If you start a buck, he must cross water to escape the island, and even alone, you'll hear him splashing (unless rapids mask the sound) and have plenty of time to get ready to shoot when he climbs out on shore. (Be careful about shooting while he's in the water—you may lose him. Also, it may be illegal in places.)

It's best to have more than one hunter on larger islands. Here, hunting is much like driving through river-bottom peninsulas. Pushers or drivers start at the upriver end of the island after the shooter has floated to the downriver end. The shooter positions himself so he can either see both sides of the island or can check each side by walking a short distance. Pushers should make a back-and-forth, S-curve path toward the downriver end of the island. Both pushers and standers should listen closely for deer in the water. If the island is large, make more than one pass through it.

While floating, watch for deer crossings and watering places. Concentrations of tracks on both shores at the same place indicate that deer cross there, perhaps to feed on the other side. If there's a concentration of tracks on only one side, deer drink there. Over the years, I've found several good and consistent crossing places. One is on the Dolores River, another on the Wyoming portion of the Green River, and a third on the Yellowstone in southern Montana. Here, mule deer either leave the heavy riverine cover or come down from nearby hills to cross the river and feed in alfalfa or hay fields.

If you find such a spot, I'd suggest spending your hunting time right there. It will in all probability be easy to collect a meat buck there; adult bucks, largely nocturnal during hunting season, are tougher to put on the ground. Still, if the river bottom is not getting much hunting pressure and either it's hot (the buck will get thirsty earlier) or he's hungry for that succulent alfalfa just across the river, you stand a chance of catching him either just before dark or for a few moments at first light. Perhaps your best odds for success involve finding a big-buck track and following it to his bed, which will be nearby. Tracking can work well because river-bottom bucks don't stray far.

In hot and dry weather, ambushing at a watering place is a good plan, especially for meat bucks. These spots are more common where a ravine leads down to the shoreline or a ledge leads back from the bottoms to the higher country. Ambush here just as you would at a crossing, and the odds are best in the evening just before dark.

Another productive and pleasant river-bottom tactic is the simplest of all—floating early and late, when mule deer feed most actively. It's tough shooting from a raft or canoe that is rocking even gently in the current (and in some places it's illegal to shoot from a watercraft of any sort), so work the raft to shore as silently as possible. Most big-game animals don't seem unduly frightened by humans floating silently in boats. I noticed this first while hunting red lechwe, a beautiful, reddish, semiaquatic antelope with lyre-shaped horns, and Cape buffalo in native dugouts called *mokoro* in Botswana's Okavango Delta. I've since floated right past bucks on the shore of several rivers, as well as moose, caribou, and even a grizzly (the griz thought the odd-shaped debris floating by looked good to eat, but two shots into the water beside his head as he swam out made him change his mind). If animals don't scent or hear you and you don't make an odd movement, they usually stand and watch.

On a brisk November morning on the Dolores River in western Colorado, I'd just pushed off from a launch point in Paradox Valley. Red rimrocks loomed above the canoe as it dipped down the gentle rapids and into the canyon narrows. The wind was blustery, and the two bucks I saw first bounded off into thick tamarisk bush. Eventually, I beached the canoe on a red-sand beach and lay down in the sun to warm up and forget the frustration. One good point, I thought as I dozed off, was that I hadn't seen another hunter. I awoke some time later to the lap of water against the canoe and the towering rimrocks and a buck staring from across the river.

I've floated in canoes, inflatable rafts, and dories, on float hunts from Colorado to the rivers dumping into the Arctic Ocean, and I prefer inflatable rafts several times over. They're dependable, resilient, quiet, and "forgiving" (meaning a hunter can screw up an awful lot before getting in serious trouble with one, and since hunters tend not to be whitewater experts, this is important). Inflatables are easy to transport, since they can be deflated and tossed into a car trunk or SUV with little trouble. Riken, Achilles, and Avon make top-quality inflatable boats.

Fiberglass and wood canoes are quiet enough, given some cooperation by the hunter, but they're not as noiseless as an inflatable. They're much less forgiving, too, especially in rough water. Aluminum canoes are too noisy for deer hunting or anything else except family Fourth of July outings. In the right hands, dories work well on larger rivers; they're too awkward and noisy for smaller rivers. They're also difficult to launch in places without a boat ramp.

Typically, autumn hunting seasons are low-water times on western rivers and streams. Here, draft is important (the distance a craft protrudes underwater). Inflatables and canoes can hold a surprising tonnage and still have relatively shallow draft.

Rivers on which I've had hunting luck include the Yellowstone in Montana, the Dolores and San Miguel in Colorado, and the Green in Wyoming. Montana has a dozen other floatable rivers in deer country, Idaho has at least the Snake and the Salmon, and other places have smaller streams with potential. With that many floatable rivers and streams in the West, floating for mule deer just might be the new technique that produces your trophy buck.

In the West, river bottoms, the most fertile of lands, tend to be private property. If it's posted, get permission to hunt; in some states, you must get permission even if it's not posted.

GO BACK

The concept of the "honey hole" is valid. We all have known guides and hunters who consistently connect year after year. They have hidden, "secret" spots that are always good for a nice buck. Over the seasons, I've found several good honey holes.

The trouble is, either other hunters find out about them and ruin the place, or the terrain or hunting are in some way altered.

The first honey hole I located was in Utah, in a rugged gorge of the Narrows of the Ogden River. Back then, in the '60s, the place was just too tough to get into, let alone pack a buck out of. Those years, I had the place to myself. If I put in the time, I could be sure of getting a thirty-inch-plus buck out of there. It took several decades, but excess pressure and unlimited license sales eventually pushed hunters down into "my" gorge. Immediately, the big bucks disappeared.

Another of my honey holes was on a high ridge of Nevada's Ruby Mountains, and another was Mill Canyon in northern Utah. With mule deer, honey holes don't last long because too many hunters in surrounding country disturb them too much. I found spectacular honey holes in wilderness Sonora years ago, but the place is overhunted now (and the price for a hunt in mediocre country is exorbitant).

The longest-lasting honey hole was on a plateau near the Utah-Wyoming border. I killed nine trophy bucks there, including one just over and one just under the B&C minimum. The place had few hunters because roads were extremely primitive, it was a long haul from anywhere else, and if it snowed heavily you couldn't get out before spring. The plateau was lousy with good deer browse; heavy cover was also plentiful, though the bucks didn't need it because they were so little hunted. Many of them were related, I was certain, because they had a cheater tine coming out of the right main beam in exactly the same place. Water was abundant, and few pesky does and fawns lived there (favorable buck:doe ratio).

The plateau seldom got hunted, and bucks had good retreat cover when it did. Soil nutrients were good, so bucks grew wide, high, and heavy antlers. The last buck I collected from the place would have weighed, I'm fairly certain, not much less than 350 pounds field-dressed. I'd weighed enough bucks and other animals over the years to get fairly good at field guesstimates. He'd have gone over 400 pounds live-weight. All adult bucks I killed on the plateau weighed well over 200 pounds field-dressed, and most possessed excellent antlers. Such normally scrubby species as sagebrush and scrub or Gambel's oak grew to unheard-of proportions. Just as important, the plateau had the right gene pool to produce big deer. Such a place in this age is one in a billion, and when it does show up it's usually destroyed within two years (I can list all sorts of examples, from an Indian reservation in southeast Saskatchewan to several places in Sonora, Mexico).

Locating a buck honey hole is tough and iffy. First, find a place that produced one or more big bucks in the past. This in itself isn't easy, since few hunters freely volunteer information about their favorite spots. One way is to study hunting data gathered by state game agencies; these, however, are not always accurate since even at state roadblocks, hunters are reluctant to share their honey hole (I know—I made up place names when asked where I killed a big buck). Less experienced hunters, however, will freely tell where they killed a buck because they are so happy and proud. Another idea is to check back issues of local newspapers, many of which publish stories of big bucks taken in the vicinity (this is less common now, with so much anti-hunter sentiment about).

Buck in the timber.

Newspapers in small towns are best. Check taverns, especially if there are buck heads and antlers hanging on the wall; we all know what happens with whiskey and veracity, but even if you can't find concrete info in a honky-tonk, you'll have fun looking.

These days especially, honey holes don't last long. Other hunters find out about them, move in, and kill off the bucks or the bucks move out. The best example is northern Mexico. For a while back in the late '80s, the entire province of Sonora seemed a mule deer honey hole. Outfitters piled U.S. clients throwing fistfuls of greenbacks at them into the *ranchos* and the same places year after year. Big bucks disappeared, and the outfitters and their clients went to new *ranchos*. The *ranchos* ran out and so did the big bucks, but the prices for hunts haven't gone down and outfitters are still making big profits because of earlier history. Sonoran hunts are several times more expensive than better guided hunts in Idaho or Wyoming, in my opinion the best states to find a trophy buck these days. In Sonora, most guides, outfitters, and clients are quite content with a twenty-seven-inch rack, a buck I would not shoot in Utah or Wyoming unless he was particularly massive. Paying six or seven grand for a twenty-seven-inch buck is throwing your money away.

I suppose Sonora may have some yet-undiscovered honey holes. Back in the '60s I saw some places so remote that I still find it difficult to believe that they have by now been exploited. But men with bulldozers and dynamite can go anywhere, and soon men in four-wheel-drives will show up and shoot at the big deer. I still think the best bet for a trophy buck is to get into the truly wild places in Idaho and Wyoming and probably other states—places where the deer are carefully managed and hunting pressure isn't too heavy.

The behavior and lifestyle of big bucks are such that only so many can exist on a given chunk of western real estate. In the arid southwestern deserts of Sonora, there isn't enough feed to support dense populations of mule deer, so the animals are more vulnerable than northern populations. Still, adult bucks are intensely sought. Kill off those bucks in a well-publicized spot in Saskatchewan or Sonora, and you're left with the same conditions that exist throughout most of the West—lots of young bucks and few trophies.

Once a honey hole is publicized, it is probably already worthless to the trophy hunter. An example was my personal honey hole in Mill Canyon off the South Fork of the Ogden River (I can name it now because it is worthless hunting country and full of summer cabins, roads, and the incessant whine of ORVs). Any deer killed in the place today is an accident and probably was feeding on rose gardens all summer and considered a pet by a little old lady with blue hair. But back in the "old days," I killed four good bucks there in four consecutive seasons. On my last successful hunt, as I packed out a buck with a thirty-three-inch spread, I noticed three hunters working a slope up the canyon. The following season, half-a-dozen hunters were in the canyon and I didn't see an adult mule deer. A season later, the place was overrun with redshirts, and that was the last time I hunted there.

Another larger and more famous honey hole was the famed Dolores Triangle, formed by the Colorado River on the northwest, the Dolores River on the southeast, and the Colorado border on the east. The place consistently produced monster bucks in the 1950s and '60s. Magazines published a couple of stories about the hunting there, and then the word was out. And the trophy buck hunting was over. I hunted the Triangle early in the '70s and spotted plenty of small bucks, but couldn't find a single adult buck track. Simply, the trophies had all been killed or chased off.

Changing environment also destroys honey holes. Mule deer habitat may undergo natural changes such as forest and range fires, which may be beneficial in the long run since deer don't eat trees and fires tend to stimulate growth of vegetation. Drought and other severe weather alter habitat, too. More commonly, though, man's interference destroys good hunting by making rough and remote country more accessible. The U.S. Forest Service and the Bureau of Land Management—through road construction often associated with logging in the case of the former, and through simple neglect and not enforcing off-road restrictions in the case of the latter—have caused hundreds of thousands of acres of remote deer habitat to be opened up to machines and machine-dependent sportsmen. And hunters wonder why trophy buck hunting throughout the West is declining.

It's best to look for less publicized and commercialized honey holes. If a good buck or two have been taken in a place in the past season or two, habitat there may not have changed and other hunters may not have found out about the spot. It's possible the big buck was just pushed into the area by hunters elsewhere, or he may be a freak onetime occurrence, but it's likely he was there for a reason. Perhaps the place was overlooked by most hunters; had good cover, food and water; or was attractive for other reasons known only to mule deer bucks. If so, odds are good that another buck will take over the locale.

In seeking locations with a high proportion of adult bucks, remember that big boys generally don't hang out where there are does and fawns unless it's rutting time. The more does, the fewer adult bucks. Places with lots of young bucks and does attract hunters away from big-buck honey holes; praise Diana for such places.

Bucks must live long enough to achieve trophy proportions. In my research, few bucks on most western deer ranges reach trophy size before their fifth birthday (exceptions exist, of course, especially in places with unusual soil nutrients, abundant food and/or a good local gene pool). Of seventy or so fully mature trophy bucks I've aged in three countries and six western states, all have been between 5½ and 10½ years old. I have it from reliable sources that exceptionally large antlers may show up on bucks 4½ years of age, too—I just have not seen them. Even in habitat devoid of humans and hunting pressure, a six-year-old buck has to be lucky to survive the winter, rutting battles, falls, diseases, parasites, lightning, and coyotes. An eight-year-old buck must be even luckier. Mule deer honey holes are most often places with little or no hunting pressure or other human traffic. In my experience, one of the best ways to locate such spots is through meticulous examination of topographic maps. If the place is in mule deer country and has no roads or maintained trails into it, check it out.

Let's say you've found a suspected honey hole, through topo-map examination, research, or word of mouth. For confirmation, look for big-buck sign—remember track sizes, rubs, scrapes, droppings, beds, and other evidence of a buck's presence. Pay special attention to scrapes; 95 percent of them are made by adult bucks, according to my data. Likewise, big tracks (forehoof length about four inches) always indicate big bucks. If there's no big-buck sign, go elsewhere.

Adult bucks in good habitat have small home ranges. If there's sufficient high-quality browse and cover in a small area and the buck doesn't need to move far to get at it, why should he? The less he moves around, the less energy he uses and the less he exposes himself to danger. I've located any number of home ranges less than a mile in diameter, and most were much smaller than that. As mentioned earlier but also pertinent here, adult bucks spend most of their time in a small portion of their home range, I call the center area. They're intimately familiar with all characteristics of this area and are thus minimally susceptible to a variety of dangers therein. Big bucks are stay-at-homes; they find a place that meets all their needs and stay there. If you kill a buck in such a place, odds are high that another will find the spot and take up residence. Then your best tactic is to return and collect another big buck.

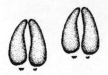

Chapter 5

The Narratives

QUEST FOR THE SHEEPHERD BUCK

In the early dawn, the buck appeared, then disappeared, ghostlike, into the thick maples half a mile down the ridge. All I could tell in the dim light was that he had an unusually widespread rack. I was hunting the heads of some draws above, places that had yielded bucks in years past. I'd hunt down toward the buck later in the day if nothing else turned up.

A few yearling bucks and does flushed out of the aspen and maple stands at the heads of the draws, but nothing of any size, so I walked slowly down the ridge toward the thick maples where I had seen the wide-racked buck earlier. The sun was coloring northern Utah's Wasatch Range to the west a rich salmon pink. I moved slowly into the maples, listening carefully, making as little noise as possible. My plan was to move whatever was in the maples down to the bottom of the ravine and then up the opposite, relatively open slope, where I could get a shot. There were subtle noises off to my left—perhaps a grouse walking on dried leaves, or maybe a porcupine. Then more noises below. Whatever it was, it was going away fast and into the bottom. If it was the big buck, my plan was working. I ran back out of the maples to a sagebrush opening. Two small bucks crashed through the aspens and chokecherry in the bottom and up the opposite slope. Then there was more movement going uphill. I ran up the slope, rounded the top of the stand of maples, and there he was, close up. I wasn't ready to shoot, though, since I hadn't expected to see anything so suddenly. In the second or so I was face-to-face with the buck, those massive, sky-scraping antlers became the stuff of an obsession. I had met the big buck of Sheepherd Canyon. And then he turned and disappeared.

The following deer season, one canyon to the south, I again encountered the myth in the flesh, the Sheepherd Buck. Several hunters on horseback were brushing the opposite slope. I watched, hoping they would scare something my way. A half-mile downslope were more horseback hunters. The first group passed a thick growth of maples. The leaves had fallen, and I figured I could see any movement on the opposite slope with binoculars. Suddenly a buck emerged from the top of a stand of brush, scarcely ten yards from where the nearest hunter had ridden. The buck wasn't spooked and moved deliberately and carefully. He followed the hunters a short distance and then moved down into the canyon bottom. He knew other hunters were riding up the canyon, and he waited until they had passed before he moved into the bottoms less than thirty yards behind them. When he disappeared into the aspens, he was heading toward a saddle sixty yards to my right.

The wind was in my favor as I jacked a cartridge into the chamber of the .270 and checked the scope. I moved a little closer to the saddle. From the new vantage point I could see the saddle and two hundred yards up the ridge. If he crossed, I'd get him. But he didn't cross. After two hours, I moved down to where I'd last seen him.

The tracks told me he'd walked about a hundred yards up from the bottom of the canyon, always keeping to the thickest oak brush. He'd bedded in the oak and was cool enough to stay put even when I walked within twenty-five yards of him on my way down to the canyon bottom to pick up his tracks. When he did move, he went silently. Then, farther upslope in thick brush, I heard the thump, thump of a mule deer bouncing to safety. I

This is the Sheepherd Buck. It took me four years to finally bag him. My emotions here were bittersweet.

knew there was no chance to catch him that day, so I headed back to camp.

I spotted him one more time that season. The sun had just set, and frost was already settling on the tawny, late-October grasses and arrowleaf. No others had hunted the small draws that emptied into Sheepherd Creek for nearly a week. Does and young bucks browsed out of a stand of maples across the draw. As the light faded, more deer fed into the open. A yearling and a four-point browsed within easy rifle range down the ridge. I stalked back up the ridge toward camp. It was too cold to sit any longer.

On a game trail that led over the top in the direction of camp, I paused and looked back. Silhouetted against the western skyline stood the Sheepherd Buck. He was a little over a hundred yards away. If there was any doubt about his identity, the right antler's abnormal sixth point erased it. I raised the rifle, but the buck disappeared. I stumbled back to camp in the near-darkness.

The next year I saw the buck on opening morning. He'd already seen me but wasn't too concerned. He seemed to know

I was too far away for a shot. He watched for a moment and then casually walked into the growth of maples where I'd first seen him two years earlier. I sat down to think out a course of action. If I went down into the canyon bottom and up to him, I'd simply spook him over the opposite ridge. I decided to hike up to the head of the draw and down the other side of the opposite ridge. Since I'd be above him, there was a chance of spooking him into the bottom and up the opposite slope, the same strategy I'd tried two years earlier to no avail. It took me an hour to work into position. The wind was in my favor. Thick, big-bellied clouds raced by overhead, seeming low enough to grab. A few big drops of rain slanted out of the black sky, making dark craters in the dry, red dust. It would snow before the day was out, but now the about-to-happen weather was making game and hunters nervous. The maples whipped back and forth in the wind. I would not be able to hear anything move in there, but neither would the Sheepherd Buck. Filled with misgivings, I looked across the canyon. There, a few feet from where I'd been sitting earlier, stood the buck. He knew I was too far away for a shot. He watched me a moment, twitched his tail, and disappeared over the ridge. Perhaps the whipping trees and gusts of wind had made it unbearable in the brush, where he wouldn't have heard danger approach and any scents wafted to him by the shifty gusts would be unreliable. But then again, maybe he had guessed my plan of attack and simply decided that the best place to be was the one I'd just come from.

The storm hit that night and dropped ten inches of snow, which prevented me from hunting for the next few days. The four-wheel-drive could get me within four miles of the big buck's haunts, but I didn't dare try to drive farther down the steep road and across the frozen creeks in the heavy, new snow. The morning dawned clear and cold. Wind shrieked across the flats as I fastened the bindings on the cross-country skis, which I figured could take me to the buck's canyon in short order. I was in place across from his favorite stand of maples before the eastern horizon

This buck was pretty typical of Sonoran mulies in the '70s and '80s. Today, decent bucks are as scarce as truthful congressmen.

turned rosy red. I scanned the canyon, searching for the buck, and contemplated the sailor's saying, "Red in the morning, sailors take warning." Finally, I saw the cream rump and black tail of a deer disappear into maples across the canyon. I had the impression of huge antlers, but it was more a sixth sense than anything concrete I'd seen. Maybe I just wanted to see the buck so badly that I had imagined it. If it was him, I didn't see how he could have detected me; the wind had been in my favor, I'd been quiet, and I hadn't made any movements. The more I thought about it, the more I became convinced that he had somehow discovered me. It was just a strong hunch. There was no evidence to support it.

As I moved down the canyon and into the maples, I deliberately kept upwind. I walked quietly toward the ridgetop, listening carefully. Stellar jays scolded vigorously from the maples. Twice I heard movements, possibly chickadees searching tree bark for insect eggs. At the top of the ridge, I found where the big buck had gone over. He had crossed beneath two spruce trees—the only route he could have taken without being seen.

Using the country and cover to my advantage, I hunted down into the next canyon, not following the buck's tracks in the snow. On the far side of that canyon, in thick brush but silhouetted against the snow, stood six bucks. One was staring at me. It was the big one, the Sheepherd Buck, my buck. I worked down toward the group, making as much use of the scrub-oak cover as possible. Five bucks were still feeding. I hadn't fooled the big one, though.

The big one was getting more nervous as I continued working toward them, and one by one the other bucks picked up on his uneasiness and stared in my direction. I was within rifle range, but the bucks were in heavy brush. My buck was keeping the other deer between him and me. I sat down to await further developments. If I went farther down the slope, I would be in heavy timber and unable to see the deer. If the animals ran, they would have to cross at least one and maybe two openings.

When they did take off, they went slowly at first, then more rapidly as they panicked. Five bucks crossed an opening two hundred yards away. The Sheepherd Buck, though, trotted straight up the hillside and through the thickest brush he could find, paralleling the other bucks' flight. If he continued in the same direction, he would still cross an opening farther up the slope. All the bucks entered a thick stand of spruce and emerged on the other side, running in open sagebrush. The Sheepherd Buck had joined the group but placed several other deer between himself and me. If I shot, I would hit one of those. Farther upslope, again in heavy cover, he cut off from the herd. It was the last time I'd see him that season as he crossed over the ridge—out of rifle range as usual—and disappeared.

Late the following summer I began to scout the big buck's country, trying to learn as much as possible about his habits, movements, escape routes, and anything else I could. I was aware that his habits would change with the shedding of velvet and antler polishing in late August, and again with the coming of deer season, but anything I could learn about the buck would help. At the same time, I didn't want to spook him or make him more alert. Each free evening I would drive my Toyota pickup up on the flat above the buck's haunts and watch his country with a spotting scope. The long August evenings yielded all sorts of information about mule deer behavior.

It was several days before I located the Sheepherd Buck. The preceding winter had been brutal, and I was glad to see the old boy had survived. It was difficult to find him now with the leaves still on the maples, aspen, oak, and willows, but I did see enough of him through August and early September to discover his favorite routes to feeding areas and cover. Not once did I see him run; all his movements were calculated and deliberate. In early September, after he had shed his velvet, I got the impression his antlers were a little smaller. If it was true, he was getting on in years, past his prime. Even so, his antlers were still huge, widespread and tall. Each evening just before dark he left his daytime haunt in a tangle of maples and willows and moved to the open slopes to feed on cliffrose, bitterbrush, and forbs. Another large buck appeared in the area, and occasionally the two fed amicably together. That would change with the onset of the rut in November, however.

On opening morning of deer season I was in place long before the eastern horizon began to brighten. I didn't have a real plan; I'd seen too many of them go awry in the past few years to have much faith in them anymore. I'd just sit down and see what happened. In the predawn half-light, while looking hard through the binoculars, I saw a movement and a silhouette on the opposite slope. Playing a hunch that it was the big buck, I moved down the ridge toward the bottom. The light was coming fast now. Down the canyon hunters were moving my way, talking, and scraping against brush. About four hundred yards across the canyon, standing in a clump of maples, was the Sheepherd Buck. I put the cross hairs on him, but there were branches in the way. I watched him through the scope, thumb on the safety. He stepped into a small opening. He had made a mistake! I held at the top of the shoulder and squeezed. At the blast of the rifle the buck leaped into the air and landed on all fours a few yards down the slope. He was staring at me and didn't seem to be hit. I held a few inches above the shoulder and squeezed again. This time, the buck leaped, bucked, and ran into the brush. I was certain I had heard the bullet slap flesh. Seconds later the buck was running toward the ridgeline. In a moment he would be gone, and the brush was too thick to shoot into. As the buck dodged through the trees, his great rack sagged, slowly at first, then quickly as he fell.

I ran up the opposite slope to where the animal had been. His tracks were easy to follow in the snow. He had run thirty or forty yards, paused and begun to bleed, and then tried to run over the ridge. He died trying.

The first shot had grazed the brisket, and the second had entered an inch and a half higher and gotten the heart.

I was so full of adrenaline that the mile-long drag up the ridge seemed like child's play. Later, with the head caped and the antlers free, I measured the trophy. He had a high-reaching rack and a spread of thirty-four inches. I again had a feeling he wasn't quite as large as he'd been a few years earlier when he was in his prime. However, he was one of the best of the forty or so mature bucks I'd taken up to that time, and was certainly the one that had given me the best hunt.

Later, I cut a cross-section of one of his teeth and counted the rings. There were nine. He was an old buck, past his breeding prime, and possibly would not have survived another winter.

I had hunted the Sheepherd Buck for four seasons and had seen him each year. He outsmarted me every time. And though I had taken a good buck at the end of each of the previous seasons when it was clear that I wouldn't get the monarch of Sheepherd Canyon, that big, elusive animal was always there to haunt me. Now that I had won the game, I was almost sorry. I would miss the buck and the quest he had given me.

GROWING UP WESTERN

In 1825, mountain man Peter Skeene Ogden entered the valley through the canyon across the street; he left his name for the town that would come. In 1869, the Union Pacific and Central Pacific

Winter-killed doe, and the winter bottleneck in action.

ends of the great transcontinental railroad met forty-five miles to the northwest at a place called Promontory Summit; on a clear day, an Ogden resident could look across the Bear River Marsh, which became world-famous for its waterfowl gunning, and see where the golden spike had been driven. In 1955, Jack Kerouac mentioned the Kokomo Club on "Two-bit Street" in his novel, *On the Road*. Two-bit (25th) Street began at Ogden's Union Station, the railroad depot, and in Mormon Utah, the area's fallen angels and saloons were scandalous. And busy.

In the dusk of New Year's Day, 1962, I walked from my house across the street and into the fruit orchards that carpeted the highest foothills ringing Ogden. Big mule deer ghosted through cherry trees in the foot-deep snow and fading light, some with antlers as big around as my adolescent wrist. That day seemed to be some kind of turning point.

By summer, I had talked my dad into buying a "deer rifle," an army surplus Enfield .303. In the predawn darkness of opening day, we crossed the street and hiked through the orchards and then up the canyon until the trail gave out, then climbed a scree slope and perched on a ridge overlooking the face of a mountain. Neither of us had the faintest notion of how to hunt deer. Deer made their way across the slope toward us, and Dad handed me the gun. When they were close enough, I pulled the trigger and, in my buck-ague, missed clean. I fired again as they raced across the slope, and an immense buck fell. Later, he dressed out at 268 pounds; back then, weight was more significant than antler size. Kammeyer's, the local sporting-goods store, sponsored a big-buck contest based on weight. The winner that year weighed 245 pounds, and won a brand-new Savage Model 99. I was sick about it, because we hadn't entered.

I'd occasionally ditch high school and hop a freight train moving slowly out of the rail yards west toward places like Plain City (just a collection of farms). I'd jump off before the train hit the trestle out across the Great Salt Lake, and by then the train was going too fast for me to keep my footing, so I'd pick a soft place to roll. Often I'd ride farther out and jump off near the marshes along the lake. Waterfowl shooting there was so good you wouldn't need decoys. In the evening I'd slog to the nearest dirt road and thumb back into town; farmers in old pickups always gave rides to kids with shotguns and loads of birds.

Dad and I built a cabin along the South Fork the next summer. When not nailing down decking or shingles or fly-fishing for cutthroat trout, I explored the canyon. By autumn I had become familiar with deer hangouts and friendly with the sheepherder who ran his bands through the sagebrush flats and aspen and fir forests. He waived the $2.50 trespass fee, and I had a new place to hunt. Then, deer hunters were few and deer plentiful enough that hardly anyone would pay to hunt, so I pretty well had the canyon to myself. My first few bucks were small, but I killed one with a thirty-one-inch spread and became a minor high-school hero. From then on, I wouldn't shoot a small buck unless it was the last day.

At Christmas break I drove my Willys pickup across the Wyoming state line, bought a $25 nonresident deer tag at a honky-tonk and hotel in Evanston, and drove north to Big Piney. On the back pages of outdoor magazines I had seen ads from outfitters with pictures of big bucks strung along game poles like stringers of trout. Several had Big Piney addresses, and that was good enough for me. On the first day, I collected a good four-pointer (today that would be a five by five) in twenty-below temperatures and thirty-knot winds. It was so cold I stayed in a $4 hotel room. The entire trip cost $37, but that was a considerable sum to a soon-to-be college freshman who had to come up with $120 for the next year's tuition.

A buddy and I spent the following autumn hunting and fishing throughout the West ("Endless Autumn," *Field & Stream* 1994). The next year, I worked full time and attended college and by autumn had booked a combination hunt in British Columbia. The rate was $35 per day, and I had booked two weeks for the unheard-of (and ridiculous, I was told) sum of $490. I bagged two trophy goats and a big mule deer, passed up several moose, and chased black bears that always seemed to get away ahead of dogs that always got lost—until they got onto a grizzly, which killed one of them. On another of those chases my horse slipped on a steep slope and rolled over me, shoving my head a full foot into the snow; when I cleared the mud and snow from nose and ears, I was all right. Charlie, my Shuswap Indian guide, thought it was a good joke and was nearly helpless with laughter, but after my wind came back and my nose quit bleeding, we were again in the saddle helling through blowdowns after the baying black-and-tans. The bear got away, but as always the thrill was in the chase.

I'd developed the habit of taking the autumn off from work and college classes to go hunting. In the early days of the Vietnam draft, that was a bad habit to get into; the draft board simply did not understand the importance of hunting and threatened to revoke my student deferment. When I returned from Canada, I still had the rest of the fall to hunt and fish, a little left in my savings account, and a Wyoming antelope tag in my pocket. The notice from Selective Service remained unopened on the kitchen table.

There's a wide place in the blacktop on the north edge of Wyoming's Red Desert that over the years became one of my favorite places. A cold wind would whip dust steadily out of the northwest and bang the sign that hung above the saloon. On Friday afternoons, old Willys and Chevy pickups would spill out of the hardpan parking lot and into the rabbitbrush desert. Most of them belonged to cowpunchers and sheepherders, but during hunting season there were a few new rigs with license plates from Texas or California. Inside the saloon, men in frayed denim and dusty buckaroo hats drank quietly at a fir-slab bar entertained by George Jones on the jukebox (seven plays for a quarter), the click of pool balls, and the beery smell of empty longnecks. Old-timers with sheep dogs played pinochle at a back table. The odd plaid mackinaw told you who owned the exotic license plates. I ate my sixth pickled egg—they cost a nickel—and took it all in.

Deer trying to survive the winter.

I killed a 16½-inch buck the next morning, then camped on the prairies, broiling prairie-goat chops over sagebrush coals, shooting at distant jack rabbits, and listening to coyotes yelping off toward the Sweetwater. The only person I saw in three days was a lost rookie game warden so happy to find someone he didn't check my license. Back then, game wardens didn't automatically assume every hunter was guilty of something and were as apt to share a thermos of coffee as check your tags.

I spent another week back then in the ancient cottonwoods along the Green River and fished for big rainbows, landing a dozen over five pounds that sucked smoke-colored dry flies from between golden, floating leaves. It was the best trout fishing I ever had, before or since. I hunted out from camp and bagged limits of sage grouse that lumbered into the sky in noisy confusion, then baked them in a Dutch oven half-buried in cottonwood coals. The river bottoms were private property, but back then there were no posted signs and it was not expected that anyone would even ask to hunt. You simply closed gates, didn't litter, stayed on established roads, and didn't shoot out ranch-building windows. Common sense.

On the way home, I stopped at a noisy honky-tonk in a mining town and ordered a 20-cent beer and talked of fishing and debated with local hookers the best way to cook an antelope roast.

That December, near the South Fork cabin, I shot limits of ruffed and blue grouse that were so innocent it was hard to get them to fly. I hunted in the half-frozen Bear River Marshes and always got limits of ducks (as I recall, the limit was eight) and often of geese and pheasants.

Eventually, other, less-important things came along—graduate school for one—and there were years gone and a wife somewhere, and by the time I looked again, it had all changed. Now the Ogden rail yards are silent. Promontory Summit has become the Golden Spike National Monument. Two-bit Street is lined with espresso shops. Those foothill orchards have been replaced by subdivisions of clone houses.

And Wyoming nonresident deer tags are issued by complicated lottery and cost $150.

Like most important lessons, I learned this one later than I would have liked. The bachelor uncles and grandparents were right, though—the old days were better.

SANCTUARY

I left the truck and the ridge about midday and walked down the bare, dusty slope to the edge of the trees and then into the cold shade of the spruce. Behind me, on the other side of the ridge, was Skull Crack Canyon, thick now with summer cabins and bulldozed roads where once you could have hunted deer in trailless country all season without ever seeing another man. Beyond Skull Crack to the west were more canyons pockmarked with cabins. And beyond that was the city-choked Wasatch Front.

I looked east, down through the trees and the canyon I would descend, to the great limestone fold of rock across the gorge. It was at least a mile long, shaped like a giant gray bow. Invisible below it, perhaps one thousand vertical feet down, was the cold, clear stream that ran through the gorge. The stream had cut quickly, in geological time, through the eroded limestone plateau and formed the gash—"canyon" was too mild a word—that had become the gorge.

It was warm in the sun, and I removed my wool jacket and stuffed it into the pack. I took a drink of the clay-tasting water that seeped from beneath a great moss-covered limestone slab. Years ago I had named the slab Gravestone Rock, and it had become a landmark to those I had brought hunting and fishing in this country. Many of them had become friends, but friends who now were distant, having gone on with their lives in directions other than mine. I would return to this Rocky Mountain country for a few months of the year to hunt deer, to write, to read, and to rekindle old friendships with the people and with the land. But each time, it seemed, the old friends were more distant, other friends had gone, and much of the land had changed.

Only you haven't changed, I told myself as I walked down the slope. *You and the gorge.* Truthfully, I wasn't sure about either.

The hike down to the gorge was a pilgrimage of sorts to a place that was unchanging. Or so I hoped. The weight of the pack and rifle felt good on my back. In the deep shade of the gully bottom, the autumn frosts had not melted and the hard-frozen soil offered no purchase when I tried to dig the edges of my boots into it on the steep slopes. Too many years had passed since I had been in the gorge. It was a sacred place to me, a place where I had been baptized into the secrets of the wilderness and into the ritual of opening day.

Now, as I descended, I remembered deer hunting in the gorge. The first buck I'd killed there had been a three-pointer, and I had quartered it and packed it out of the unbelievably steep canyon, sweating heavily in the midday sun, vowing never to kill another buck in the gorge unless it was the granddaddy of all deer.

As I contoured down the steep slope toward the even steeper drop-off where the game trail went straight down a talus chute between the seemingly impenetrable wall of thousand-foot limestone cliffs, I heard the sound of a distant engine. I had been walking, alone and happy in the solitude, having forgotten about the ruined canyons to the west, and the sound made me angry.

A few trails had been pushed down the finger ridges that ran off the big ridge I had been descending. The trails would mean more places where men could take their machines. Down one of the trails a four-wheel-drive pickup descended slowly, its bed bristling with red-shirted men. Road hunters. I spat out the grass stem I had been chewing. The low whine of the truck's compound gear floated to where I had been contouring down the canyon. The truck reached the end of the trail and stopped, its engine idling. I could hear the voices of men a thousand yards across the canyon. I looked back down toward the gorge. And then they began shooting. It was a fusillade. The truck emptied of redshirts, and eight or ten red specks scattered along the slope below the trail and fired across the canyon. I heard the crack of bullets and the sound of the air being torn overhead, and I jumped behind a big Douglas fir, unsure of where the men were shooting.

This buck is browsing frost-killed forbs—ensilage—which are important food items for all mule deer.

When the shooting stopped, I could hear the men laughing and talking loudly. Apparently they had seen a buck, frightened out of its bed by the grinding noise of the truck gears, and had tried to hit it with a lucky shot across the canyon. Then the truck bed filled again with red and ground its way slowly back up the trail. The road hunters weren't going to cross the big canyon to see if they had wounded the deer.

I was glad when the truck finally crossed the main ridge and was gone. In a while, walking down the canyon and anticipating the gorge, I was content again. I spotted the first drop of blood squarely in the dust of the faint, rough game trail that wound through stands of thick oak scrub and tangles of chokecherry. More blood and a tuft of hair lay on a stub of a blowdown that lay across the trail, where the deer had fallen. And more blood. They'd hit the deer after all.

I followed the blood spoor down through the canyon bottom to the edge of the cliffs, and down the steep chute toward the bottom of the gorge. The buck switchbacked down the talus. Occasionally he would fall and there would be a twenty-yard smear of blood down the shale rock, and then the buck would bleed more freely as he made his way ever downward. This was not what I had wanted. I didn't want anything spoiling my trip into the gorge.

Dusk had closed on the shadowy bottom when I followed the blood trail across the icy creek and then contoured up the opposite slope. I would take it up again in the morning, find the buck, and finish the job the others on the ridge had started.

In the morning, I followed the blood trail up the bushy, gray-talus slope, the blood spots black now and hard to see. The buck had bedded in a thicket of oak scrub within sight of my camp. A large, not-yet-dry clot of blood lay on the shriveled brown oak leaves in his bed. I had spooked him off with my approach, or maybe he had moved off when the first light had made its way into the gorge depths. The buck would be still, and he wouldn't move far.

The trail led across the slope toward a great limestone monolith. At its base was a thick tangle of mahogany and oak scrub. I was sure the buck would be in there, that the steep rock slide upward would be too much for him. Perhaps, too, he would know there would be more hunters on the ridges above.

I circled around and above the monolith to get above the buck so I wouldn't start him upward. No need to punish the deer, and I didn't want to leave the solitude of the gorge. After my climb, I looked over the cliff rim. The buck stood beneath a juniper a few yards below. He'd seen me. The buck had a monstrous, many-pointed rack. He was no longer afraid and seemed to accept his fate, whatever it might be. He could go no farther anyway, and if he were to die, let it be here away from the ridges above and near the food and water he'd need to survive.

I put the cross hairs between the big buck's shoulders and thumbed off the safety. Better to put him out of his misery. The antlers could never be a trophy to me, having to kill him this way, and the meat would be strong and tough after his run into the gorge. It wasn't right to let him suffer. He turned and limped slowly down the hill toward the water he needed very badly. He moved carefully, favoring his right rear leg, but the bone didn't seem broken. Perhaps the bullet had passed through the ham without shattering bone or severing the femoral artery or cutting a nerve. I thumbed the safety back on and watched the buck walk stiffly and painfully, picking his way between the boulders and shrubby junipers, toward the cool shadows of the bottoms. The buck seemed to have a chance to survive. Who was I to decide he didn't?

The buck took up residence on a small willow flat around the bend from my camp. I saw him there a day later. He'd bedded at the bottom of the slope in the willows. He stared at me and I at him from less than thirty yards. The buck had selected wisely. In the gorge, he, too, was seeking something— a place of peace, a place of survival. Up the slope from his bed, good browse grew in thick pockets. The nutritional bitterbrush and mahogany would help him mend. His bed was within a few yards of the stream, so he could replace the fluids he'd lost and those he would need to heal. There would be no other hunters down here in the deep, steep gorge. We both relied on that.

I saw the buck mincing and favoring his leg on the slope above the willow flat three or four times during the next week. He moved slowly and stiffly, though perhaps less so. He was still using his injured leg, a good sign, and seemed to favor it less. I felt the buck might survive if he was lucky and the coming winter not too harsh.

The sun didn't find its way into the gorge until late in the morning. I'd spent one morning hunting some draws that led east toward the ridge above—without ever getting near the ridge, where

I might run into other hunters—and had just returned to the stream as the sun was melting the frosts on the tawny grasses in the bottom meadows. The buck had just descended the slope where he'd been feeding. He had waded into the shallows and was drinking, his injured leg lifted slightly so it wouldn't be hurt by the slippery footing in the creek. He raised his head to stare at me as I sat on a boulder and watched, then lowered it again and finished drinking. The buck knew he could not get away from me with his injured leg, and seemed to know that if I hadn't killed him by now, I would not. He stumbled a little as he climbed the two-foot bluff. He lay down in the willows facing me, and we looked at each other.

I spent the entire deer season in the gorge, mostly fishing for the small native trout but deer hunting, too, if a bit halfheartedly. The stay in the gorge had been good. It had been good for the buck, too, and he moved with less pain. His chances seemed better.

One morning, wanting to see the buck at least once again before I left, I walked up the stream to the willow flat where he had stayed. I had to leave the following day. The buck was gone. I waited most of the day, but he didn't return. Upstream, I found his tracks on the talus and dust trail that contoured along the slope above the creek. Miles upstream was an open basin with a wide, south-facing slope. Moose and elk wintered there, but deer died if they tried it during a hard winter. I'd found the antlered skulls of bucks that had died when the early winter snow had been heavy. The wounded buck had probably gone there, knowing he couldn't survive in the perpetual cold and ice in this part of the gorge during winter. He would take his chances on the south-facing slope in the basin above the forks, preferring that place to the ridges he would have to cross to get to the low canyons where his ancestors had wintered since before humans had come and made college campuses and suburban houses.

Late the next morning, I hiked slowly up the steep talus chute out of the gorge, taking my time. I was thankful that the chute was in shadow, but even so I was sweating with the exertion of the climb. The gorge had not changed since I had last visited it those years earlier, but I knew it would not remain that way. Its ruggedness couldn't save it. It was only a matter of time, and from the looks of things on the ridges and in the canyons to the west, time was running out.

It was late afternoon when I climbed the last slope to the truck on the ridge. I was glad I hadn't killed a buck and had to pack it out. I took a long pull from a can of warm beer I'd left in the cab and stared off down the canyon I had just climbed, toward the great, gray limestone bow on the other side of the gorge. Likely, this would be my last trip into its depths. The buck lived in that world. He would not outlive it, whether he died in the winter or survived another year or two. I lived in two worlds, the one I had just left and likely would outlive, the other I was moving toward and which would change more and leave me behind. As I stared down the canyon, I wished the buck a mild winter and that he cover more does in the years to come.

The following winter was hard. Perhaps the buck lived through it in spite of the wounded leg. He had already survived a bullet. But in the spring I didn't go to the basin where he probably wintered. I didn't want to find that he hadn't survived. And I wanted to remember the gorge as it had been.

THE LAST BUCK

The first thing you noticed were his eyes. They were dark and fierce, and they looked through or beyond you. They were good eyes to have in a friend, but frightening in an enemy.

I'd been sitting on a ridge waiting for the orange in the east to broaden and lighten so I could see into the tangle of aspen and willow below me. He was beside me before I was aware of it.

"Good four-pointer in there," he whispered. "Beds in the willows at the head of the draw." He turned those eyes from me and gazed up the ridge, waiting, I think, to see what I would do.

It was my third mule deer hunt. The season before, I'd killed a good buck on the edge of the Mormon town down the valley that was eating up a hundred acres of deer winter range a year. It had been luck that had put me in the cottonwoods along the

I'm saddling a mule named Snickers for a day's hunt in the Gila country of southwest New Mexico.

trail down which the buck bounded after other hunters had jumped him from his bed.

"You'll never be able to sneak up on him in that tangle," I whispered back, a bit put out that someone had invaded "my" stand.

"Mind if I try?" he asked. What could I say?

I shrugged, and he moved silently down the slope and into thick brush. I was glad to be alone again and away from the eyes that looked through you. I figured he would push game out of the draw and up the opposite slope, where I would get a shot across the tops of the aspens. No man could move quietly enough to avoid spooking everything out, but no deer flushed. An hour later I heard the flat report of his carbine.

I saw him again in the afternoon as he packed out a buck with a thirty-inch spread on his buckskin mare. I recognized the mare. I'd seen him on it during the summer, checking the sheep band that grazed the mountain. I spent my summers wandering around the mountains, watching deer. I tried not to work when school let out for the summer, but when I did, I took seasonal work—picking fruit, loading hay—that would not last long so that I could get back to wandering.

When we'd met on the ridge that morning, he recognized me as the boy who roamed the mountain. He was the man who lived in the small cabin on the timber trail and who, along with his brothers, owned this land.

"There's another good buck that hangs out in the oak scrub at the head of Rattlesnake," he said. I knew of the long ravine that was almost a canyon and that was named after a snake den in a rock slide. He had seen me gazing at his buck and was making me a gift of his knowledge.

The big buck was there in the oak brush, but I wasn't good enough to kill him. Toward the end of the deer season, I bagged a yearling buck. It was the best I could do.

The following summer I was camping at a spring high in the timber when the man rode into camp. He swung stiffly from the saddle and extended a callused hand. His handshake was firm and suggested great strength. I still could not look into his eyes for any length of time. I offered him a cup of bad coffee.

"Drop in to the cabin," he said when he'd finished the coffee and swung onto the buckskin, "when yer in the neighborhood."

I did the following day. It was a classic old log cabin with a sod roof and a great rock fireplace occupying one end and a big wood-burning range dominating the corner he called the kitchen. Old photographs framed in ornate gold hung here and there. One, dated 1899, showed a man and a woman dressed in denim and flannel surrounded by three boys and a girl. But the things you really noticed were the deer antlers. Great racks hung about the walls, all with spreads of thirty to more than forty inches. In a deer-foot gun rack was a Model 94 and a .30-40 Krag with a split stock. He was a deer hunter.

We talked of deer hunting, of the big buck that had browsed on the west ridge all summer, about the buck that forded the creek above the forks in the late dusk and fed during the night on bitterbrush on the south slope. And of the yearling that fed out of the timber in front of his cabin each evening. Next to him, I knew little of deer hunting.

I asked about the largest of the great racks that hung on the walls and on the front of the cabin. Many, I knew, would score high in the Boone and Crockett record book, but he had not listed any. The biggest had bases as big around as my wrist, with the heaviness carried well out toward the tips. Its spread was forty-one inches. It was the largest typical deer rack I had ever seen or heard of. He'd stalked the buck to its bed in a stand of fir. Another buck, with a total of fifteen long and heavy points, lay on a bare, high ridge and he had spent an entire morning creeping up on it. He could remember the wind directions, the weather, and the peculiarities of each buck as if it were yesterday. He commented that the biggest bucks were killed longest ago, that nowadays there were no more forty-inchers on the mountain and that thirty-inchers were rare. He stared out the window in the gathering dusk, waiting, I think, for the yearling buck to feed out of the timber.

"Cattle, sheep, and people use up the ground," he said. "Doesn't grow big deer like it used to. We take from the land and put nothing back." He was staring at the little buck that had appeared in front of the cabin.

His grandfather had tied up this land a century ago and had run cattle and sheep on it. Then his sons, one of them the Deer Hunter's father, grazed livestock on it, took timber from it, and sold some land farther down the valley to be farmed (and where the farms became smaller farms and later subdivisions of look-alike houses and where deer in a hard winter died on highways and of starvation). On the lower slopes, wheatgrass and bitterbrush had already given way to cheatgrass and juniper. He knew he was part of the problem. His sheep grazed the slopes of the mountain. But he tried not to overgraze the land, and he hadn't, he said, sold his share to be cut into farms and subdivisions and summer home sites like his brothers had. On his land, there would be a place for the deer. But his land did not take in all of the mountain and its valleys and meadows. And each year his brothers sold out more to the developers so they could live in bigger houses in town and drive new cars. He looked as tired as the land he spoke of as he stuffed a piece of oak cordwood into the old stove.

In the fall, he told me where and how to get a big buck that lived far up the mountain. I followed his instructions, stalking up the draw as the morning light came and the cold, dense air drifted slowly downhill, wearing wool so branches scraping against it would make no noise, having a cartridge in the chamber and my thumb on the safety, staying ready, always ready. And suddenly the big buck was there, staring hard in the gloomy half-light of the timber, its nose working to find what made it uneasy. And then my rifle was up and the shot blasted the life from the buck as it bunched its muscles to jump. It was bigger than any buck I had ever even come close to bagging. I'd followed the Deer Hunter's instructions.

A day later he killed his buck, a granddaddy with five long, even points to the side and a thirty-three-inch spread. It dwarfed my buck.

Coyotes, a major predator of mule deer in both summer and winter take an especially heavy toll during winter, when mature bucks are worn out from the rigors of both rutting and surviving.

And that was the way it went through the years. We never hunted together, but I learned from him. And we always compared notes before and after the hunt, often after each day's hunt. But he always bagged the bigger buck. My largest was smaller than his smallest.

Sometimes in the summer, I'd ride the sheep with him. The big bucks were becoming scarce in the country as more land was used up. New roads had been bulldozed and summer cabins built on the big south slope—the best winter range for deer and elk. Timber was cut from the deep canyon on the west face—always a good cover to find a buck or bull elk. Each time he saw this ruination of the land, he shook his head tiredly, as if to say he could do nothing. And he was slowing down. Age, he said, and old injuries. Once, he told me, a horse had thrown him down a talus slope and broken his neck. It was two days before his brothers found him, and a year before he could sit on a horse again.

"I can remember when the grass was stirrup-high down there. The bucks would come out in the evening and eat the grain-heads." He shook his head imperceptibly as his eyes followed the newly bulldozed road through the ruined red soil of the meadow. A few bunches of cheatgrass grew in the dust. Farther up the valley, the road led to new cabin sites. His brother had sold the canyon the year before.

It was the last summer I could spend on the mountain with the Deer Hunter. I would leave for college in the fall.

"Stay for dinner?" he asked as he got stiffly off the mare in front of the cabin. He lifted the stirrup and loosened the cinch and belly straps, freed the saddle, and hefted it onto the porch railing. I did the same. I led the horses into the aspen-pole corral, and he climbed laboriously up the porch steps and disappeared into the dark of the cabin.

It was late the following summer before I again visited the Deer Hunter. When he opened the door I again saw those dark, falcon eyes, and for a moment it was years earlier. But he did not move like he once had. He shuffled painfully across the floor and took a bottle from the cupboard. He poured a splash into two tin cups and brought one to me. "You're a college man now," he said and handed me the cup. It was sad to see him move now with that peculiar, painful shuffle, or look into his aged, gray face. But you forgot all that when you looked into his eyes.

That previous winter had been hard, he told me, and too many deer had died because there was nothing to eat on the old winter range. Houses now grew where savannas of oak and bitterbrush and sagebrush once fed the winter-arriving deer. And he'd hired another herder to watch his sheep band because he couldn't get out and ride like he used to. He hadn't seen a buck around the cabin all summer. As he told me this he gazed out the window, as if to confirm the truth, or perhaps hoping to refute it by miraculously seeing a buck in the meadow out front. He wanted to know if I would be around for the deer hunt. I said I would try, that perhaps I could take a few days off from classes and come down. He smiled, and I felt good that I would hunt with the Deer Hunter again.

I couldn't make it for opening day because of a trig exam, but I was there for the second weekend and the last few days of the season. I arrived late one afternoon. Blue smoke curled from the stovepipe above the sod roof. I knocked and entered. He was sitting next to the stove and staring out the window. A pair of crutches leaned against the table. He saw me notice them.

"Falling apart," he said with a laugh. The laugh was hollow. He glanced quickly out the window and picked up the cup on the table. "Dinner's in the oven." He took a sip from the cup.

He'd hunted earlier in the season, for a while on the mare and later on crutches through the stands of spruce and aspen around the cabin. He'd seen only one yearling buck. He had never had to shoot a yearling yet, he said, and he'd be damned if he'd start now. I laughed. He seemed to be in a better mood, and the sadness that was there when I entered had gone. Now his illness and failing body were a joke. I poured him another splash of the whiskey and one for myself, and we sat next to the warmth of the stove and waited for the roast to finish cooking. It was good sitting there, warm, watching the late October afternoon fade into dusk and then darkness, talking about old hunts, about old bucks, about bucks that got away. His eyes danced as he talked about working up the draw in the morning on the crutches and seeing if there was a good buck in the tangle of willows around the spring there. There just might be, he said thoughtfully. There was a sense of excitement and urgency I had never noticed. In past years, there was only certainty.

When I returned from hunting up the mountain the following evening, the Deer Hunter had not returned. It might take him a while to work back down the trail on the crutches, I reasoned. I built up the fires and put some water on. I began to worry when he still hadn't returned an hour later. It was getting cold and frost had settled on the meadow grasses when I walked out on the porch. I saddled his mare and led her up the trail toward the willows he had wanted to hunt.

"Over here," I heard him say as I hurried up the trail. He was sitting off the trail beneath a fir tree. "Just gave out," he said. I asked if he could ride. "Just gave out," he said again, apologizing, embarrassed about what had happened to him. I helped him onto the mare.

He shook his head and smacked his lips and said, "Damn!" He shook his head again, took the reins, and headed the mare down the trail. I followed, understanding his frustration.

At the cabin, I fed him soup and helped him onto the bunk. He was exhausted. He'd lost weight in the last year. I banked the fires and crawled into my bedroll on the couch in front of the fireplace. It was a long time before I fell asleep.

"Go hunting," he told me early in the dawn, long before the eastern horizon had begun to lighten. "I'm all right." I knew he wasn't, but there was nothing I could do anyway. And I knew he would feel badly if he were the cause of my not hunting.

He was worse that night, and though he tried to take care of the light chores himself, it was too difficult for him just to get around the cabin.

I hunted the following day with no luck and, concerned about the Deer Hunter, returned to the cabin in the afternoon. It had been my last chance to hunt. He sat by the stove staring out the window. The battered .30-40 Krag was propped against the wall next to him. He saw me notice it.

"It was my father's," he said. He turned again to gaze out the window in the gathering dusk.

I brought in an armload of wood and stirred up the fires and started dinner, then sat across the table from him. He watched intently out the window. He was hunting, at least with his eyes.

I pause by a beaver pond in northern Utah deer country.

"Saw him at the edge of the timber," he was saying as if he were carrying on a conversation that had been interrupted earlier, "a big, old buck. Been shot in the hip—hiding in that timber hoping he'd be overlooked." He'd seen the wounded buck the evening before, and now he was hoping it would come out again.

He watched intently, almost willing the buck out of the shadows and into the open next to the creek. And then it was there, in the shadows along the edge of the timber, wraithlike in the fading light. The buck dragged its useless leg behind as it made its way to the water. The Deer Hunter picked up the rifle from the wall and walked, without the crutches, to the door. I felt like I didn't belong, and it was almost like watching a film from the back of the theater.

When he heard the creaking of the cabin door, the buck lifted his head and stared. The animal was not frightened. The Deer Hunter shuffled as quietly as he could down the stairs and away from the cabin. It would not be right to shoot the buck from the porch. The buck watched as he limped across the opening in front of the cabin, then sat heavily in the frost-covered grass. The buck collapsed at the shot.

The Deer Hunter stood and walked over to the buck. It was the best he had moved in more than a year. I stood a short distance off as I watched him open the buck and spill the guts on the grass, setting the liver and heart aside. Then he tried to drag the buck toward the cabin. He moved it a few feet before he fell. I helped him back to the cabin. I was part of the scene again.

"Wouldn't have survived the winter with a wound like that," he said as I helped him into a chair beside the stove. "He's a good buck." He stared out the window into the near-darkness where the buck lay dead in the grass.

Later, I dragged the buck to the big tree in front of the cabin and hung it. We'd skin and butcher it in the morning.

"Not that bad of a set of antlers," he said as we stood on the porch the following afternoon. I had to leave. He leaned on his crutches and picked up the gnarled old set of antlers, then put them down again. He extended his hand. His eyes were still the eyes of the hunter—they held none of the worn look of his gray face and hunched shoulders.

A few days later, at college, I heard the Deer Hunter was dead. I talked with his sister, the only one of his siblings who had understood anything about him for many years now. She had arranged for one of the herders to bury him in the stand of timber above the cabin. It would be kept quiet—it was against county regulations, she told me.

I left school again to visit the Deer Hunter. His grave was a collection of rocks over freshly turned earth beneath the big fir and spruce trees, the only old-growth timber left in the valley. I was glad there was no cross. He wouldn't have liked it. He had often talked to me about taking from the land—too many people took the land for houses, grazed too many cattle and sheep on it, took timber from it— without ever putting anything back. Now he had put back into the land.

The last buck's antlers were still on the porch of the cabin. I picked them up and carried them up the slope to the grave and placed them between two large shoots of a fir tree. In time, the tree would grow around the antlers and lock them there. It was more fitting than a cross or headstone.

THE SPIRIT OF SONORA

The twentieth century—not to mention the twenty-first— was gone now. It had begun to fade as the battered Jeep crossed the border and clattered south over the rutted, sometimes missing volcanic cinder track to the tiny Tepecano village cringing in a thorny acacia and saguaro desert between jagged, looming, red volcanic mountains. The dry wind that rattled corrugated metal roofs on crumbling adobe shacks blew away the century's remains. Scraggly dogs, bloat-bellied *ninos*, and chickens wandered the single dusty street. In spite of the dismal setting, I hadn't munched an antacid since leaving the pavement in Arizona.

We'd seen him first the previous year. Paquito, a diminutive Tepecano, and I had found him while searching remote volcanic ranges for prehistoric rock art and ruins. I was armed only with a camera, and when we jumped the huge desert mule deer, I was so awed I forgot to trip the shutter. He dwarfed the other big bucks we'd seen, and his heavy, even antlers certainly spread more than forty inches.

He'd been a thing to think about through the following interminable year, but now we were back, slogging through the flat, ankle-deep sand of the desert, dodging spiny acacia or jumping cholla that seemed to attack the ankles. If one attacked a burro, we had a rodeo, and unless the cholla detached itself, we had to throw the burro down to get it off; we packed pliers and heavy gloves for such occasions. Then we led the packstring up a deep, boulder-strewn, volcanic canyon, its dust pocked with the tracks of peccary, deer, desert bighorn, and puma. It took three days to worry the laden burros through and around boulders and ledges. With machetes we hacked through acacia and mesquite tangles along the arroyo bottoms until the grade eased. The bisnaga, cholla, and organ-pipe cactus disappeared, and we topped out into a forest of pinyon, juniper, and ponderosa pine. We camped in a brown, grama-covered basin, and Paquito tethered the burros by twisting goat-gut hobbles around the front feet. We baked frijoles and tortillas in a coffee can over pine coals and seasoned them with garlicky wild *ajo*. Paquito brewed a vile, potent coffee in a pounded-out hubcap he'd brought. We settled back beside the fire and listened to the wail of coyotes and the *chir-r-ruping* of quail.

The following day we continued along the top of the range until it became a heavily forested mesa. By then we were days into the nameless volcanic peaks and ancient ponderosa and pinyon forests, and a lifetime away from civilization, where even such ordinary gadgetry as phones and televisions seemed the stuff of science fiction. Finally we crested a pass and gazed into the big, lonely basin where we'd seen the enormous buck.

It felt as if we were staring far back in time. Desert sheep grazed on the grama grass between towering, brown lava pinnacles, and lower down a *lobo* ghosted across a grassy basin and into the ancient forest. On a distant slope, a black bear dug into a rotted fallen pine for termites and big mule deer walked into sight from around the shoulder of a hill. I half expected a band of Yaqui hunters to stalk out of the timber, and I wouldn't have been surprised to see a Mexican grizzly wander out of history.

At the edge of the pines we rigged a shelter (against what?) out of two pack tarps and scrounged dead pinyon for the fire. While we arranged camp, the band of rams stared and the mule deer browsed. As Paquito rustled up frijoles and tortillas, I sat with my back to the fire and stared across the basin as the sun set and the air chilled. In spite of the wildness, I had never been more at home, anywhere.

In the dawn, we started out from camp to hunt. Puma tracks wandered here and there, and once we found a bigger, more splayed cat track—"*Tigre*," Paquito said to indicate that it was

Shuswap Indian guide Charley taking a lunchtime break in British Columbia.

the spoor of a jaguar. We hoped the big cats wouldn't make a meal of the tethered and helpless burros. We stalked a band of bucks at the top of a volcanic slide, but the big one wasn't there. Two of the bucks had spreads in the mid-thirties, but we held off for the big one—or perhaps to prolong the hunt.

We didn't find him in that basin, so we packed deeper into prehistory to the head of a titanic gorge that dropped five thousand feet to its cottonwood green bottoms. From the rim we saw a distant growth of willows and cottonwoods, which indicated water. Paquito had never been to the gorge or heard of its existence. Along the rim we found wolf tracks, spotted a black bear and flocks of wild turkeys and Coues whitetails and big mule deer, and found three sets of puma tracks. At the second camp, two *lobos* barked at us like dogs from the woods fifty yards away. While I hunted the big buck, Paquito killed a young turkey with a .22 and roasted it over pine coals.

We stalked and passed up too many bucks to count, and frequently would noon in a protected alcove littered with stone and mud mortar ruins and heaps of broken pot shards. I would photograph the ruins and the ancient petroglyphs and pictographs. But we didn't glimpse the big-antlered buck.

Eventually—out of frijoles and tortillas and tiring of a steady diet of turkey and quail—we were forced back through the Pleistocene, back into the first basin where we'd seen him. As we descended to the desert floor, I glanced back one last time. I was sure that was him standing on a ridge half a mile off. Through binoculars I thought I could see heavy tines and an incredible spread of antlers. Nothing could be that big. But we were out of food and had to hurry to make it to a place where we could camp before nightfall. I turned away with reluctance.

Paquito killed two tiny Coues whitetails at camp and broiled the backstraps over mesquite coals, seasoning them heavily with salt, pepper, and *ajo*, and nothing ever tasted better. He'd take the rest of the meat back to his protein-starved village, where he'd be a hero. He was a hunter, so he was already a hero there.

I came back the following year, bringing three big crates of canned food, which Paquito distributed to the ecstatic Tepecanos. Then we packed into the long canyon and back to the plateau and prehistory. The game was just as it had been for ten thousand years. Reddish *lobo* wolves howled at us from the ridges, and the tiny *cola blanca* bounded from the thickets and up the slopes between the candelabra cacti and acacia. An immense ram stared from a volcanic outcropping, and puma pugs and scrapes in the dust of the arroyo made the burros jump at shadows.

In the same camp at the edge of the towering ponderosas, I simply gazed at the autumn-browning grama grass and the old trees. Two big mule deer bucks browsed at the edge of the trees, and both spread thirty inches. Though I've hunted mule deer the rest of my life, I never again passed up thirty-inch bucks. More bucks bedded in a manzanita thicket at the edge of a rock slide. Big antlers rose above the shiny red bark and broad evergreen leaves. I circled the hill and left Paquito with the burros. In close, I could see that one buck spread better than a yard. Still, he wasn't the big one. I would never kill that one if I didn't hold off.

That late October was similar to the one before. We saw desert sheep, bears, turkeys, quail, *lobos*, Coues and mule deer, and two big pumas on the edge of the gorge. We lived on frijoles, tortillas, quail, and turkey, and we couldn't find the big buck. In the end we were forced out of the place again, the country affirming its power as it pushed us away. On the trip out, we again killed two whitetails for the villagers.

When I'd seen the huge buck last, he was fully mature, so possibly the *lobos* or lions had killed him. He might have died of old age, though with all the big predators around, very few edible creatures got a chance to die of old age. Since breeding bucks mature early and die young, he might have fed a lion or wolf. On the other hand, he'd been healthy when we'd seen him. I couldn't forget him, but mostly I couldn't forget the wilderness. I'd try again.

By the next season, my optimism had drifted away like an illusion. Still, we packed back into that older, truer place. The

My Jeep in the once-famed Triangle deer country. The big bucks are gone now, and so is the Triangle's fame.

game was there, gazing at us with what could only be described as curiosity. We found good bucks in that basin, and drifted to sleep each night to the hooting of horned owls and the howling of *lobos*. A black bear ambled through camp, frightening the hobbled burros off across the basin. We could spot deer simply by looking. We didn't pack farther in, or try to find a way into that mysterious gorge, because we didn't know if the buck was still alive. We stayed so long after the frijoles and tortillas disappeared that even Paquito began to lose flesh, and he didn't have any to spare.

I wasn't surprised or disappointed not to find the big buck. I was surprised, however, that it didn't matter. True, the buck would have been the trophy of a lifetime, and yes, the long quest would have been rewarded, but I collected a better trophy—a good look at the happy hunting ground. That too-brief glimpse is more than any trophy I'd hang on a wall.

I've often thought of returning, seriously enough to put aside two months and enough money to hire Paquito and his burros, but I've had the wisdom not to. Better not to go back than to spoil a dream already lived.

DRIFT LIKE SMOKE

There had been no revelation in the killing of the big goat. It had been too physical and too dangerous and there had been no pitting of the self against the game, only the shots across an avalanche channel and the goat tumbling through the powdery snow. And there had been no blood on the hands and face, either, no throat-cutting, no ritual of any sort, only the shooting and caping and packing. And we'd need luck to make it back to camp at all, working along avalanche channels and across the creek where the ice sagged, groaned, and gave, plunging me waist-deep into the numbing waters that froze solidly within minutes. We made it back, but there was no revelation, only a hard-won trophy.

But the buck was different.

I had taken good bucks before by myself, so I had begun the journey, as Charley would have said it, though I wasn't aware of any journey. It was only after a hunt by myself, perhaps in a camp as wet snow slanted out of the darkness to sizzle on the hot rocks of a campfire, that I had any intimation of any kind of epiphany. And it was more than shooting and killing and hanging antlers or horns on a wall.

"A man can have a wall full of horns and never be a hunter," Charley had told me that first night out, in a wall tent sagging with the new wet snow and smoky from the imperfect oil-drum stove. His English, like the oil-drum stove, was imperfect, and from time to time he would pause and search for a word or lapse for a moment into the guttural, glottal, tongue-clicking Shuswap. Though I could mostly understand his words and intent, even when he lapsed into the tongue of the grandfathers, as he called it, often I was not quite sure of his meaning. I sensed, though, that to be a man one must become a hunter, and not everyone who killed game became a hunter, even with the killing of hundreds of bucks or bulls or billies.

There had been no luck with the moose in the high valley, perhaps because I was not yet ready. Charley had sent the second guide and wrangler back to base camp, and we had packed down through the forest of birch and spruce and fir to below the snow line. And as we moved, hunted, and slept in the damp, sagging tent smelling of old canvas and the spruce boughs we laid on the ground for beds, I learned. In a real sense, Charley taught me the "bush" (as it was called there, but which in reality was all prairies and forests and mountains and streams and all that wandered in them) or at least started me on the right path. As I look back now, three decades later, it seems the classic mythical tale of the mentor and the apprentice, though at the time I had no idea that that's what was taking place, and I think even now Charley would laugh at the notion. But consciously or unconsciously, it happened.

It was more peaceful, quieter in more than just noise level, with the wrangler and assistant guide gone, and the hunting was more in tune with the big, dark spruce and fir trees. It was as if the bush watched, judging almost, as we moved through it. The killing was no longer important; we'd already taken one trophy anyway, and that was as much as one could expect from a hunt. It was the hunt itself, a sense of moving through and understanding and feeling the bush. It was hunting with Charley, even though I understand now I was not yet a hunter, and following him as he drifted quietly through the woods working a track or testing the wind or straining to see into the gloom of the forest. And each day my senses became more keen and my mind more aware as I moved slowly toward the state of awareness Charley hunted in always. I found I could actually scent a bull moose or black bear, and especially a buck (they were coming into rut now and smelled of musk and urine), something I'd never been aware of before.

We tracked bucks to their beds and jumped them during the week or so we hunted like this. Always they were up and over a blowdown in little more than the time it takes to bring the rifle to the shoulder, but always Charley would say, "Not yet. Not this one." We were going through the motions of the hunt without killing, I realize now, so that I might learn something. I still don't know if it was a conscious mentoring effort on Charley's part or something instinctual, internal, embedded in his genetic makeup to immerse the young hunter in the ways of hunting as his grandfathers had done it. And I did not mind that we did not kill, even though it would have been unthinkable a few weeks earlier. Some of the mule deer bucks we'd jumped had carried antlers so large they'd had to twist their heads sideways as they fled between the close-growing trees.

Always, when tracking or simply moving through the gloom of spruce and fir, Charley would test the wind by dropping a pinch of dry spruce needles or caribou moss he'd crumble with his fingers, or lint from pockets of his wool pants if the needles or lichen were damp. And he did not always hunt into the wind. Just as often he hunted downwind, using our scent to drive game to a place he knew, and mostly he could predict where the animals would go. I learned that we hunted individuals with wills and thoughts of their own, not robots that would behave the same as every other member of its race would behave, so his predictions weren't always right. Once, we jumped a good buck from its bed, and my rifle was up quickly as the buck fled through the trees, angling away, and Charlie said, "Not yet." Somehow I had expected him to say that, so I hadn't even thumbed off the safety.

"He'll circle and come back before midday."

We sat with our backs against a centuries-old fir across the trail from the buck's cover. No sun brightened the gray, late-autumn days, and even if it had, it wouldn't have penetrated the gloom of the old-growth forest. The spires of the ancient spruce and fir were somehow holy, the silence that of a medieval cathedral, and somehow all creatures in it, including us, were hallowed. There existed an overwhelming feeling of rightness, of belonging to all of it. At least here and now, killing was no longer the goal of the hunt, only a part of it no more important than the beginning, or the tracking, or the living in a tent.

And then the buck was there, coming easily down a game trail that had been used for centuries by its ancestors. His dry reddish-brown hide almost glowed against the wet black of the forest. He moved down the trail, nose raised to test the wind, large ears pivoting, straining to sense anything out of the ordinary, anything that didn't belong. But there was nothing that did not belong. We had blended into the time and place so well we were as much a part of it as the buck or the trees. When the deer had walked to within ten yards, Charley raised his hand and said something in the guttural Shuswap. The buck did not run, but only turned to look at Charley more specifically, then walked easily down the slope and disappeared into the trees. I could have shot him a dozen times, but it didn't enter my mind.

I asked Charley to teach me his techniques—how he knew where game would go when he let them catch our scent, how he could predict when a buck would return, how to track as he did—but all I could get was a wave of his hand, as if those things weren't important, and were individual matters. And then he would hold his hand over his stomach—not to say that hunger was more important but rather to convey some feeling, perhaps some sixth sense, that came from his core. Then he would say something mysterious, or something that didn't make sense to me.

"Drift like smoke," he would say. Other things he said at such times held no meaning for me, so I did not remember them.

We moved camp again to a broad valley with a steep, heavily timbered east-facing slope and a west slope that had been burned off years earlier. There was a heavy growth of young poplar, birch, willow, and other shrubs Charley said were good food for deer and moose, and sometimes, during a hard winter, even for caribou.

"Good place," he grunted as he drove in a spruce stake with the flat of an ax.

An iron frost had settled the next dawn as we hunted up the valley along the willow flats toward the big burn. We stalked quietly, or at least I tried to, stopping to watch a cow moose and her calf browsing on willows.

Then we came upon a track in the steel-hard-frozen spruce duff, made before the morning frost had settled. It was as big as any we had seen, and it headed in the direction of the old burn and the thick browse.

I had begun to tremble, to shiver almost, even before Charley pointed at the track and said, "This is the one."

By the time we trailed up to the old burn and the thick tangle that had grown up in it, the ground had begun to thaw and soften, making the walking quiet, except where I scraped against a bush. Charley followed the track without pause and almost without glancing at it, as if he knew where the buck would be. He was hunting in the old way, following no set of rules, hunting as the best hunter in his tribe had done since he could remember and as his grandfathers had done

Buck "tending" a doe during the rut.

since before he could remember. It was instinctual, something that came without thought (unless he was forced to speak to me, which he hadn't done in some time). It was as much a part of him, perhaps, as his gray-streaked hair (not so much a symbol of age as of timelessness) or ageless face that carried always the look of the hunter. He drifted, as surely as it is possible to do so, and there was no hesitance in anything he did. The sureness carried over to me, and I knew we were bound somewhere to something.

Looking back now, years later, I do not know how Charley knew that this was the buck, or the time. I did not know whether he had selected it or perhaps the forest had chosen us. But there was no doubt then that it was the time, and from time to time, as we moved easily and quickly through the gloom of the ancient bush, I would shiver uncontrollably, and not from the cold breeze or the light sleet falling out of the fog.

At the edge of the thick brush in the old burn, the buck's tracks, what was left of them and what hadn't filled with sleet, turned upward, skirting the thick stuff. He was not stopping to feed or to rest or for any other reason, but moving steadily, unhurried. Charley scarcely glanced at the tracks now, seeming to know where the buck was going, and even what would happen.

We stopped once, and he turned to me and said, "When he runs, shoot fast and easy."

At that moment I knew what all the tracking and flushing of bucks and shouldering the gun without shooting in the past weeks had been for, at least in part. But there was another part I was not sure of then, though I am now. It was learning to hunt without taking a trophy, without killing as the only goal, without the thought of acquiring something. It was learning to become part of the bush.

The day had become darker with thickening fog and snow, and the buck's tracks were barely visible indentations now. But none of Charley's sureness had left, and we moved as purposefully as ever through the late autumn day, still convinced we were going somewhere.

And then the buck was there in the damp gloom of the fog and forest and Charley was no longer there but off somewhere to one side and the gun was coming up in seeming slow motion, and still the buck stood, a glowing, dry, warm gray-red-brown presence in the wet black-and-white woods. And then he was bounding away and the cross hairs were on his shoulder and then slightly in front and then there was silence and a pinch of deer hair hanging in the breeze and Charley walking toward where the buck had been. I didn't remember the shot, and the forest was eminently silent as I followed and started to shiver again.

It was a good buck, but no better than others we had seen. Charley had his hand on an antler as I walked up. There was no mark visible on the buck—he'd fallen on the bullet hole, and he was in such contrast to the wet, black ground that he seemed almost alive.

Then Charley pulled the buck's head back by the antlers, tilting his chin up and drawing the knife quickly across the taut throat. Charley had been a guide for many years and knew better than to ruin a cape that way, but we both knew this was different—this was no mountain goat shot across an avalanche channel, no bull killed on a Colorado elk ranch.

Ritually, Charley dipped the tips of his fingers into the dark venous blood oozing from the deer's throat and touched them to my cheeks, and I felt something beyond the warm, sticky blood. I did not understand, then, what it was. It took a score of years to see that I had been painted not only with blood and not only for a few hours, but with the essence of the bush and forever. It was then that I became a hunter and, by definition, at least to Charley (though he never would have voiced such things) and me, a man.

We broke camp the next day and turned the packstring down the valley toward the log-cabin base camp on Crooked Lake. And as we rode, there was that feeling of understanding. In later years I'd feel it again in rare, uncluttered moments when I realized that Charley had hunted not only for game but also for meaning.

And probably I'd feel it most intimately when alone in a wilderness after having hunted hard and fairly for something, whether or not I'd killed it.

FARTHER AND HIGHER

The good thing was that early blizzards had kept other hunters out of the high country. Most wouldn't go if they couldn't drive close. Even the hardiest horsemen wouldn't force mounts through stirrup-deep drifts, and it was too cold to sit in a saddle all day. I had the place to myself.

The bad thing was that fog and snow reduced visibility to a few score yards. A hunter had to step on a buck to see it. And it was cold. On the ridges, windchill would freeze flesh in minutes. It was so dangerous that a few days later, during a break in the weather, two mountain bikers tried to ride across the crusted, wind-glazed snow; one staggered back to the road, the other froze to death under a tree where a few days earlier I had eaten lunch.

A young buck browses on willow shoots during winter.

So on the next to last day of the season, I trudged through thigh-deep snow up a ridge two thousand feet above my house in northern Utah. I no longer had much faith in my chances and was simply going through the motions; even hunting without hope is better than no hunting at all. I'd seen only one yearling buck all season. I plunged my mittened hands deep within Canadian army arctic pants and pulled the balaclava down over my face to protect it from the driving snow and wind. "No sane buck would be up in this." When I'm out alone, I talk to myself.

Something moved in the maple growth thirty yards ahead; then a titanic buck bounded and wallowed into the open. By the time I'd pulled my hands from the pockets, gotten the sling off over my head and the rifle to my shoulder, the buck had disappeared below the curve of the slope. If only I'd been ready.

Though the fog and low clouds hadn't lifted, the snow had quit, so it wouldn't fill in the tracks. The buck bounded down the slope—it would have been too exhausting for him to wallow through the drifts upslope. I followed, the rifle in my hands and a cartridge in the chamber. The buck slowed to a less-tiring trot. He couldn't bound long in heavy snow, even downhill.

The trail led straight down and into a canyon. If the buck kept descending, he'd hit the snow line three thousand feet below and I'd lose him in the rocky terrain. But the buck veered across the slope to the east, slowing to a less-energy-consuming walk. The trail led downwind, so the buck would scent me as I followed. He'd stay downwind as much as possible to keep track of me, and I anticipated an all-day stalk. I hoped he'd eventually make a mistake and give me a quick shot if I kept at it.

The trail stayed inside heavy oak brush; when the buck came to an opening, he'd skirt it in the cover of the scrub. Later, the buck buttonhooked to be directly downwind of me and waited in the oak; I read in the tracks that he'd scented me at some distance and bounded off through knee-deep snow. But he quickly slowed to a trot again to save energy, and then to a fast walk. He continued downwind, stopping often in the heavy cover until he caught my scent, then racing off again. He'd survived enough deer seasons to know that moving during the day in the open was a certain way to get shot at, so he stayed to the brush.

A mile farther on, the trail led into a maze of other tracks where four deer had browsed in a patch of chaparral. Bits of leaves and bark littered the snow. I slowed so I wouldn't get off on the wrong trail. The big buck's tracks led in a straight line through the meanderings of the others, and no other hoofprints were as large as his four-inch track.

The trail turned back uphill into deeper snow, tangled brush, and shrieking winds. It wouldn't take long for the wind to obliterate the trail. The tracks zigged from one tangle of brush to the next. The buck tried to scrape me off the trail in heavy thickets as he might an irritating tick on a bush. We climbed into fog so thick I couldn't see a dozen feet ahead. The snow started in earnest again. Before long, it would cover the trail. He climbed straight toward the ridge above—no more circling downwind to catch my scent, because he was sure I was following. He intended now to outlast me.

As the trail approached the ridgeline, it abruptly turned downwind and downslope. He knew I was still on the trail, so he hadn't turned downwind just to scent me. Instead, he'd become nervous in the open near the top of the barren ridge. While trailing, I had forced the buck to do two things totally against his experience: move during daylight and cross openings. I knew there weren't other hunters this high in the stormy weather, but the buck didn't and he hadn't gotten big by acting dumb, especially on this overhunted bit of public land. He wanted to get back into heavy cover and shake me so he could bed safely until dark.

The snow quit again, and the buck slowed to a walk once he made the oak cover. Instead of the three-foot stride of a trotting buck, the walking strides were closer to two feet and the hind hoofs printed neatly in the tracks made by the forehoofs. The buck would bound only after he sensed me at close range; bounding took too much energy, and he couldn't keep it up in heavy snow. No mistaking the bound, either—all four hoofs struck the ground close together, with the hind ahead of the forehoofs and the left hoof slightly ahead of the right. On dry, level ground a buck's bounding stride measures twenty-two to twenty-nine feet; in heavy snow the bounding stride is closer to sixteen feet.

The trail meandered as he searched for a bed or a place to watch the backtrail. I waited. Better to let the buck settle down and find a place to bed than to keep pushing him. I'd have a better chance for a shot if I could jump him from his bed. I built a fire under a big spruce and ate lunch. The smoke drifted east toward the buck, then a crosswind carried it up the slope and away. He couldn't scent me, so possibly he'd settle down.

My dilemma was that I wanted to give the buck time to quiet down without using up all the daylight. I hadn't made much progress, and losing the light was becoming more and more likely. After a quick lunch, I took up the trail again.

The tracks meandered down the slope, and the buck had waited inside an oak thicket to scent me. If he had smelled me, he'd have raced off in that characteristic, stiff-legged mule deer bound. But he paced east again, toward a saddle that led into another canyon. The fog hadn't lifted, but from time to time it tore apart briefly and showed the opposite slope of a canyon or a ridge above. Then it socked in again. Though I'd often trekked throughout the area, in the fog I had no idea where I was. No matter—I'd stay with the trail until dark if necessary, then hike down toward civilization or build a fire under a big fir tree and spend the night.

The trail led down the slope, then buttonhooked back uphill across the wind, paralleling his downslope trail two hundred yards off; he was hoping to catch my scent as I followed, I suppose. He hadn't scented me—perhaps because I was later than expected after the lunch break—and he continued on at a fast walk. Then the trail went through a saddle on a low ridge. As I followed, the fog broke long enough for me to see him cross the ridge three hundred yards above. I brought the rifle up and thumbed off the safety, but the fog closed. The antlers pushed

Buck and doe during the rut. The buck is exhibiting flehmen, and determining if the doe is ready to breed.

thirty inches in spread. I forced myself to wait and give the buck more time to calm.

The trail led over the saddle into another canyon and a stand of Douglas fir. The buck had stood and paced, then begun hoofing a bed in the fir needles under the big trees. But he'd had second thoughts and walked on, contouring the slope toward another ridge.

The trail skirted a meadow, beyond which the buck stopped and waited to watch his backtrail. When I didn't show in what the buck considered an appropriate time, he'd walked downwind toward the ridge and begun taking short meanders as he searched for a bed. He wasn't as worried about me, but he still had doubts. He wouldn't chance bedding just yet. I stopped and waited another twenty minutes to give the buck time to settle down a bit more. The earlier lunch break had made the difference between trailing a spooky buck that knew I was on his trail and one that was no longer ready to bolt. Another pause might make a critical difference later, especially if the buck bedded down. I'd catch him then, but whether or not I got a reasonable shot depended on where he bedded and how ready I was when he jumped. I was glad other hunters weren't this high up to complicate the tracking. It was just me and the buck.

The fog was just as thick as ever. Visibility was seldom more than thirty yards and often less than that. Judging by the quality of light, morning had become midafternoon. It would be dark in a few hours. Then I'd hike downhill in darkness to whatever civilization I'd find. Pausing now was risky. I might not catch the buck before dark.

The trail led to the top of a small ridge, then angled downhill into another canyon and up into a tangle of aspen saplings, where the buck had stood again and watched his backtrail, then walked on. He'd relaxed enough to browse frost-dried forbs in a small ravine, he hooked a small fir sapling with his antlers in passing; shreds of bark and needles lay on the snow. Then he'd circled downwind and upslope, waited and watched, then walked on.

I found the bed under the umbrella canopy of spruce trees. Nearby, droppings steamed faintly in the fading light. "He's spooked again," I told myself, but the buck had left at a walk. I hadn't frightened him after all. Apparently, the bed just hadn't felt right. He'd bed again soon. I blew snow off the scope and stuffed my right mitten in a pocket to free my trigger finger.

He bedded the second time in a tangle of chokecherry and scrub aspen. He had been in it long enough to melt the snow two inches deep. This time, though, he'd left at a bound. He'd scented me, and I was no closer now than when I'd begun. The buck bounded down the slope and across toward the bottoms. I floundered through the snow. With the waning light, I'd have to hurry. I no longer had time for finesse.

As I climbed a bluff, the fog lifted momentarily. Through the binoculars I followed the animal's trail in the snow down the slope and then up the creek until it led out of the bottoms and climbed the opposite slope. Then I spotted the buck, or his rump, in a willow thicket. In the glasses I found antlers, but as I brought the rifle up, the buck stepped into cover. I put the cross hairs on an opening a few yards higher, waited, and prayed the fog wouldn't close again. He skirted the opening, and for a moment I saw his outline, put the cross hairs on a brushy tangle just ahead, and pressed the trigger. The bullet slapped, and the buck leaped and bounded downhill into fog.

I wallowed through the snow to the bottoms and picked up the trail in the dusky half-light. No blood. No hair. No faltering stride. I'd missed. But that bullet slap—did I hit a branch? The trail went on—fifty yards, one hundred yards—as I hurried to beat the darkness. Then the buck stood and bled. Forty yards farther on, I found him fallen under a tree.

I gutted the buck in the dark, then turned the carcass over and urinated on it to keep off the big scavengers. I trekked down the canyon in the night made even darker by the fog. Three hours later, I oriented on a farm and, after two more hours of fighting brush, staggered home. In nearly eighteen hours I hadn't seen a human track.

FLAT TOP MOUNTAIN

Most true hunters have had their own wild classroom, whether it was Grandpa's bottom quarter-section or the Bob Marshall Wilderness. Mine was Flat Top Mountain.

Nothing to my credit, but back in the days before the road, I was a pioneer of sorts on old Flat Top, and I'm glad I had a place to learn and be free in. The young need that freedom, as well as a place to make and learn from mistakes. What good is freedom without a place to be free?

In that Utah valley you'd walk through autumn-tawny wheatgrass and slate-blue sagebrush beneath a lapis lazuli sky, but you couldn't ignore Flat Top on the horizon. You'd see it towering above the valley on a moonlit night, and it caught the first vermilion rays of a new sun. Once on top, you sensed the mountain in the barn-stink of a September elk wallow, a flapjack-sized cougar pug, or the distant twilight wail of a coyote.

I was fourteen when I started wandering Flat Top, as insignificant as a protozoan on the back of a whale, and learning of its gorges and fellow organisms—grouse, elk, deer, and the rest. I learned, too, about dealing with Flat Top and its citizens and, by extension, about the ethics of living.

There were grouse on Flat Top—ruffs low down in the cottonwoods in the canyons that cut down its flanks, blues in the spruce and fir on the north-facing slopes, and sagehens on top. Few hunters chased birds up there, and the grouse were so plentiful it was impossible to imagine they could ever be scarce: Flocks of sagehens numbering in the hundreds lumbered into the crystalline autumn sky as if in slow motion, and in places blue grouse were so thick in the firs you couldn't take a step without flushing birds. I occasionally shot over the limit, more birds than I could possibly eat, and sometimes they'd spoil before I could clean and freeze them. But when I did that, something bothered me. It was wasteful, of course, but it eventually dawned on me that seeing and listening to birds out there in the sagebrush and spruce was worth more than a bunch of dead ones in the neighbor's hog pen, no matter how much I loved wingshooting.

When you hunted ducks and pheasants down there in the valley, how many you shot was important. You were a high-school hero if you could boast of and prove shooting half-a-dozen pheasants or more on a weekend. That scorekeeping carried over to Flat Top, too, to the extent that it didn't matter how you got them, just as long as you did get them. Shooting naive blue grouse perched on a branch was acceptable because it increased your bag. About the same time as I began to understand that bagging too many grouse was a waste, I also realized that the final tally was less important than how you did it. There was no real fun in shooting grouse on the sit anyway, and it didn't improve your wingshooting skills.

I learned other lessons up there on Flat Top. I was good with a rifle on the range, but in that youthful time, if a big buck got up, I occasionally got too excited and blasted away. Once, I jumped a good buck from a tangle of spruce, and as he bounded into the ravine and up the opposite slope, I opened fire, really too excited to know where I was shooting. On the third or fourth shot, the buck staggered and was gone. I trailed him for much of the day, laboriously unraveling the twisted trail, occasionally finding a blackened splatter of dried blood on sliderock or a scuff in the fir-needle duff, until I caught up to him. As I squeezed off one final time, it truly hit me how much the buck had suffered. In a moment of rare insight, I felt the pain. I agonized over it for weeks. I almost never again shot at an animal without being sure, and sometimes that required counting to ten to let the excitement abate.

On Flat Top I learned the basics of tracking bucks and, later, the finer points of the art. I learned first to identify a mature buck or bull's track; then his stride; how to age a trail by clues given by the wind, temperature, moisture, sun, and weather; and finally how to interpret an animal's state of mind by his trail and ultimately to predict what he'd do next. Once, I spent four days tracking an enormous buck, carefully following the trail over ridges, down canyons, and through aspen tangles, returning to camp each evening to doze fitfully until the light would come and I could take up the trail again. I knew that he'd eventually reach a refuge and stop, and he did just that, and he was the best buck I ever earned.

I learned by trial and error how to approach game close enough for a shot, which meant considering wind direction and intensity— not only because it carries scent but also because it carries sound. I learned of silence and wearing quiet wool and moving slowly. I learned patience. I made my mistakes and flushed huge bucks in heavy timber before I was close enough or ready to shoot. Ultimately, through years of practice, I found that if I really concentrated, paid attention to all details, and stayed alert, I could kill bucks in their beds, often at fifteen yards.

Like most hunters, I passed through the gadgetry phase. I tried Day-Glo camos, practiced with deer bleats and other trendy game calls, experimented with scent concoctions guaranteed to bring a buck into your lap, shot with hot cartridges and high-magnification riflescopes. I found that these "aids" to bush lore were really only substitutes for it, and that to consistently bag good bucks, you had to fall back on still-hunting, tracking, and stalking.

Flat Top taught other lessons, too, like always to check for blood spoor whenever you shoot. I once fired at a buck across a canyon, had felt good about the shot, but the buck hadn't reacted. When he walked into the woods, I shrugged, cussed, and guessed the bullet had been deflected by a branch; not wanting to climb down into the bottoms and up the steep opposite slope to check for blood, I went on about my hunting. But the decision had been too comfortable, and something nagged at me all day. The hold, after all, had looked and felt just right, and the rifle was still zeroed perfectly. In the end, I went back, followed the scant blood trail, and found the buck dead in the trees a hundred yards away.

I learned up there that other things are more important than shooting deer. I learned the pleasure of solitude, the silence of wilderness, and the awe of walking through old-growth forests that had never felt an ax or saw. I found that you didn't need to carry a gun to appreciate an aspen campfire warming your backside on a crisp October night, the libidinous bugling of bull elk causing you goose flesh in the half-light of dawn, or the adrenaline-pumping crash of a

I'm sitting on a mule named Slick as we cross the sierra in a rare snow.

jumping buck. On some things I am a slow learner, but Flat Top taught me finally that you don't need to bring back a buck as proof that you had a good hunt.

Flat Top Mountain changed, as all wild places must. Cattlemen bulldozed a road up its flank and onto its top, and Herefords grazed the wheatgrass and grama down to dust; people and machines raced over the new road, and forest grouse became scarce and the sagehens disappeared; the few bucks and bulls that survived became nocturnal and died young. Another lesson learned up there says not to return to once-wild places. You'll not only ruin a trip, you'll destroy a memory. The more brilliant the mountain larkspur was, the surer it will have been picked, if not yanked up roots and all.

A final lesson learned up there is that we all need a Flat Top Mountain. The young need a classroom to develop abilities and learn values, and it's up to us, the elders, to preserve pieces of wild lands for future lessons.

SIERRA MADRE DREAMS

The rancher couldn't see us after sundown when we had our evening swim in his pond. In the dark, we sat on the earthen dam using willow saplings as rods and poached some of his trout, each stick bobber making a "slurp" in the blackness when a fish pulled it under. Then we'd hike down the dry arroyo to camp in the moonlight. Night birds made wavery calls from the mesquite thickets on the foothills, and big owls hooted farther up in the pines. Coyotes yelped below on the flats, and beyond was the glitter of the little town of Sierra Vista, which means "mountain view."

Butch fed twigs to the coals on the sands of the dry wash bottom, and Kit gathered deadfall out in the dark and said he hoped he didn't step on a rattlesnake. Gordy cleaned the trout and threw the guts into the black acacia on the other side of the last drying pool in the wash. Little Bob rummaged in the packs for his stuffed Mickey Mouse and whimpered.

This was our last outing of the summer. Next week we would begin the nine-month routine of climbing onto the yellow bus and rattling into town and down the broad dirt road to the school out on the greasewood flats. In school, we would not have been friends, probably, without sharing these adventures in the arroyo. Butch was sort of the organizer, and he pretty much quit school in the spring so he could go out to the arroyo when there was water to draw frogs and other animals. He was older, the oldest in his eighth-grade class; he had been for several years.

Little Bob had gotten over his homesickness by the last day, mostly because Butch had taught him to shoot the .22. We had been living on trout and jack rabbits, with canned peaches for dessert. On the last night, we watched a scrawny, spitted jack rabbit sizzle and brown over the mesquite coals.

The big stars pulsed like animated jewels. We had been trying to count them in a strip of sky between black hills. Kit had read that Genghis Khan had navigated by constellations to cross Asia, and Gordy had heard that all the best pirates navigated by the stars.

"If we followed that big star in the east down the arroyo until we hit the San Pedro River, where would ya wanta go from there?" Butch asked.

"I'd just go north into the White Mountains and hunt them big deer up on the Apache reservation," Gordy answered. He was still gloating over shooting the jack rabbit that was slowly getting closer to being our dinner.

"How 'bout you, Kit?"

"I'd walk up to Benson and hop the freight train east as far as San Antonio and see the Alamo." Kit had a coonskin hat and watched the Davy Crockett show religiously, even the summer reruns. He wanted to kill a bear with a Bowie knife and hunt deer with a muzzleloader.

Little Bob just wanted to visit Disneyland out in California, so we didn't pay him any attention.

"You're next, Butch," I said.

"Well," he said, pausing and considering the best way to tell it, "there's this place down in Old Mex. You climb from the desert up through canyons so thick you have to hack the acacia and mesquite with machetes to get the burros through."

Butch's father was a prospector who came into town, usually in the back of a rancher's stock truck, only when he had a broken leg or something else that needed fixing. Then he was gone again. He'd told Butch about a secret place deep in the Sierra Madre.

"Then there's a steep canyon you climb, with springs where desert sheep and jaguars drink, until you come to sheer cliffs that climb straight up out of the ponderosa pines. At first, it seems like you can't get through, but Pa found a way, on the north side, where he could get the burros up narrow crevices if he removed their packs, and then up another arroyo. Then he'd hook a block and tackle over a juniper on a cliff above and hoist them forty feet up there. He had to blindfold them burros or they'd kick their way out of the sling or scare themselves to death. Once on top, there's rolling grama-covered hills and basins and forests of old-growth pine and white oak. Pa's shot bears up there big as a horse, and cougars, and once he got an old jaguar that killed one of the burros. And he's shot deer and a bighorn ram. He camps around a pond that has some strange fish he'd never seen before; you could wrap a piece of wool yarn around a hook and catch them. He says it even snows as early as September, and that a man never needs to go nowheres else, once he gits up. There are old Indian ruins with walls still standing and corn cobs in old rock and mud granaries and arrowheads and cliff paintings and pots and baskets in the ruins, at least in those where the roof ain't fallen in."

"How'd they get that town up there?" Little Bob asked. His eyes were as wide as when someone talked about Disneyland.

"They built it right there, out of the rock and mud that's all about."

"But how did them people get up those cliffs? There musta been some old and sickly ones." Kit's eyes were wide as Little Bob's.

Butch began again. "Prob'bly only healthy ones clumb up in the first place. Them people had been there for hundreds of years, mebbe thousands. Pa said that when the summer monsoon comes, the lightning crackles and bounces off the rocks in a frightful way, and that mebbe them old Indians got 'lectrocuted. He found a herd of mule deer bucks that had died and they were all lying there like they'd just gone to sleep, 'cept the hair was burnt. Pa figgered lightning hit 'em."

We sat saguaro-straight, staring at Butch. Everyone had forgotten the jack rabbit on the spit.

"There couldn't a been many people," Gordy said, "or they would have eaten up all the game."

"There's so much of it you don't have to hunt. Pa says that you just take a walk with a gun and before long you'll collect one of them big mule deer bucks, or mebbe a turkey or bear. Pa says that if you ain't careful, you git fat up there and can't climb back down through the crevices."

A big, dark bird glided over in the firelight and down the arroyo toward the star in the east.

"The Papago says those kinds of things are omens, and that if you know how, you can tell the future by 'em," I mentioned, then poked a stick at the jack rabbit. "It must be midnight."

Buck browsing rose hips in Montana. He's competing with black bears and grouse for the nutritious hips.

Kit cut up the jack and put it onto tin plates. Butch filled the porcelain cups with Kool Aid.

"Butch, when you go down there, will you take me?" Gordy asked. "Me, too!" we all chimed.

I drifted off to sleep thinking of that place down in the Sierra Madre. Toward dawn, I sat up and looked at the boys sprawled on the sands around the glowing coals. As I watched, the owls hooted, then the sky lightened, and then the doves began to mourn, and then suddenly flies buzzed and the primrose blossoms closed up in the daylight.

More than a decade later, I went back. In the southern distance the Huachuca Mountains climbed into the desert haze, but the roads were paved and thousands of glittering houses climbed far up the foothills, almost to our arroyo. The school had been enlarged, and the town had engulfed it and spread out beyond into the greasewood desert. Gordy had become a banker and wouldn't go anywhere his big, polished pickup truck wouldn't take him. Kit had married a big-boned woman from Bisbee and lived in a trailer house on a dusty lot beyond the city limits and had so many children I couldn't keep track of them. Little Bob had become Big Bob and weighed three hundred pounds. "You can find Butch in the honky-tonks," he told me.

"Couldn't git beyond ol' Miz Fasenmeyer's eighth grade," Butch told me. "She had it in for me. Pa never come back from one of them prospectin' trips, neither." That led to talk of that place down in the Sierra Madre, and the old snap came back into his eyes. "Mebbe I'll git my Model 94 out of hock and go. I still got Pa's map. Mebbe Pa's still down there. Mebbe he struck the mother lode."

"Let's do it," I said, "seriously."

Butch stared into the half-empty beer mug, then at the mirror behind the bar, then at a couple playing eight-ball in the back. "Can't. No money." He looked into the mug again, relieved. "Mebbe in the spring."

"I've got money," I said, "and think of them big bucks."

He looked at me, then across the bar and back to the pool players, then out the door at the cars in the street. He wiped his palms on his jeans and ordered another beer and said. "Damn," not quite under his breath. "Once, I hocked everything I owned to git to La Paz for festival. Pa said the senoritas were always friendly to gringos, and there were days of parades and parties and free food, and deer hunting in the jungle and fish that jumped three feet when ya hooked 'em. I got some kind of trots the first day and missed the whole thing."

Then, "Ya don't know why Kit never went to the Alamo, or Little Bob out to Disneyland, or why Gordy never got up to hunt those big deer on the Apache reservation, do ya?"

He drained the beer, stood up, and walked out the door and across the street in that disjointed saunter he had, and disappeared into the gloom of the Dry Gulch Saloon.

Nocturnal moths are attracted to the blossom of the evening primrose, which blooms only at night. One grew in a beer pitcher behind the bar, its dreamy white petals spread wide in the dim tavern light.

THE TRACK

It's a familiar theme—returning to places that were important to you when you were younger and always finding the same thing: they've changed. I'd come back to Weber County, Utah, where I'd learned to hunt deer and hunted sporadically for the better part of four decades. I'd seen the county change from a near-wilderness with only a few rugged four-wheel-drive trails used mostly by sheepherders to a place where a road ran down nearly every ridge. As the country changed, I kept moving— first to Mill Canyon, which now bristled with summer cabins and where I'd killed a handful of big bucks, several over the magic thirty-inch spread; then to the Narrows, once too rough until young hunters had been pushed into it by crowds in more accessible places; and then to some hidden draws in Magpie Canyon, which had now been discovered by platoons of

These two bucks are about to spar—that is, put their antlers together and shove. Sparring averts potentially serious dominance battles later on as the rut approaches.

horseback hunters who combed it in posses as if hunting outlaws. As the people came to these places—almost following me, it seemed—the big bucks disappeared and I moved on in search of another canyon or plateau that was too rugged for weekend hunters. Now there were no more places to go.

The track led upward, through a thicket of oak scrub, occasionally leaving a big print in a patch of snow left over from the storm a week earlier. I paused to look at one track—it was longer than a .270 cartridge. "There is a big one left," I told myself, though I'd known it since the evening before, when I'd watched the big buck make his way cautiously up the slope. He was on the move, and knew deer season would be soon underway; he'd heard the parade of four-bys and motorized tricycles and was looking for a hideout. Probably he had one in mind.

It was late in the morning and I was making my way slowly through a big stand of Douglas fir. The slope faced north and there were still several inches of soft snow in the shadows and the tracking was easy. I'd been on the track for five hours, and it showed no signs of slowing or circling as if the deer might be searching for a bed; except where it meandered in a patch of shiny-leaved chaparral, where the buck had fed, undoubtedly in the dark, it was still leading purposefully southeastward. He knew where he was going.

It was easy to lose myself in the track, to begin to think like a deer, or at least try to, and forget about the roads that ran now on almost every ridge. It was easy except when the distant sound of grinding gears floated to me on some errant zephyr. Then in my mind I would leave the track and there would be only helplessness and anger. But soon the sound would die again and I would be there on the track, trailing the buck again, a buck that was more than meat and antlers.

I trailed slowly up out of a big shadowed canyon, and still the track showed no sign of stopping or slowing. I was surprised to see that it had begun to be evening; I'd been so lost in the track that I'd forgotten time. The mellowing sun was only a finger's width above the great purple peaks of the Wasatch fifteen miles to the west.

Following the still-old track, still trying to think like a wise old buck, I realized with a start that I wouldn't catch him that day. It didn't change anything, though; I was hunting honestly now, not merely wandering around looking for some yearling buck (virtually the only ones left in the country since they'd been fawns the season before and illegal to shoot). It was the first time in years that I'd lost myself in deer hunting this way, and I wouldn't have given it up even if I'd known; somehow there was no way to catch the buck. As it was, I knew my chances were slim. (But this was the way to hunt, like that time several seasons earlier when I'd seen the big buck across the canyon. I was sure it was this same one. I'd crossed the canyon that year and found the trail in the heavy, fresh snow and followed it for two hours—had unraveled it when it doubled back, then when it lost itself in a maze of other deer tracks, then again when it disappeared completely and I was able to find it again only after half an hour of puzzled circling where the animal had leaped thirty feet down a slope and landed in a maple thicket. Then, concentrating on the trail, I'd walked into the buck at twenty yards. He stood momentarily in a tangle of chokecherry with his rump toward me, staring back over his shoulder. Could his antlers really have been that big? I wondered, after he'd leaped a blowdown and disappeared down the slope.) Since, I had been searching for that buck in my dreams, and now I felt sure I was on his track again.

I left the track in a saddle where the trail had begun to drop into another canyon. It would be a good place to pick it up again in the morning. In a sense, it was unimportant whether or not I got the buck, whether I even caught up with him. In that sense, the hunt was the important thing. In another sense, at another level of thought, that rack of antlers had become the most important thing in the world to possess. I puzzled at the paradox as I walked down the ridge and across the flat to camp.

It was dark when I left camp the next morning, moved across a broad plateau, through a small canyon, and then down a ridge to the saddle where I'd left the track. To the east, the sky began to lighten, and in the distance to the north, lights bounced along ridge roads. I could hear the grinding of gears or the hum of an engine, but then the wind would change and bring me the deep hooting of a horned owl on a spruce snag to the east.

The track was just where I'd left it, all right, next to a boulder I had put on top of another as a marker. It hadn't been a dream, then, or imagination. As I set by the campfire the night before, with no one to talk to about it, it had all seemed too good to be true, and I'd begun to wonder if it had really happened or whether the track was really that big. I put my finger in it and traced its outline. "No dream," I told myself.

The trail led down into the canyon. On the open slope I could follow it in the dawn, but where it disappeared into the shadows of the timber, I had to stop and wait for the light to come. Then, too slowly, it was light enough and I moved off through the trees and along the track. Except where the buck stopped to vigorously horn willows as big around as my forearm, leaving shreds of bark on the snow, he was still moving with purpose. I picked up strands of curled bark and put them in my pocket. At night, in camp, I would look at them to dispel the doubt that probably would come again.

The track wasn't hard to follow in the needle duff amid the spruce or in the snow or on soft soil, but from time to time it would cross a rocky slope or a place where clay wet from the earlier storm had dried out and been baked hard by the sun. Then I'd lose the track and have to spend time circling to pick it up again on ground where the big animal could leave a clear print.

By afternoon of the second day, the track seemed no fresher than it had the day before. It was frustrating: For two days now, my world had been limited to the ground a few feet in front of me, and though for those two days I'd never been more content, it didn't seem like I was making progress. Part of me wanted the track and trail to go on forever, but I wanted to get to its end, too.

I found his first bed early that evening. He'd used it the day before, and it was underneath the low boughs of young fir trees. From the bed he could have seen his backtrail, the slope below and the road across the canyon, and with one jump been lost in a tangle of maple and spruce. I was glad I hadn't caught him there; I wouldn't have had a chance.

Clearly, I wouldn't catch him this day, either. And, it was four miles back to camp.

In camp hours later, I was glad for the foil-wrapped burritos and hardboiled eggs and instant cocoa. I could wolf a quick dinner and crawl into the tent without worrying about a campfire and cooking. I held for a while the strips of willow bark I'd picked up that day, then tossed them aside. It was real, all right.

I awoke in the dark, somehow knowing it was time to go. By late morning I was on the track again. The buck seemed to be wandering now, looking for something. Before long, I came across his bed in the shadows of big spruce trees. There was heavy frost in the bed and, in its center, a single big track. The buck had probably used it the evening before. Possibly he'd been traveling all night; more likely, he'd need to stop and eat. If he spent much time feeding, I'd gain on him. I'd brought food in my daypack this time in case he led me too far afield to make it back to camp that night.

The trail led onto an open slope and over a ridge. He had meandered on the slope, through thickets of serviceberry and into chaparral and from one bitterbrush to another. He was feeding, all right, but how long had he been at it? How much time had I gained? In the shade there was still frost on the edges of the freshest tracks where the soil had been pushed up by his weight. That meant he'd made them before the heaviest frost just before dawn, after which the tracks would have been only depressions with cracks radiating outward through the frozen soil. I knew he'd hide again as soon as it began to get light—he was too smart to show himself in daylight during deer season.

The trail led into another canyon, thick with maples and chokecherries and dense with stands of big timber, broken by towering pale limestone cliffs and fractured scree slopes. I

I'm crossing a river, which is a rare occurrence in desert mule deer country.

eased down the steep slope, still concentrating on the track; I lost time again where it crossed a talus slide, then picked it up once more on the other side and followed it into a stand of timber where the tracking was easy again on the dark loam and spruce-needle duff. I'd been concentrating so hard on the trail that I hadn't noticed the country. It seemed vaguely familiar. Then it was familiar. I'd hunted the canyon years earlier. Unless I missed my guess, it was too rough for motors to get into. I knew, though, there were now roads on ridges not too distant. I hoped no one had spooked the buck; he was wary enough as it was.

I continued on the trail, excited now, feeling sure this was where he'd been going all along. It had the right feel to it. If I was right, there was a good chance of reaching the end of the track before dark. His droppings were fresher here, and the top pellet hadn't dried from the sun and wind.

The trail was twisting now, first one way, then another—he was looking for a bed. I'd have to start being more careful about wind direction and to think ahead. I hadn't had to worry about the wind before because the track had been old, but things had changed. The trail was getting fresher all the time. The buck would almost certainly bed where he could watch and scent his backtrail—I'd have to anticipate where he'd be.

The track turned downslope and moved across the wind. Then it moved across the slope, into the wind again, the buck making sure no danger was ahead. Then it twisted off in still another direction. He was too careful. There'd be little chance of killing him in his bed.

I no longer carried the rifle slung from a shoulder. I had it in both hands, ready as a grouse hunter is ready, my thumb near the safety and the sling tucked away in the pack. It could be any time now, but I couldn't anticipate him, and I was too keyed and liable to make a mistake. I sat down and gnawed a chunk of jerky. I'd come too far to blow it at the end of the trail. "Calm yourself, calm yourself," I chanted in cadence with the chewing.

I took up the trail again, and now it was leading down. The country had opened, and for the first time, I could see across the canyon as I contoured across the slope, off the track now and trying to anticipate where the buck had gone. I didn't want to be caught on his backtrail, where he'd expect trouble. I'd have a better chance of surprising him from where he didn't expect anything. At least there was a chance for a shot that way.

A nice buck and yours truly.

I had to sit and calm myself again. "No good to be so tight you explode when he breaks for it," I told myself softly. I took a deep breath and picked up the trail again. As I eased through the brush, I spotted two does staring from just across the canyon. One was very nervous and stamped a forefoot.

"Just what you need," I told myself. I'd taken up talking to myself in the second person.

The nervous doe started up the slope, at first trotting stiff-legged and then, as her panic increased, bounding frantically. The other doe followed somewhat reluctantly. Then I sensed something just at the edge of my vision. It bounded the stream at the bottom, then crashed up toward the willow patch the does had vacated. It was the buck, all right—nothing else could be that big.

I threw the gun to my shoulder and put the cross hairs on him as he came into the open and started up the trail the does had followed. He'd seen them run and it had made him nervous, even though he still didn't know what the trouble was. The cross hairs wobbled all over the buck and nearby slope. Three days of concentration and tension burst like a balloon, and I missed clean. Then I breathed deeply, feeling myself go cold inside and freeing the emotional part from the body that would press the trigger.

The buck was trotting straight away up the slope when the .270 went off. He bucked heavily, and a moment later came the slap of bullet against flesh. Part of me knew the buck was already dead, but I was taking no chances and held the cross hairs above and ahead of the still-trotting animal and pressed the trigger again. The buck went down suddenly, and then there was that second shot slapping into muscle and bone. Then the cold calm was gone again and I was on an adrenaline high and shouting inside.

I like to think of that track as a farewell gift from the country, more important, even, than the trophy. Each time I stare at the buck's head gracing the wall of the great room, I remember vividly the dawns and the frozen track and the smell of the buck. I know I will never return again, and that hunt was the best way to remember a place and all the years I spent hunting and camping in it.

A SPECIAL KIND OF ANGUISH

Antihunters won't understand this story; in fact, they might consider it more grapeshot for their cannon of misinformation. Their collective mind is made up, and nothing anyone can say will change it. No matter, this story isn't for the antihunter; it's for the hunter, because he understands that someday it will happen to him, and when it does, he will feel more than regret for a lost trophy—he will know a special kind of anguish.

I was younger then, fresh from the range and the benchrest where the 7mm magnum had printed sub-minute-of-angle groups, a bit cocky and sure of my ability with a rifle since in the past season I'd killed four heads of game with as many shots. I spotted the big mule deer buck in the half-light of dawn across the canyon, one of the best bucks I'd seen. I fought back the pounding in my ears and the ox kicking in my gut, forced myself to go slow, took off my jacket and rolled it across a clump of brush, then eased the rifle onto it and held high for the distance. The buck minced toward the timber, aware of the coming day, forcing me to hurry the shot. The rifle spat flame and punched into my shoulder, the shot echoed across the canyon in the silent dawn, and the buck hunched, stumbled, regained his feet, and wobbled into the trees before I could jack another round into the chamber. At first, I was sure he was mine, but a deeper, more rational voice said something was wrong.

I found the light-colored underfur on a sagebrush and a watery, greenish splatter of blood. The hair came from the belly and the greenish blood from the gut. I was sick about it as I waited for the light to come enough so I could follow the trail into the deep shadows of the timber. I hoped the buck would lay up and stiffen. I should have taken more time, but those antlers were absolutely immense! If I didn't have it, I shouldn't have shot. Why? I asked myself, furious that I'd screwed up and at the same time sick for the buck. I didn't even think of those antlers, which were probably gone anyway.

The light came slowly, and when there was enough of it I followed the trail into the trees. I was already weary from what I'd done, and I knew that both the buck and I would suffer for hours yet, since there would be little blood sign to follow and the trailing would be slow and laborious. I wanted to suffer, too; I deserved it.

The buck stumbled for the first fifty yards, and the trail was easy to follow in the shadowy half-light of thick fir and spruce. Then his stride smoothed out and there was no stumbling or kicked-up black loam on fir needles and he was trotting in a straight and determined line. I'd at first hoped that the buck wouldn't go far, that the bullet had clipped an artery and he'd bleed out, or that maybe he'd holed up immediately, too sick to continue on, and then I could finish it quickly. But this

My new Jeep in Nevada's Ruby Mountains, top deer terrain.

determined stride told me he'd go on and that I'd be lucky to catch him, and even if I did, it wouldn't be for hours. On this trail, unlike my shooting, I'd need to take my time and be certain not to lose the spoor.

The trail led through the big stand of fir, then down a steep, brush-choked ravine. If he had continued in a straight line, he'd have crossed an open slope, but he still had his wits about him and was wise enough not to. He was keeping more or less downwind, so he'd scent me if I got too close. He wasn't hurt so badly that he'd lost the learned caution of an old, veteran buck, and he certainly wasn't panicking and apt to make a mistake. For a while I wondered if he was really seriously hurt; his trail was smooth and his route through the brush downwind and calculated. Maybe he was all right. Possibly I'd just nicked him and he'd be OK. But then I remembered the watery, greasy blood, and I knew I'd been rationalizing and that he would die and that it was up to me to speed it up and end his suffering.

Now I was sure I wouldn't catch the buck soon, if at all. I wondered if he had any idea I was on his backtrail.

The trail led into the canyon bottom, and the buck had made a short dash across an open meadow to the trees on the other side. There I found more blood. He'd stopped and bled where he'd watched his backtrail; the sprint across the meadow had opened the wound. Then the wound closed again and there was nothing but the walking stride contouring down the slope and through the timber.

I wished it had never happened. I should never have taken that shot. I shouldn't have been so damned sure about my shooting. I wanted to smash something. I let go a string of expletives that would shock a railroad man, and I felt better.

It took two hours of trailing the buck through the timber to cover a mile. By that time I'd developed a "feel" for the trail and begun to think like the buck, and I anticipated where he was going as much as I actually followed the tracks. He continued on as if he knew where he was going, but maybe he was just running from the pain. Then he crossed a scree slope in the trees and I lost the trail. He was no longer bleeding, so there was no black splatter of blood here or there, especially on the light, jagged sliderock. I crossed the slide, then cast for sign like a pointer seeking bird scent. It was some time before I found the trail again, and I was convinced it was his only an hour later when I found a blackened smear of blood on a blowdown.

The trail crossed a ravine, then angled up into trees. I was watching the ground when I heard him go just ahead and glimpsed the black-tipped tail and heavy, widespreading antlers. He trotted into the trees and disappeared. He didn't gallop or bound, something a healthy buck would do. There was a dried clot of black-green blood on the brown fir needles where he'd bedded. He wouldn't survive, I was doubly sure.

I jumped him again within a mile, from a thick tangle of willows and chokecherries, and there was no chance for a shot—wouldn't have been even if I'd known he was there. I just saw a flash of tan and heard the popping branches and he was gone, leaving the watery clot of blood on the dried leaves. He's feeling it now, I thought, and he isn't going far between stops.

I followed the trail for hours, understanding it was far from finished. It would have been easy to give it up there and pretend it had never happened. Finally, his walking strides shortened and became uneven, and I pictured him sick and felt the burning in my belly just as he did. I felt myself weakening, too, because I'd eaten nothing since the night before, and my leg muscles were fluttering. It was right that I should suffer, and I even took pleasure from it. It was bush justice.

I jumped him again in some trees, and as he stumbled off I took a snap shot that did nothing but topple a willow. I followed quickly, since he was stumbling and the churned-up tracks were easy to follow on the fir-needle duff. For the first time, I felt like I might get him, though I was beginning to wonder if I'd give out before the buck. I was stumbling more often, too, as the late afternoon sun dropped toward the peaks of the Wasatch in the distance to the west. I had to beat the darkness now. I tried not to think of the long hike up the canyon to the truck miles and three thousand feet above.

I was dehydrated, too, knowing that a drink from a water hole in this sheep and cattle country was almost guaranteed to give you a giardia infection. My legs ached, my skull pounded, and my belly burned from anger and worry. I thought of the buck out there bedded in the trees somewhere, sick and watching his backtrail. I worked a cramp out of a thigh and started off on the trail again. He stumbled and his stride was uneven. He was weakening, but the sun was westering. It had become a race with darkness.

I glassed the opposite slope of a ravine. The buck walked slowly across an opening and disappeared in the trees before I could shoot. I jumped and slid down the ridge, pumped full of adrenaline at the sight of him, and quickly climbed the opposite slope to his trail. I'd gained time that would have been used tracking him that distance, and I knew now he was just ahead. The trail led into thick stuff where it was impossible to follow without spooking him off. Something told me to circle ahead and below, so I followed the hunch, which was getting stronger by the moment. I stalked down into the timber below the tangle of brush, moving slowly, keeping the rifle ready. Then he was there, unaware, walking slowly down a ravine toward the bottoms. I eased the rifle up as he jumped instinctively, and held low on his shoulder as he trotted down the slope. He fell at the blast, and I hit him again as he struggled.

The twilight thickened and became darkness, and still I stood staring at the buck, relieved he was no longer suffering. Only that was important. The antlers were nothing, though they were huge. I felt in the darkness a formal, quiet feeling, the same kind you get after having four wisdom teeth yanked and you walk out of the dentist's office, happy it's done. I sat awake next to a small fire most of the night, staring at the buck and feeling hunger, thirst, and cold and deserving my suffering. I climbed back up to the truck in the morning.

The buck's head hangs on my wall now, dusty and worn with time. Usually, it's just part of the wall, as trophies eventually become, but every once in a while I look up and think about it and I feel again the guilt and it reminds me to go slow and to think carefully whenever I draw a sight on an animal. I hope never to feel that kind of anguish again.

I FOUND A TRACK

Dark clouds drifted from the northwest and snuffed the red flare of the sun before it could rise. A warm south wind had begun to melt the snow in the dawn of the last day of the season. I was hunting country new to me—the place I'd hunted since boyhood had been leased now and was overrun with ORVs and redshirts. I'd been forced onto a strip of public land sandwiched between private properties, along with hundreds of other hunters. Worse yet, the preceding winter had been so long and brutal that 90 percent of adult bucks, going into the winter weakened from rutting, had died. And with the burgeoning northern Utah human population, winter range had become golf courses, lawns, and campus parking lots. I had little faith in finding a buck, but any hunting was better than no hunting.

So on this last day of the season I had hiked along an icy snowmobile trail and then dropped into a steep canyon, more out of ritual than any real expectation. I was startled to find the big track. I measured it against a 7mm-08 cartridge, and it went four inches, indicating a fully mature buck. The print had been made the evening before in soft, thawed snow that had frozen hard, leaving a clear impression. The trail was old, but the buck wasn't traveling seriously. The trail meandered through bitterbrush and mountain mahogany. Shiny evergreen leaves littered the snow where he'd browsed. The cuts on the bitterbrush had oxidized to brown, confirming my judgment that he'd made the trail the evening before. I straight-trailed, paying little attention to wind direction. I wasn't close yet.

An hour later the trail became fresher. It had been made in the frozen snow before the dawn's thaw. Crumbly ice crystals fell into the prints where the buck had broken the crust. The trail wandered where he'd fed, then led into a stand of aspens. Here the wind shifted and quartered across the trail and wafted uphill. I looped downwind of the trail to offset the adult buck's habit of buttonhooking and bedding downwind of its backtrail to scent danger that might be following. I returned to the trail every hundred yards or so for confirmation that I was still going in the right direction. The buck had bedded briefly in the aspens before daylight, then gone on. The tracks still had those ice crystals in them; if he'd made them after the dawn thaw, the snow would have been soft and the prints clear and clean. The air was now warming and drifting uphill.

The tracks showed that the buck had turned downwind a few yards and then buttonhooked back along the backtrail to check for anything following. Was he suspicious, or just habitually cautious? I hoped it was the latter, because if he suspected something was following, he would be twice as jumpy.

He had continued on before I'd gotten close enough to scent. He wasn't hurrying—he was still walking, I could tell, because the hind hoofs printed in the tracks made by the forehoofs. The strides were measured and short. The buck walked south and seemed to know where he was going. I wondered if he'd been pushed out of another area by hunters, or if he lived in this country and was familiar with the terrain. If he were a newcomer, I'd stand a better chance. He wouldn't know the best cover and escape trails.

Half a mile farther on, the buck again doubled back on his trail, but again continued walking before I'd gotten close enough for him to scent me. Then he'd climbed a slope east for half a mile, keeping downwind so he could scent anything following. Apparently, I still wasn't close enough to be scented. Then he'd turned back south and across the wind, keeping to the thickest cover and avoiding all openings; when he came to one, he circled it in timber or brush.

As I trailed, I forgot my bitterness over the lost hunting grounds and the crowds. Catching the buck became my entire focus.

The tracks turned downwind again. When I saw the start of the buttonhook, I backed off quickly, hoping he wasn't close enough to scent me. When I was far enough back, I circled downwind and eventually picked up the trail again—he had indeed buttonhooked along his backtrail and stood and waited in a tangle of mahogany. He'd caught my scent, probably just where I realized, too late, that he had moved downwind.

From the mahogany hideaway the buck had trotted uphill, keeping downwind to be sure no one was following. He wasn't badly frightened, I could tell, because he wasn't retreating in that characteristic, panicky, stiff-legged bound in which the hoofprints are close together and the hind hoofprints ahead of the forehoofs. Probably he'd reasoned, in whatever way deer reason, that I was simply one of the random humans he had run into over the seasons.

He slowed to a walk within two hundred yards. The strides were shorter, the hind prints tracked into the front ones again, and the hoofs were no longer splayed. I sat on a deadfall and ate lunch to give the buck time to settle down. He'd need to make several backtrail buttonhooks and find no one following for him to calm enough so I'd have a chance at him. I was pretty sure he was looking for a place to bed.

When I thought the buck had time enough to settle down, I started off on his trail. I grimaced at the squeak of snow compressing under my moccasins (I'd hung the boots around my neck to trail the buck more quietly), and cringed as a chunk of bark I'd loosened dropped to the snow. But these were natural sounds, and they wouldn't frighten the buck unless he could associate them with a human.

I trailed for hours, straining to spot something in the close-growing aspens and tangles of scrub oak ahead and to the sides. The trail led through a small opening where the buck had trotted quickly, then into a tangle where he'd slowed, comfortable again in the cover. I slowed even more, because it was impossible to move with any speed through the gnarled oak scrub that grabbed and scraped at my clothes.

Two hours later, I looped uphill to clear a particularly thick tangle and then continued on above a cliff that dropped into a steep ravine. When I climbed out on the other side, I sat down to think it out. I'd have crossed the trail if the buck had turned uphill, so he was either down the slope or bedded somewhere behind. I inched a hundred yards down the slope, then cut across the ravine and the wind but found nothing. I cautiously returned to where I'd lost the trail. The buck had to be behind, perhaps in that thick oak tangle.

I eased just downwind of where I thought he'd be. Then, while crawling beneath a deadfall, I sensed rather than saw a slight motion just at the edge of true vision. Was it a chickadee searching the tree bark? A dead leaf fluttering in the breeze?

I scanned very slowly for long moments before spotting a subtle, constant motion in some branches. It wasn't the breeze, because it continued after the wind died down. Eventually, the branches became heavy, dark antlers sticking up from a

Buck in big sagebrush.

blown-down tangle of brush. The breeze brought me a heavy, pleasant musky scent.

The buck was staring off at his backtrail and, judging by the slight, rhythmic movement of the antlers, placidly chewing his cud. I inched closer, keeping the wind in my face and a fir tree between us so he wouldn't pick up any movement. I paused at every step, trying to find more than antlers to shoot at.

He was still undisturbed at twenty yards, but I could see nothing but those antlers. I sat down quietly in the snow, hoping it wouldn't squeak and give me away. Better to wait for the buck to make an undisturbed move that might give me a considered shot than to frighten him and hope for a quick one in that tangle. I'd outwait him.

Moments dragged into minutes and then hours as I lost track of time. After what I later figured was three hours, the buck finally stood. He stretched and urinated, keeping just enough behind a screen of scrub to prevent a sure shot. I told myself to wait. Then he hoofed out a new bed in the snow and lay down again. I had to keep telling myself not to force it. He lay facing me.

Dirty cotton clouds drifted through the peaks, and the gray day turned to grayer dusk. The chill sank its fangs into me and hung on like a badger. A snowmobile whined along the ridge far above, breaking my concentration. Outside thoughts forced their way into my consciousness, and I shivered. The air got colder.

I shifted my weight and hoped the buck wouldn't notice. But he did. He'd seen only the slight movement behind a screen of brush, perhaps nothing more than a chipmunk might make, but he was alert, and the snowmobile had made him nervous. The light was going, and the cold and inactivity made it difficult for me to move. If I remained motionless much longer, it would be impossible to shoot.

I raised the rifle a centimeter at a time, until the buck stood. He'd expected nothing. To him I must have seemed a haunt risen from the earth. As he bunched his muscles to jump, I pressed the trigger. He soared up into the dusk and then stumbled and fell down the slope.

As the buck's eyes glazed, I felt the same mixed feelings as I'd had that dawn. I wondered about my part in it; he was one of the few old bucks to have survived the winter, and probably the only one left on this badly pummeled strip of public land.

But this was better than to be pulled down by dogs or hit by a car when heavy snows forced him down from the mountains to filch a living in suburban foliage and ornamental hedges. In my mind's eye, I saw again the drifted-over deer carcasses that accumulated in highway borrow pits each winter. I inhaled the buck's musky odor and marveled at the depth of his chest. I ran my fingers over the heavy antlers and whistled softly in awe.

Clouds and snow closed on the mountains, and lights flared through the brown air from the city of Ogden four thousand feet below.

As I honed the knife in the near-darkness and wondered how big the buck really was, a doe with twin fawns stepped from the timber and stared. The larger fawn had the deep chest and developing proportions of a buck. It stamped a forehoof at me, and then they bounded into darkness.

LATE SEASON

Soon now, I'd dip down the rocky track, no smoother now than it had been. The old and familiar sensation had been repeated each autumn for a quarter-century—the plunge off the high plateau, the truck jarring over each boulder as it nosed down the grade to the saddle and then out over the flat at eight thousand feet, the headlights cutting through predawn darkness and showing

The two racks on the left are hunter kills from the '80s. The bottom one spreads 24 inches and is about as good as you can hope for in Mexico these days.

electric-blue deer eyes that fired back at you, moving past the water hole to where the flat dissolved into the big, dark Douglas fir trees that flowed down the north slope into that big, once-quiet canyon.

At first I'd come in an old Willys, too young to hunt or to drive but doing them anyway; there'd be no law out there, or other hunters, either. There were only coyotes wailing out of the black-icy nights, the elk tracks that circled camp in the darkness and new snow, and the deer. Each season I'd leave with a decent buck, almost as sure a thing as the early snow, having learned my hunting and everything else I considered important then from O'Connor, Trueblood, and trial and error. I killed bucks not with skill and finesse but with bullheaded, stubborn persistence. That, and bucks were more plentiful and naive and often stared at you in curiosity, something they never did now. The few big ones that survived had become nocturnal during hunting seasons. The Toyota bounced as smoothly as anything could over the rocky road.

Over the years, though, the same thing had happened there as eventually happens to all wild places—people came. It's a familiar story to every hunter over forty. First just a few, then more with their machines; the big bucks disappeared, and hunting became a competition.

Then, just a few years ago, I walked from camp down the canyon again through the timber and into that big canyon, once silent and, surprisingly, silent once again. I still-hunted idly through a foot of new, wet snow, deer staring from the slopes in curiosity just as they did back then, and there was that same sensation—as if I were the only hunter on the planet and there'd be no disturbance, no ATV grinding its way into the bottoms and spooking the deer, no fool blasting at something six hundred yards off across the canyon. It was 1962 and I was eleven again, and there'd been no Vietnam, no Dallas, no hordes entering "my" deer country. I had that same feeling of anticipation so strong in my guts it was all I could do to keep from shouting. The only difference was that now, instead of a Model 700, I carried a .54 Hawken; but that wasn't important—it was only a tool, anyway.

The late muzzleloader season was first held a few years before I tried it, and it started well after the centerfire redshirts had gone home for the year. The weather was harsher then, dipping to near zero at night, with storms and squalls that would snow you in. The deer believed that the shooting was over and all they'd have to do was feed to survive the coming winter. It was Edenic hunting, really, just as it had been back then, and what bucks were left browsed during daylight, something they never did now during the regular season. But more important, you had the hunting to yourself, and you could rely on your skills in tracking and still-hunting and compete only with the quarry, not other hunters.

Stalking and still-hunting were as pleasant in the open bottoms as they had been then, too. You'd search into the timber on the north-facing slopes and up the open south-facing slopes where scores of deer browsed as dawn mists lifted. You didn't need complicated tactics and tricks; simple still-hunting was enough, just as it had been those years ago. Deer were everywhere, and it didn't matter that most were out of range of the muzzleloader. Shooting seemed minimally important; just being there and going back to your youth, to the hunting of the old days, everyone's fantasy, was enough. But you had to hunt to keep the fantasy. And maybe you'd kill, too, but that was in the future, and at that moment it didn't seem important.

As I drifted down the creek, gawking at deer on the slopes, awed by a silence I hadn't known in the canyon in decades, I realized I didn't have a buck in the freezer (if it stayed that way, I'd miss an important part of my winter). But it didn't really concern me then— I was strongly against any form of goal-orienting. I was a trophy hunter at other times, but now it didn't matter. What was important was to hunt without hurrying, to savor it.

Fresh buck tracks had been made in the new snow within the hour, and they were bigger than anything I'd seen during the regular hunt. Does and small bucks browsed in bitterbrush and mountain mahogany on the open slopes, but I felt no urge to make a stalk yet, to close the distance and kill, because then the bubble would burst and I'd be back to reality. There was no hurry, too, because there'd be no one here to spook the deer and make them more wary and difficult to approach. This leisure, this time, was a luxury, something you never had during the regular deer season. Then, it was kill a buck as quickly as you could or someone else would get it, or at least scare it into the next canyon.

A week went by that way, without urgency, and the bucks still stared from slopes or far meadows. I made three unsuccessful stalks, not really minding that they'd failed, until I realized one evening that it was nearly over and I didn't have freezer venison (it was more than just meat—it was a symbol and omen for the coming year). But at least the mulies were as plentiful and unconcerned as on that first day. I stalked down into one of the timbered ravines that dropped off the big plateau, does and a three-point buck flushing from maples below and up the opposite slope, too far for a shot.

Bucks browsing on frost-killed forbs in October.

Later, as I eased out of a stand of timber, a good buck stood from his bed and stared. The Hawken was up as I thumbed back the hammer and set the fore-trigger, and when the bead was right on his shoulder, I touched the set trigger. A cap-gun pop—a misfire! The buck stared through the drifting light snow as I fitted another cap—and had another misfire. I hissed unprintable words, forced a wire into the nipple to clear it, fitted another cap, and pressed the trigger again. *Another* misfire, and the buck trotted across the slope as I lowered the gun—and then it fired into a clump of sagebrush. I swore vehemently, but a moment later laughed at myself.

"Well," I said aloud as I turned for camp, "that's it." The first late-season hunt fantasy was over. I climbed out of the ravine and walked across the flat, already thinking of chores I'd neglected, then paused to load the gun just in case. Two hundred yards from the tent, three yearling bucks browsed up onto the flat at the edge of the fir trees, and as quickly as I spotted them, I dropped into the waist-high sagebrush. They fed toward me as I rammed a wire into the nipple and around it to be sure it was clear of condensation and ice, fitted a fresh cap, and thumbed back the hammer. When they were eighty yards off, I set the trigger so only a touch would fire the gun, and waited. The bucks now quartered away as they browsed, so they'd come no closer. I eased the heavy Hawken up, rested elbows on knees, and prayed the blunderbuss would fire. When the sights were aligned just so on the leading buck's shoulder, I touched the hair trigger. I heard the .54-caliber ball strike as I squinted through blue smoke, and all three bucks bounded into timber. Then I followed bright, frothy, crimson splashes on the snow to the buck piled up under a deadfall a hundred yards below.

There were other late seasons after that. Some years I would kill a buck and some I wouldn't, but that wasn't really the attraction. I got close to trophy bucks several times, only to have the Hawken misfire; wet weather and temperature changes caused condensation that froze or blocked the spark path through the nipple or dampened the powder. Each time, I painted the air blue and laughed at myself afterward. And I learned as I hunted, exactly as I had back then. But more important, during those seasons I had the place to myself and there was no competition or rush, and I always recaptured that feeling of going back, of being young again, full of anticipation at the years to come. Even with frustrating misfires, there's no better reason for hunting the late season.

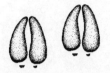

Afterword

TROPHY BUCKS ARE WHERE YOU FIND THEM

Because I have already published two books on hunting trophy mule deer (*Stalking Trophy Mule Deer* and *Mule Deer Strategies*), and because I have written more than forty feature deer articles in hunting magazines, mostly in *Field & Stream* and *Outdoor Life*, and because I have who knows how many whopping buck heads and antlers in my house, I am considered a mule deer "expert." I suppose this is a bit like being a "woman expert." Just when you think you have the answers, you find a woman, or a buck, that completely makes a fool out of you. I might be a little like those stock-picking experts in the early 2000 bear market: Many of them lost a fortune (an acquaintance told me he lost roughly the amount of the wages he will have made over his entire working life if he retires at age sixty-five—I told him to go deer hunting).

The difference between me and many of these experts on the stock market or on women is that I know it's impossible to be an expert on mule deer. They're simply too unpredictable.

Still, I suppose I know more about mule deer biology (you can't spend nearly two decades studying them formally without learning something!) and about mule deer hunting (here, it's more than three decades) than some other experts. Which leaves me open more often than I like to a common question asked by would-be trophy buck hunters: Where should I go to kill a big buck?

Let me try to answer that question with three examples.

The first involves the Dolores Triangle. As mentioned earlier in this tome, the Dolores Triangle is formed by the Colorado border on the east, the Colorado River on the northwest, and the Dolores River on the south. The country therein includes the northern foothills of the La Sal Mountains and a lot of pinyon-juniper and rimrock country. Hunters there find river bottoms, decent feed, and too many four-wheel-drive roads for comfort. In about the mid-1900s (it's still difficult to refer to the 1900s as the "last century"), the Dolores Triangle became noted for huge bucks, with good reason. I remember reading stories of the place in the big outdoor magazines, and lusting over the photos of big bucks taken from the area. Hunters heard about it, moved in, and killed off the big bucks. Within a few years, the Triangle had no more trophy bucks than

This Sierra Madre tom puma won't eat any more venison. His gut, however, was full of javelina, the little desert pig. They're easier to catch than deer. My guides and pals are vaqueros Armando and Jesus, and they're just as proud of the puma as I am.

overhunted places elsewhere in Utah. Since I'd heard about the Triangle throughout my youth, I still had to try it. I didn't get there until the early '70s, but I managed to draw on an early rut hunt. Deer were plentiful, including young bucks from 3½ years of age down to yearlings. In five days of hunting, I did not see a mature buck or find a single big track. Hunters were packing deer out of the Triangle, but a state conservation officer said he hadn't checked out a single mature buck. I didn't even bother shooting one of the little bucks and left disgusted. There are two lessons here: First, don't visit a place with too many expectations; you're likely to be disappointed. And second, with mule deer, if everyone has heard about a "hot spot," it's already too late.

The next example is northern Mexico. In my opinion, northern Sonora was once the greatest and largest trophy mule deer spot on the continent. In the 1970s and '80s, forty-inch bucks were still coming out of the place with enough regularity to make any buck hunter's adrenaline kick into hyperdrive. By the early '90s, results had slowed considerably and forty-inch bucks were rarer than black diamonds. Still, the Sonoran deserts were producing thirty-inch bucks. Used-car-salesmen types outfitted the place in droves. They'd bring in any and all hunters they could with no regard for future seasons. Sonora is largely privately owned by big ranchers—cattle are Sonora's gold. Hunting was only lightly controlled by government agencies, and was mostly an anything-goes proposition on the big ranches; once there, do what you want. Often the outfitter didn't buy the hunting licenses and tags the dude had paid for until the animal was already in the bag, on the chance that the client would be unsuccessful and the outfitter could pocket the extra gringo dollars. This left the innocent client hunting illegally and without the required licenses. This scam is still common enough in current-day Mexico; Homero Canedo Carballo, an outfitter out of Hermosillo, did it to me (his company, last I heard, was Sierra Madre Hunting). It took me two hunts with him to figure it out.

Homero (and others) often bribe peons to let them on a ranch that is otherwise closed to hunting, with the owner none the wiser. Instead of paying the landowner a $500 or so trophy fee for a buck and daily use fees, Homero would pay the *peon* $100 and bring hunters in the back door for several seasons until big bucks played out. The farm worker is happy with the situation because often he gets paid as a guide for a few days, too. Homero kills as many bucks as he wants at a much reduced price, and the client and landowner know nothing about the arrangement. Unfortunately, this leads to severe overharvesting of adult bucks—and ultimately their disappearance.

These days, trophy bucks are as scarce in Sonora as in other overhunted parts of the deer's range in Utah or Colorado. Even respectable outfitters are only taking bucks in the mid to upper twenties, with thirty-inchers the exception rather than the rule it used to be. But Sonora's reputation is hard to kill, and U.S. clients continue to pay seven-grand-plus for a "trophy" buck hunt with less chance for an exceptional animal than they would have in the U.S. for a fraction of the cost.

The genetic makeup of the mule deer in Sonora is alive and well. If the government and landowners could get together and closely manage the herd by reducing permits, reducing season lengths, and discontinuing hunting during the rut, the Sonoran mule deer herd could come back more rapidly than in other places because it is not faced with the "winter bottleneck." I'd like to see this happen, and I have hopes that eventually it will. The first step is for gringo clients to quit hunting south of the border; this would send a clear message to both the Sonora pro-hunters association and the Sonoran government. I've talked with young and savvy modern Mexican outfitters, and a fair percentage of them agree with me, even though taking action would pull money out of their pockets. This, above all else, gives me hope for the Sonoran mule deer. My role in promoting Mexican deer conservation is to discourage Americans from hunting down there; the hunting now is largely inferior to trophy buck hunting in many western states. Why pay $6,000 to $8,000 for a hunt that you could duplicate for $2,000 in Idaho or Wyoming, with more chance at a trophy buck?

One note to the Sonora mule deer story: Big bucks—and I mean animals with spreads into the upper thirties and Boone and Crockett scores over 185—still show up on Sonoran ranches. If Sonora is overhunted, how so? The answer almost invariably is that a new ranch has just opened to hunting. One such place was my friend Enrique Zepeda's ranch near Caborca. The first year it opened, and that was only two seasons ago as I write this, hunters took bucks ranging from twenty-nine to about thirty-six inches in spread. All had balanced antlers with good mass and long points. Enrique sent me a photo from long ago of a mule deer buck killed on his property; it was a nontypical with a forty-two-inch spread and about twenty-six points and would make any hunter's jaw drop to about beltline. It was difficult to tell how old the photo was, but it was ancient. I assume the buck was the only one taken from the place until Enrique opened up the hunting recently. It's my understanding that the second season's hunting was not as good and the bucks were much smaller; he's not hunting the ranch any longer and is prospecting for other areas. And so it goes with mule deer hunting. I'd been trying without luck to find a good place with a high probability for big bucks for several client-friends for the 2000 season. Enrique is pessimistic about finding thirty-inch bucks on his ranches, as are the other reputable outfitters in Sonora.

Example three: Half-a-dozen or so years back, an Indian reservation in southwestern Saskatchewan decided to encourage U.S. hunters to harvest its big mule deer. An editor of a fledgling hunting magazine in Utah and several others heard about the place and hunted there. The hunt was late, with heavy snows, and bucks were at a disadvantage. They were naive, having been hunted only lightly by the Indians. Most of the bucks taken were exceptional, most of them, if memory serves, measuring between thirty and thirty-nine inches in spread. As soon as hunters heard about it, they were literally throwing their money at the Indians for the next hunt. I know, because I tried, but no more permits were available. Just after the first hunt, the plains suffered a severe winter, which affects adult bucks most because they enter winter exhausted from rutting, so the second season was a dismal failure. Several U.S. hunters, after learning of the poor results in the early part of that second season, tried to peddle their tags to me (apparently, I was on some sort of list at the reservation). The few bucks killed that year weren't trophies, and the new "hot spot" drifted into obscurity. It's my understanding the hunting still has not "come back."

So, then, where does one go to collect a trophy mule deer buck? It's easy to tell a hunter where to hunt for a big Stone ram, a brown bear, or a great whitetail or pronghorn. Yet after having hunted and studied mule deer for more decades than I am going to mention, I still can't answer that question. Places produce well for a season or two, hunters find out about them, and each spot becomes just another overhunted deer range.

Of course, if a hunter could only find the right spot, the big bucks would run right in front of him, right? Maybe not. So the better question is not where but *how*. As mentioned often in these pages, trophy bucks have become nocturnal and secretive during hunting seasons. More ranges than we may think contain an adult buck, but they are simply among the toughest animals on the planet to kill (see my "how-to" section for ways to go about it).

I've mentioned the seventy or so mature bucks I've bagged over my hunting career. Most were collected within fifteen miles of my house along the badly overhunted and overpopulated Wasatch Front in northern Utah. Until this year (2000), resident licenses for deer were unlimited and schools had the eve of the deer opener off so kids could hunt with their families.

The local mountains and canyons literally bristled with redshirts. In the predawn, the headlights of pickup trucks and ATVs bounced down every ridge, and there was a steady stream of traffic on the highways. The deer hunt was an institution, and opening weekend a carnival.

Yet by hunting carefully in various localities within this big deer-hunting stadium, I collected some huge racks. I didn't do it by sitting on a ridge or bouncing about on an ATV; I did it by hunting hard on foot, by employing a variety of tactics discussed in this book, and by persistence. Only a few hunters have the dedication necessary to hunt this way in this day of quick fixes and pills for anything, so the few cagey adult bucks that do survive are in no more danger than they ever were, and there will always be a big buck in this canyon or under that ridge ten miles across the valley. To get one of these superbucks, you just have to work harder.

This answer isn't going to be satisfactory to some hunters. I still haven't told them where to go. If I must be pinned down, so be it. The Kaibab of northern Arizona still produces excellent bucks, as does the remote Salmon River country of central Idaho and remote places in western Wyoming. Draw a tag, and hunt hard.

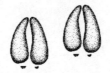